The Local Impact of Globalization in South and Southeast Asia

In the past two decades, several millions of IT-enabled services jobs have been relocated or 'offshored' from the US and Europe to, in particular, low-cost economies around the world. Most of these jobs so far have landed in South and Southeast Asia, with India and the Philippines receiving the bulk of them. This has caused profound changes in the international division of labour, and has had correspondingly wide social and economic effects.

This book examines how this 'next wave in globalization' affects people and places in South and Southeast Asia. It brings together 12 case studies from India, the Philippines, China, Hong Kong and Thailand and explores how and for whom services offshoring creates opportunities, triggers local economic transformations and produces challenges. This book in addition compares how different countries take part in this 'second global shift', investigates service-sector driven economic development from a historical perspective, and engages with the question whether and to what extent services offer a new promising avenue of sustained economic growth for developing countries. It argues that service-led development in developing countries is not easy for all the workers involved, or a guaranteed path to sustained economic development and prosperity.

This volume stands out from other books in the field in its exploration of the social and economic outcomes in the cities and countries where services have been located. Based on cutting-edge empirical research and original data, the volume offers a state-of-the-art contribution to this growing debate. The book provides valuable insights for students, scholars and professionals interested in services offshoring, socioeconomic development and contemporary transformations in South and Southeast Asia.

Bart Lambregts is post-doc researcher with the Amsterdam Institute for Social Science Research (AISSR), University of Amsterdam, and lectures urban planning at the Faculty of Architecture, Kasetsart University, in Bangkok.

Niels Beerepoot is assistant professor at the Department of Geography, Planning and International Development Studies of the University of Amsterdam.

Robert C. Kloosterman is Professor of Economic Geography and Planning at the Amsterdam Institute of Social Science Research (AISSR), University of Amsterdam.

Routledge Studies in the Modern World Economy

For a complete list of titles in this series, please visit www.routledge.com.

150 Moving Out of Poverty
An inquiry into the inclusive growth in Asia
Jonna P. Estudillo and Keijiro Otsuka

149 The Local Impact of Globalization in South and Southeast Asia
Offshore business processes in services industries
Edited by Bart Lambregts, Niels Beerepoot and Robert C. Kloosterman

148 Low-carbon, Sustainable Future in East Asia
Improving energy systems, taxation and policy cooperation
Edited by Soocheol Lee, Hector Pollitt and Park Seung-Joon

147 Corruption, Economic Growth and Globalization
Edited by Aurora Teixeira, Carlos Pimenta, António Maia and José António Moreira

146 Chinese Entrepreneurship
An Austrian economics perspective
Fu-Lai Tony Yu and Diana S. Kwan

145 International Trade, Competitive Advantage and Developing Economies
How less developed countries are capturing global markets
Caf Dowlah

144 The Global Commercial Aviation Industry
Edited by Sören Eriksson and Harm-jan Steenhuis

143 Decentralization and Infrastructure in the Global Economy
From Gaps to Solutions
Edited by Jonas Frank and Jorge Martínez-Vázquez

142 Poverty, Inequality and Growth in Developing Countries
Theoretical and empirical approaches
Edited by Atsushi Maki

141 **Banking on Equality**
Women, work and employment in the banking sector in India
Supriti Bezbaruah

140 **Irish Economic Development**
Serial under-achiever or high-performing EU state?
Eoin O'Leary

139 **Capitalism and the World Economy**
The light and shadow of globalization
Edited by Toshiaki Hirai

138 **The International Monetary System, Energy and Sustainable Development**
Edited by Sung Jin Kang and Yung Chul Park

137 **Crises in Europe in the Transatlantic Context**
Economic and political appraisals
Edited by Bruno Dallago and John McGowan

136 **Measuring National Income in the Centrally Planned Economies**
Why the west underestimated the transition to capitalism
William Jefferies

135 **Comparing Post War Japanese and Finnish Economies and Societies**
Edited by Yasushi Tanaka, Toshiaki Tamaki, Jari Ojala and Jari Eloranta

134 **The Economics of Cooperative Education**
A practitioners' guide to the theoretical framework and empirical assessment of cooperative education
Yasushi Tanaka

133 **The Geographical Transformation of China**
Edited by Michael Dunford and Weidong Lui

132 **Japan's Aid**
Lessons for economic growth, development and political economy
Edward M. Feasel

131 **The Economics of Knowledge Generation and Distribution**
The role of interactions in the system dynamics of innovation and growth
Edited by Pier Paolo Patrucco

130 **The Open Society and its Enemies in East Asia**
The relevance of the Popperian framework
Edited by Gregory C.G. Moore

129 **International Remittance Payments and the Global Economy**
Bharati Basu with James T. Bang

128 **Innovation, Globalization and Firm Dynamics**
Lessons for enterprise policy
Edited by Anna Ferragina, Erol Taymoz and Kamil Yilmaz

The Local Impact of Globalization in South and Southeast Asia

Offshore business processes in services industries

Edited by Bart Lambregts, Niels Beerepoot and Robert C. Kloosterman

Routledge
Taylor & Francis Group
LONDON AND NEW YORK

First published 2016
by Routledge

2 Park Square, Milton Park, Abingdon, Oxfordshire OX14 4RN
52 Vanderbilt Avenue, New York, NY 10017

Routledge is an imprint of the Taylor & Francis Group, an informa business

First issued in paperback 2020

British Library Cataloguing in Publication Data
A catalogue record for this book is available from the British Library

Library of Congress Cataloging in Publication Data
The local impact of globalization in South and Southeast Asia : offshore business processes in services industries / edited by Bart Lambregts, Niels Beerepoot, and Robert C. Kloosterman.
pages cm. -- (Routledge studies in the modern world economy)
1. Offshore outsourcing--South Asia. 2. Offshore outsourcing--Southeast Asia.
3. Service industries--South Asia. 4. Service industries--Southeast Asia.
I. Lambregts, B. W. II. Beerepoot, Niels. III. Kloosterman, Robert C.
HD2368.S64L63 2015
330.95--dc23
2015012642

ISBN: 978-1-138-77726-2 (hbk)
ISBN: 978-0-367-66871-6 (pbk)

Typeset in Times New Roman
by Fish Books Ltd., Enfield, Middx.

Contents

List of figures

List of tables

List of contributors

Niels Beerepoot is assistant professor at the Department of Geography, Planning and International Development Studies of the University of Amsterdam. His research focuses on service-sector growth in the Philippines and India. Since 2011 he has been the project leader of the NWO-WOTRO Integrated-Programme project on understanding the local outcomes of the emergence of the offshore service sector in Mumbai and Manila.

Neeraj Hatekar is Professor of Econometrics, Department of Economics, University of Mumbai. He is the Coordinator for the Centre for Computational Social Sciences, University of Mumbai. He has been the Smuts Visiting Fellow at the University of Cambridge and has taught courses on Indian economic development at the university. He is a prolific writer and has contributed to many peer-reviewed academic journals and the *Economic and Political Weekly*.

Chie Iguchi is Associate Professor of International Business and Global Innovation Management at Keio University Faculty of Business and Commerce in Tokyo. She obtained her PhD in International Business form the University of Reading Business School, UK. Her research interests include the roles of R&D, technological upgrading, innovative activities and knowledge-creation activities in host Asian countries, particularly Japanese MNE's behaviours in Thailand, Malaysia, Philippines, Taiwan, Singapore, India and Indonesia, as well as issues of head-quarter and subsidiaries relationships. Besides her professorship at Keio University, she is a board member of EAMSA, AJBS, AMNE and National Representative of Japan of EIBA.

Jana Maria Kleibert is a PhD candidate at the Department of Human Geography, Planning and International Development at the University of Amsterdam. She holds an MSc in International Relations (cum laude) from the Graduate School of Social Sciences of the University of Amsterdam. Her current research project focuses on the emergence, evolution and developmental impact of the offshore service sector in the Philippines and India. In particular, she uses the global production network approach to analyse changes towards local embeddedness and upgrading into higher value-added service activities. Her broader research interest are globalization, economic geography and development studies.

Robert C. Kloosterman is Professor of Economic Geography and Planning at the University of Amsterdam. He is Honorary Professor in the Bartlett School of Planning, University College, London and held the Franqui Chair Entrepreneurship at the Faculty of Business Studies, Hasselt University (Belgium) in 2012. He is fascinated by cities and how they work. More specifically, he is interested in what kind of economic activities take place in contemporary urban environments and how they are related to other aspects, such as institutional frameworks and the historical legacy in terms of economic orientation and urban morphology.

Sandhya Krishnan is currently a PhD candidate at the University of Amsterdam and University of Mumbai under the project 'Understanding the Current Wave in Globalization'. Her research looks into the rise of the new middle class in India with a special focus on the contribution of the offshore services industry to the formation of the class. Sandhya completed her Masters in Economics at the University of Mumbai in 2009. Since then she has worked as a researcher at the Economic and Political Weekly Research Foundation, Mumbai and at the National Institute of Public Finance and Policy, New Delhi.

Randhir Kumar is a PhD candidate under the project 'Understanding the Current Wave in Globalization' at the University of Amsterdam and the University of Mumbai. He completed an MA in Globalization and Labour Studies at the Tata Institute of Social Sciences in Mumbai. Before Randhir started his PhD research, he worked as a Research Associate at the Indian Institute of Management-Ahmedabad in Gujarat. His research interests include international development economics, entrepreneurship and labour relations.

Bart Lambregts is post-doc researcher at the Amsterdam Institute for Social Science Research (AISSR) of the University of Amsterdam and lectures urban planning at the Faculty of Architecture of Kasetsart University in Bangkok. He holds an MSc in Urban Planning from Delft University of Technology and a PhD in Human Geography from the University of Amsterdam. His current research concentrates on the role of services industries in processes of globalization and local/regional development, sustainable urban mobility issues and the interdependencies between urban development practices and climate-resilience building.

Mary Leian C. Marasigan is a researcher at the University of the Philippines School of Labor and Industrial Relations and a PhD candidate at the University of Amsterdam, the Netherlands.

Kishore More holds an MA in History and currently works as a project fellow in the Center for Computational Social Sciences of the University of Mumbai. He is also a PhD scholar in History at the Department of History, University of Mumbai.

Rene E. Ofreneo is Professor and Former Dean of the School of Labor and Industrial Relations (SOLAIR), University of the Philippines. Rene Ofreneo has a Certificate in Development Economics, an MA in Industrial Relations and a PhD in Philippines Studies (Labour and Economy). He has written extensively on the labour and industrial relations issues in Asia. He sits in the board of several journals dealing with labour and management issues in the Asia-Pacific such as *The Journal of Industrial Relations* (Sydney) and the *Asia-Pacific Review* (London). He is three-time recipient of the International Publication Award of the University of the Philippines.

Antoinette R. Raquiza is Associate Professor at the Asian Center, University of the Philippines Diliman where she teaches Philippine and Asian Studies. Her research interests include Southeast Asian politics and governance, comparative political economy of late-developing countries and the changing configuration of national and global capitalism. Her book, *State Structure, Policy Formation, and Economic Development in Southeast Asia: The Political Economy of Thailand and the Philippines*, was published by Routledge in 2012.

Thomas Sigler is a lecturer in Human Geography in the School of Geography, Planning and Environmental Management at the University of Queensland in Brisbane, Australia. He holds a PhD and an MS in Geography from Pennsylvania State University, and has worked in several different contexts including the US, Australia, Panama, Honduras and Congo. Dr Sigler's research focuses on understanding the interface between globalization and urbanization, primarily as an outcome of inter-urban networks that are formed through historical, economic, political and cultural networks.

Emeline Vogelzang holds a Masters degree in International Development Studies at the University of Amsterdam. For her Masters thesis she conducted research on the role of the business process outsourcing sector in the formation of a new middle class in Iloilo City, the Philippines.

Xu Zhang is a PhD candidate in Human Geography and Planning at University of Amsterdam. He is an urban geographer interested in the transitions of Chinese cities and regions under conditions of contemporary globalization. His current research has focused on the development of advanced business services and the impacts of these activities on the economic and spatial restructuring of metropolitan areas in China.

Simon XB. Zhao, PhD, is founding Director of the International Center for China Development Studies, HKU. He specializes in urban regional studies, geography of trade and finance and the development of international financial centres. He is an editorial board member for two international journals and has published more than a hundred papers in international refereed journals. Dr Zhao was a member of the Central Policy Unit, HKSAR government and provides consultancy services to national and local governments in China and the private sector. Currently he co-leads the HKSAR RGC Theme-based Research Scheme Project 'Enhancing Hong Kong as Leading International Financial Centre', and HKU Strategic Research Theme Project 'China's New Round Urbanization'.

Acknowledgements

This book emanates from a longstanding interest of the editors in the economic and social transformations taking place in South and Southeast Asia. Over the years and during many visits we have become witness to countries and cities in the region becoming affected by what is starting to become popularly known as the latest wave in globalization. This wave, which is largely services driven and essentially entails the relocation by firms of information technology-enabled services and business processes from advanced to developing economies, is starting to make serious impacts. It causes profound changes in the international division of labour and triggers a range of highly interesting and potentially important social and economic transformations in the economies where the work lands. These fascinate us and are therefore the focus of this book.

More specifically, this book is the outcome of the seminar 'Creating and capturing value in the next wave of globalization: experiences in (offshore) services production from India, East Asia and Southeast Asia' that was held in Bangkok on 25–26 April 2013. The seminar brought together a group of scholars from the Netherlands, India, Japan, Thailand, Indonesia, the Philippines, Singapore, Hong Kong and Australia to discuss service-sector driven growth and its local outcomes in different parts of Asia. We acknowledge the support of the Netherlands Organisation for Scientific Research-Science for Global Development (NWO-WOTRO) whose financial support (grant number W 01.65.329.00) enabled us to organize the seminar and produce the book. We are furthermore grateful to Kasetsart University (Faculty of Architecture) and the Netherlands embassy in Bangkok for their contributions in kind to the success of the seminar.

Our special thanks goes out to the book's contributing authors for their enthusiasm, commitment, determination and willingness to share their expertise. It has allowed us to compile a volume that draws from academic fields as varied as economic geography, economics, political science, labour studies and international business studies, and we hope that the book will attract readership from at least as many disciplines. We would also like to thank Puikang Chan of the Amsterdam Institute for Social Science Research of the University of Amsterdam for financially managing the NWO-WOTRO research project from which this book results. Finally, we would like to thank Laura Johnson, our contact person at Routledge, for the very pleasant collaboration and her admirable patience.

Bart Lambregts
Niels Beerepoot
Robert C. Kloosterman

1 The local impact of services offshoring in South and Southeast Asia

Introduction and overview

Bart Lambregts, Niels Beerepoot and Robert C. Kloosterman

Services offshoring and its local impacts

Services offshoring in context

Mushrooming office parks, omnipresent recruitment signs, crowds of nightshift workers celebrating the end of workdays with food and drinks at sunrise, booming catering, leisure and retail businesses: in cities such as Mumbai, Bangalore, Gurgaon, Manila, Cebu City and various others it is hard not to notice the impacts of the unfolding shift of services production from the Global North to the Global South. Services offshoring, as the process is called, has gained substantial momentum since it surfaced in the 1990s. What started with a trickle of low-end information technology (IT) functions being moved from the United States (US) to India has grown into the large-scale migration of multi-various service production activities from advanced to emerging economies. Several millions of services jobs in the Global North have already been affected (Fernandez-Stark *et al.* 2014) and there is potential for many millions more to follow (Blinder 2006, 2009). The underlying restructuring process and the resultant social and economic effects are far reaching and according to some observers indeed radical enough to justify the use of powerful labels such as 'globalization 2.0', and 'the second global shift' (Bryson 2007, Freeman 2005).

To be credited for the global shift in services production is the increased tradability of various services products, enabled by important advances in information and communication technologies (ICT). The latter, over the past 25 years or so, have paved the way for the massive digitization of business processes and the electronic transfer of the associated services products. Helped further by diminishing trade barriers and the rise of a well-educated and IT-literate labour force in the Global South, firms today enjoy literally a world of opportunities to engage in labour arbitrage and expand their production networks. The IT-enabled unbundling of service production processes allows for such processes to be outsourced and/or offshored. While outsourcing refers to the migration of production activities across a firm's organizational boundaries (i.e. contracting out a business process to a third party), offshoring concerns the relocation of activities overseas. Offshoring may or may not involve outsourcing. The former is often referred to as 'offshore outsourcing', the latter as 'captive offshoring'.

Since its inception, services offshoring has become an increasingly complex phenomenon. Initially, work mainly flowed from the Global North to the Global South. Today's movements are more intricate, with investments and jobs also migrating in the opposite direction and between countries in the Global South itself. Patterns of specialization emerge in result, sometimes based simply on the kind of language that is locally mastered (e.g. English, Spanish, French, Japanese) but increasingly informed by more sophisticated differences in skills availability (e.g. analytical and creative skills). Motives to engage in services offshoring have become more variegated too. While initially offshoring was primarily about achieving cost benefits through labour arbitrage, an emerging motive these days is for firms to source skills that are increasingly hard to find 'at home' but still in abundant supply overseas (Bunyaratavej *et al.* 2011).

The past years also have seen an impressive increase in the variety of services activities being offshored. No longer does it concern customer relations services (call centres), data processing (back office activities) and relatively simple IT services alone. Today's offshorable services are increasingly knowledge intensive and include a choice of financial, legal, engineering, design and medical services, along with an expanding array of ever more advanced IT services (such as application development) and even research and development. In tandem with the proliferation of offshorable services, a fairly complex nomenclature has developed. The literature is peppered with acronyms such as BPO, KPO, LPO, BPM, IT-BPO, ITES-BPO and others, with BPO standing for business process outsourcing, KPO for knowledge process outsourcing, LPO for legal process outsourcing and BPM for business process management. Each refers to different subsectors or segments of the business process outsourcing industry. The acronyms IT-BPO and ITES-BPO emphasize that services outsourcing and offshoring are strongly information technology-based, with ITES standing for information technology enabled services. In this volume ITES-BPO is used to refer to the industry at large, while other acronyms may be used to identify particular subsectors or processes.

The above goes to show that services offshoring is a rapidly evolving practice. On the back of the previous wave – the global reallocation of industrial production – it deepens the international division of labour, further extends and refines global production networks, and affects the lives of people and the fate of places in myriad ways. Unsurprisingly, the trend, also dubbed 'the next wave in globalization' (Dossani and Kenney 2007), is increasingly recognized as one of global consequence. The number of periodicals, blogs, conferences, consultants and scholars engaging with the topic is growing rapidly. Political attention has become considerable as well, notably in the most affected countries (e.g. the US, India, the Philippines), but also beyond those. International development organizations have become aware to the development potential as well and have emerged as active contributors to the debate (see e.g. Asian Development Bank 2011, 2012, Ghani and O'Connel 2014, UNCTAD 2005, UNESCAP 2011, World Bank 2007, 2009, 2011, 2012).

Much of the academic debate so far has essentially centred around two major themes. A first body of literature approaches services outsourcing and offshoring from a business management perspective. It concentrates on the logics for firms to engage in outsourcing and offshoring, explores the challenges involved and develops advice mainly targeted at business practitioners (see e.g. Bäumer *et al.* 2012, Berry 2005, Brown and Wilson 2005, Couto *et al.* 2007, Eltschinger 2007, Kobayashi-Hillary 2008, Metters and Verma 2008). A second debate focuses on the question how services offshoring affects the economies of the countries and regions from where the work departs. A central question here is whether offshoring of relatively low value-added tasks creates opportunities for the 'freed' labour to engage in higher value-added activities and (thus) strengthens the (global) competitiveness of local firms, or whether the trend primarily adds to local unemployment problems (see e.g. Bardhan *et al.* 2013, Breznitz and Zysman 2013, Levy and Murnane 2005, Massini and Miozzo 2012, Milberg and Winkler 2013, Rubalcaba 2007).

Concentrating on local impacts in the Global South

This volume engages with a third dimension of services offshoring, and one that so far has remained little studied. It concerns the local impact of services offshoring in the economies where the work lands, with a focus on South and Southeast Asia: the part of the world that attracts most of the services offshored (Tholons, 2014). A trickle of publications addressing the effects of services offshoring in the Global South has started to emerge (e.g. Ahmed 2013, Amante 2010, Beerepoot and Keijser 2014, Benner 2006, Fernandez-Stark *et al.* 2010, Graham and Mann 2013, James and Vira 2012, Ofreneo *et al.* 2007, Taylor and Bain 2005). Many issues, however, remain underexposed – a deficit this volume aims to address.

As noted, in ITES-BPO hotspots such as Mumbai, Manila, Bangalore, Gurgaon and Cebu City it is hard not to notice how the arrival of thousands of export-oriented services jobs brings changes to the city. Most visible of course are its physical manifestations: the mostly newly built office towers and business parks, often well-guarded and surrounded by restaurants and shops catering to the office workers; the manifold recruitment signs and activities (e.g. walk-in interviews in popular and accessible places); and of course the bustle created by the crowds of office workers either on their way to work, during break times or after work hours. Yet, beyond these a range of other, less clearly visible but perhaps even more far-reaching effects can be conceived as well. First of all, services offshoring, in the same way as manufacturing offshoring has done and still does, pulls local economies into the global economy. ITES-BPO firms, be they the result of foreign direct investments or be they home grown, are fixed or flexible parts of the global value chains (Gereffi and Fernandez-Stark 2010) or global production networks (Coe *et al.* 2004) of multinational corporations (MNCs) and their likes. Essentially, the arrival of an ITES-BPO industry means that a local economy and its actors assume a role in specific, global value creation processes. While this creates opportunities, it also introduces dependency (decision-making power in global production networks often is not located where the ITES-BPO activities take place) and other challenges. Assimilation into the global economy by way of the arrival of an ITES-BPO industry can be seen as a process of 'strategic coupling' (Coe *et al.* 2008, Kleibert 2014, MacKinnon 2012), or in other words as a process, involving both local actors and global producers/investors, in which local assets are purposefully linked with the needs of global producer capital. How this process plays out bears relevance for the way a locality becomes inserted in the global production networks (e.g. its value creating role, its degree of control over affairs, the resources supplied, the return on resources received, its potential to not only create but also to capture value) and as such determines the potential for realizing local and regional development.

Yet, to a certain degree irrespective of how the strategic coupling process plays out, the arrival of an offshore services industry creates opportunities for a local economy. These of course include employment opportunities for those who are interested in and qualify for working in an 'international' office environment, but also business opportunities and potentially more for those commanding the supply of facilities that ITES-BPO firms need. Providers of office space and information and telecommunications infrastructure, suppliers of supporting services such as security, catering, transport and housekeeping, collectors of taxes, and those that manage to appeal to the consumerist desires of those employed in the ITES-BPO industry, may anticipate business. The business generated, in turn, may result in job opportunities for others, including those who do not qualify for working in the ITES-BPO themselves. Indian and Philippine industry stakeholders estimate that every ITES-BPO job creates about three jobs elsewhere in the local economy (IBPAP 2012, NASSCOM 2014). While these represent estimates rather than proven numbers, an employment multiplier effect is likely to exist. Beyond direct employment, increased business and indirect employment, the industry is also likely to offer employees the opportunity to acquire skills and as such to contribute to peoples' employability (Beerepoot and Hendriks 2013, Marasigan in this volume) and skills accumulation in the labour force at large, which must be considered assets from social and development perspectives.

The rise of an industry that is globally connected, export oriented, relatively well paying and applying international standards in at least part of its business processes, is also likely to trigger transformations in the economy that surrounds it, especially of course if this industry manages to accumulate some volume compared to the size of the surrounding economy. Such transformations may extend to supporting industries, which may have to step up their performance in order to qualify for business (see Kumar in this volume), to government regulations, which may have to be adjusted in order to accommodate new business practices, to the educational sector, which may want to respond to new industry and labour market demands (Kleibert 2015), and so on. In addition, for ITES-BPO employees a job in a relatively well-paying, internationally oriented work environment may open the door to a new lifestyle. Competitive wages are likely to transform the lives of employees and their next of kin in various ways, and for some may bring middle-class status within reach. Simultaneously, being part of an international work environment is likely to affect workers' self-image and consumer preferences. If indeed, as for instance Fuller and Narasimhan (2007), Murphy (2011) and the World Bank (2013) suggest, services offshoring is contributing to the rise of a new middle class in the emerging economies that benefit most of the trend, the potential of the development to transform societies cannot be underestimated.

The above is not to say that services offshoring for the receiving economies represents a carefree pathway to participation in the global economy and – possibly – development, quite the opposite. There are important issues and challenges that should not be overlooked. A pertinent question for example is who stands to benefit from the trend and who not. The question may be addressed at the global level (i.e. advanced/sending economies versus developing/receiving economies) but also at the level of the receiving economies themselves. How inclusive or exclusive is access to the jobs provided (Beerepoot 2010)? Who provides the supporting infrastructure and receives the rents and fees payable by the industry? Who stand at the receiving end of the consumer spending of the ITES-BPO workforce? Do the answers to these question point at existing social, economic and political power configurations simply being reaffirmed or does the arrival of an ITES-BPO industry provide opportunities for new categories of actors to enter the playing field and/or make a step up the social ladder? Another major challenge for receiving economies concerns the question how to make sure that the arrival of an offshore services industry is going to sustainably contribute to real development and not fall into a low value-added, non-embedded services branch plant economy or worse. If regional development is at least in part about successfully progressing from making basic contributions to value creation, to being able to 'move up the value chain' or to engage in 'value enhancement', and to eventually increase the level of control over one's contributions (value capturing) (Coe *et al.* 2004), the challenges for those local economies currently producing footloose and low value-added services in foreign-controlled global production networks, become crystal clear.

South and Southeast Asia in the spotlight

Geographically, as noted, the book's focus is on South and Southeast Asia. While services offshoring is a truly global phenomenon, the largest concentrations of offshored services activities are found in this part of the world. India and the Philippines have surfaced as the world's most important locations for offshore services production (Asian Development Bank 2012, Dossani and Kenney 2007, 2009, World Bank 2007), with India distinguishing itself in the domain of IT-intensive services and the Philippines excelling in contact services. Other countries and cities in the region join in too, however, and are busy carving out their niches in this emergent global services production landscape. Malaysia takes part (Brooker 2011), China, in an attempt to diversify away from manufacturing, seeks to hook up (Freeman 2005, Zhang in this volume), Hong Kong is establishing itself as the region's foremost centre for merchanting and merchandising services (Sigler and Zhao in this volume) and Bangkok slowly emerges as a hub for Japanese contact services (Lambregts in this volume). The scene in the region is evolving rapidly. What started as a relatively straightforward cost–benefit seeking production relocation process with mostly western firms in various roles guiding the process, has gradually turned into something much more intricate. The industry still expands, but also matures and seeks for ever more efficient allocation of resources throughout the region. In result, more refined divisions of labour and more complex production networks emerge, increasingly also between and among South and Southeast Asian countries. Here, local actors gradually gain confidence and begin to assume increasingly important roles. Indian IT consulting and outsourcing firms such as Infosys, Wipro and Tata Consultancy Services, for instance, are already seen transforming into multinationals with production networks extending into both the Global North and into the wider Asian region (Beerepoot *et al.* 2014). These new developments, moreover, are superimposed on and interfere with the still evolving outcomes of the global shift in manufacturing production, which has worked to integrate (much of) the region in the global economy from the 1960s onwards (Ofreneo in this volume). By focusing explicitly on South and Southeast Asia, a regional hotspot for offshore services production, we are able to point out differences and similarities between countries as they engage with this latest wave of globalization and also reveal emerging divisions of labour and interdependencies between them.

Aims

The book's aims, finally, are threefold. First, it draws attention to this yet under-researched dimension of the global services offshoring trend: the outcomes it generates in the receiving locations, i.e. the countries and cities to where services production is moved to. The book portrays the opportunities created for local economies and their key actors, explores the factors that condition developments and touches upon the potential threats associated with the trend. Original empirical illustrations are provided and most chapters are based on recent empirical research and as such make state-of-the-art contributions to the debate. The book's second aim is to assess how the outcomes of this latest wave of globalization are helping to rebalance relationships at the regional and global levels. With new(er) divisions of labour emerging between countries in South and Southeast Asia and between these countries and other parts of the world, with local markets maturing, and with local economic and political confidence growing, power configurations in global and regional production networks are bound to change. Those involved are likely to be affected in various ways, as revealed by the empirical illustrations provided in many of the chapters. The book's third aim is to investigate the implications of the above for theories of economic development. In particular, the book examines the extent to which we are seeing evidence of a services-based development trajectory emerging as a real possibility. The road to development for developing countries conventionally has been thought to 'compulsory' run via industrialization (see Dicken 2011, Fröbel *et al.* 1980), but the stormy rise of especially India and the Philippines as exporters of services poses a challenge to this idea and raises the question whether services-led development may be a viable alternative trajectory of socioeconomic modernization (see also Rodrik 2014). By investigating different pathways of services sector development and by scrutinizing how services offshoring empowers (in terms of finance and skill development) the workers involved and affects local economies we hope to provide the beginning of an answer or at least some starting points for further scholarly debate.

Overview of the book

The above questions are explored in 13 chapters grouped in four parts. Part I essentially sets the scene. It presents a broader framework for the analysis of the role of services in development and looks into the ways the offshore services sector has developed in India and the Philippines.

In Chapter 2, Robert C. Kloosterman, Niels Beerepoot and Bart Lambregts position the rise of services in developing countries in a historical perspective and assess to what extent these activities can indeed generate sustained growth. Initially, the contribution of services to economic development was considered to be small as only manufacturing was seen as being capable of delivering sustained growth in productivity. However, since the second unbundling in the 1990s (Baldwin 2006), advances in ICT and policies of liberalization have enabled digitized services to be carved up into separate operations that can be commodified and, subsequently, traded across the globe. This has introduced greater opportunities for making productivity gains in services production and led to greater recognition of its role as a driver of economic growth as elaborated on in the subsequent chapters.

Jana Kleibert in Chapter 3 takes up the ambitious task to compare the emergence and evolution of the ITES-BPO sector of India and the Philippines. Basing her work on interviews and secondary literature she discusses the role of government policies, the education system, business associations, foreign investors, domestic firms and returnee migrants. She shows that India should not be seen as ahead of the Philippines in a singular development or pathway, but that important differences in the availability of local assets and differences in opportunity structures have led the two countries to get integrated into global services production networks in essentially different ways. While India managed to develop large domestic-owned firms in IT services, the Philippines' offshore service sector so far has remained dominated by foreign investors delivering voice-based services, which has consequences for the degree to which the countries are able to capture the gains of ITES-BPO growth.

In Chapter 4, Antoinette R. Raquiza looks into the rise of the ITES-BPO sector in the Philippines in more detail. She shows how over the past decade the arrival and subsequent boom of the ITES-BPO industry has invigorated the Philippine economy and led to a surge in the country's trade in services. The chapter argues that the proximate factors that have distinguished the Philippines as among the world's top offshore destinations for BPOs – notably, a large English-speaking, skilled work force have also promoted the export of labour – a situation producing contradictory currents in the domestic labour market. By applying a political economy approach that highlights the interactions between economic powers and state institutions in the country, Raquiza raises critical concerns about the long-term prospects of the Philippines' current growth trajectory.

When discussing the economic benefits of ITES-BPO growth and addressing the question how local embeddedness of foreign firms in this sector can be enhanced, valuable lessons can be learned from the analysis of inter-organizational linkages of Japanese multinational firms in the Philippines provided by Chie Iguchi. In Chapter 5 she demonstrates how subsidiaries of Japanese firms in the Philippines hardly maintain local input–output relations with local Filipino owned-firms. This reduces the opportunities for knowledge spillovers and increases the chance that production, once the Philippines becomes too expensive or otherwise unattractive as a production site, relocates. The chapter brings together the literatures on national innovation systems (NIS) and global value chains and should stimulate discussion on the roles of multinational company subsidiaries in an NIS.

Part II looks beyond India and the Philippines and investigates how elsewhere in the region export oriented services are produced and to what effect. As emphasized by Xu Zhang (in Chapter 6), the success of India and the Philippines in services exports has generated interest among other countries in Asia for the opportunities provided by the trade. Xu Zhang examines how the Pearl River Delta (PRD) in China aims to transform itself from the 'Workshop of the World' to the 'Office of the World'. He shows that many PRD cities' current service development strategies and programmes still rely heavily on experiences accumulated in the industrialization period. These tend to overlook the unique features of business service activities as well as the assets that individual cities dispose of. Zhang argues that more targeted and place-based service development strategies and policies are needed for cities in China, and warns that the options and measures available to local governments in building the 'Office of the World' may be more limited than they seem to think.

Next in Chapter 7, Thomas Sigler and Simon Zhou focus on Hong Kong's vital role in the global economy as an intermediary connecting China to the world at large. The authors neatly show how since the territory's decline in manufacturing in the 1980s, Hong Kong's economic growth has been driven by service exports – primarily trade-related, transport and advanced business services – and then focus on two related activities – merchanting and merchandizing – that have overtaken Hong Kong's entrepôt role since approximately 2007. Findings indicate that these services offer limited employment opportunities and primarily serve to reinforce historically dependent trade networks that benefit the upper echelons of the value chain.

Bart Lambregts, in Chapter 8, examines the rise of a small but interesting concentration of Japanese call centre activities in Bangkok, Thailand. The conditions for non-English-speaking economies such as Japan and Thailand to engage in services offshoring are more challenging than for English-speaking nations. The limited availability of Japanese language skills abroad, for instance, seriously restricts opportunities for Japanese firms to offshore voice-based services. Japanese firms negotiate this condition by offshoring voice-based services to low-cost destinations and by hiring Japanese staff at local wages. Bangkok, a city that otherwise has remained relatively untouched by the services offshoring wave, is such a destination. The chapter explores both the firms' strategies and the motives of the Japanese workers filling the cubicles.

Part III concentrates on workers engaged in the next wave of globalization and how transformations in labour markets impact on their position and bargaining power. The ITES-BPO sector is considered to provide the much-preferred white-collar jobs for an increasingly college-educated labour force but it is criticized for providing employment to only a narrow segment of workers.

Rene Ofreneo, in Chapter 9, argues that many workers in Asia have not benefited from recent and current economic growth. These include workers in Asia's huge informal economy and in domestic-oriented industries. He uses the metaphors 'Factory Asia' and 'Service Asia' to describe how Asian countries have become integrated in global production networks of industrial and services production. Taking a union perspective, he critically observes how in both cases large segments of the labour force have remained excluded and that those who do work in export-oriented production are increasingly confronted with flexibilization and contractualization of work. According to Ofreneo, optimistic projections by international agencies about the shift in economic power towards Asia and the emergence of a so-called new middle class ignore how in various Asian countries growth is uneven and exclusionary, and in many cases takes place at the expense of labour rights.

In Chapter 10, Leian Marasigan uses the concept of employability to examine the employment and job search experiences of former ITES-BPO workers in Metro Manila. She finds that the knowledge, skills and other experiences gained during employment in the ITES-BPO sector are not always recognized in the tight local labour market that exists outside the ITES-BPO sector. Many workers also appear to view BPO work as short-term job experience (a 'transition stage') rather than as a serious career. The chapter argues for a more nuanced view of workers' employment prospects post-BPO and lends support to the view that contextual conditions are important factors influencing employability and the longer-term prospects of those working in the ITES-BPO sector.

Randhir Kumar in Chapter 11 shows how in Mumbai the growth of the ITES-BPO sector affects those involved in support services. More sophisticated demand from ITES-BPO companies for support services such as security have changed both the characteristics of what are traditionally regarded as low-end services and the industry that delivers them. The emergence of multinational corporations in low-end service production intensifies competition and makes it harder for local firms to partake in the profitable market segment provided by ITES-BPO firms.

Part IV for the book focuses on the wider societal implications of the growth of the ITES-BPO sector, in particular by raising the question whether it adds to the formation of a new middle class in the countries and cities concerned. The rise of the ITES-BPO sector is commonly associated with the emergence of a new consumerist force. Neeraj Hatekar and Kishore More in Chapter 12 show how the middle class in India has substantially expanded in the early 2000s. At least 600 million Indians are now considered middle class, and are spending substantially more on education, health, consumer services and durables than they did earlier. In overall terms, the ITES-BPO sector, although often regarded as a main driver of new middle-class formation, adds only marginally to this major transformation in the Indian society. However, at local level the new spending power of ITES-BPO workers can incite major transformations. As demonstrated by Sandhya Krishnan in her research on ITES-BPO workers in Mumbai, in Chapter 13, as well as Niels Beerepoot and Emeline Vogelzang who focus on a smaller provincial town in the Philippines, in Chapter 14, the development of a consumerist culture is part and parcel of employment in this sector. Employees in the ITES-BPO industry in Mumbai have experienced several changes in their consumption practices. Many report to have become more brand conscious and to have developed a taste for new cuisines and more luxurious modes of transport. The chapter shows that the new middle class produced by the ITES-BPO industry should rather be seen as a privileged section within the middle class itself and identified by its new and expensive forms of consumption. Beerepoot and Vogelzang in turn show how the ITES-BPO sector is expanding to smaller provincial towns in the Philippines. These cities essentially skip the industrial stage of development and instead become part of global services production networks. The new employment opportunities generated by the sector, however, seem to be to the direct advantage of a selective group of workers only.

The book ends with an effort by the editors to pull together the key messages emerging from all this work and to identify avenues for future research.

References

Ahmed, G., 2013. Global value chains, economic upgrading, and gender in the call centre industry. In: C. Saritz and J.G. Reis (eds). *Global Value Chains, Economic Upgrading, and Gender. Case Studies of the Horticulture, Tourism, and Call Center Industries.* Washington, DC: World Bank, 73–106.

Amante, M.S., 2010. Offshored work in Philippine BPOs. In: J.C. Messenger and N. Ghosheh (eds). *Offshoring and Working Conditions in Remote Work.* Geneva: International Labour Organization, 101–134.

Asian Development Bank, 2011. *Asia 2050: Realizing the Asian Century.* Mandaluyong City: ADB.

Asian Development Bank, 2012. *Asian Development Outlook 2012 Update. Services and Asia's Future Growth.* Mandaluyong City: ADB.

Baldwin, R.E., 2006. Multilateralising regionalism: spaghetti bowls as building blocks on the path to global free trade. *The World Economy*, 29 (11), 1451–1518.

Bardhan, A., Kroll, C.A. and Jaffee, D.M. (eds) 2013. *The Oxford Handbook of Offshoring and Global Employment.* Oxford: Oxford University Press.

Bäumer, U., Kreutter, P. and Messner, W. (eds) 2012. *Globalization of Professional Services – Innovative Strategies, Successful Processes, Inspired Talent Management, and First-Hand Experiences.* Berlin: Springer.

Beerepoot, N., 2010. Globalisation and the reworking of labour market segmentation in the Philippines. In: A.C. Bergene, S.B. Endresen and H.M. Knutsen (eds). *Missing Links in Labour Geography: The dynamics of economic space.* Aldershot: Ashgate, 199–210.

Beerepoot, N. and Hendriks, M., 2013. Employability of offshore service sector workers in the Philippines: Opportunities for upward labour mobility or dead-end jobs? *Work, Employment and Society,* 27 (5), 823–841.

Beerepoot, N. and Keijser, C., 2014. The service outsourcing sector as driver of development: The expectations of Ghana's ICT for accelerated development programme. *Tijdschrift voor Economische en Sociale Geografie*, DOI: 10.1111/tesg.12122.

Beerepoot, N., Roodheuvel, I. and Jacobs, F., 2014. *Integration of Indian Service Providers in the Dutch Outsourcing Market.* Amsterdam: Report for Platform Outsourcing Nederland, Amsterdam Institute for Social Science Research.

Benner, C., 2006. 'South Africa on-call': Information technology and labour market restructuring in South African call centres. *Regional Studies,* 40 (9), 1025–1040.

Berry, J., 2005. *Offshoring Opportunities: Strategies and Tactics for Global Competitiveness*. Hoboken, NJ: Wiley.

Blinder, A.S., 2006. Offshoring: the next industrial revolution? *Foreign Affairs*, 85 (2), 113–128.

Blinder, A.S., 2009. How many U.S. jobs might be offshorable? *World Economics*, 10 (2), 41–78.

Breznitz, D. and Zysman, J., 2013. *The Third Globalization. Can Wealthy Countries Stay Rich in the Twenty-First Century?* Oxford and New York: Oxford University Press.

Brooker, D., 2011. Servicing a world elsewhere? Examining everyday work practices in the emerging economic spaces of Malaysia's business process outsourcing industry. *Singapore Journal of Tropical Geography,* 32 (2), 141–154.

Brown, D. and Wilson, S., 2005. *The Black Book of Outsourcing: How to Manage the Changes, Challenges, and Opportunities*. Hoboken, NJ: Wiley.

Bryson, J., 2007. The second global shift: the offshoring or global sourcing of corporate services and the rise of distanciated emotional labour. *Geografiska Annaler*, 89B, pp. 31–43.

Bunyaratavej, K., Doh, J., Hahn, E.D., Lewin, A.Y. and Massini, S., 2011. Conceptual issues in services offshoring research: A multidisciplinary review. *Group and Organisational Management.* 36 (1), 70–102.

Coe, N.M., Dicken, P. and Hess, M., 2008. Global production networks: Realizing the potential. *Journal of Economic Geography.* 8 (3), 271–295.

Coe, N.M., Hess, M., Yeung, H.W., Dicken, P. and Henderson, J., 2004. 'Globalizing' regional development: A global production networks perspective. *Transactions of the Institute of British Geographers.* 29 (4), 468–484.

Couto, V., Mani, M., Seghal, V., Lewin, A., Manning, S. and Russel, J., 2007. *Offshoring 2.0: Contracting Knowledge and Innovation to Expand Global Capabilities.* Durham: Duke University CIBER/Booz Allen Hamilton Report.

Dicken, P., 2011. *Global Shift: Mapping the Changing Contours of the World Economy*. 6th edition. London: SAGE Publications.

Dossani, R. and Kenney, M., 2007. The next wave of globalization: Relocating service provision to India. *World Development*, 35 (5), 772–791.

Dossani, R. and Kenney, M., 2009. Service provision for the global economy: The evolving India story. *Review of Policy Research*, 26 (1–2), 77–104.

Eltschinger, C., 2007. *Source Code China: The New Global Hub of IT Information Technology Outsourcing*. Hoboken, NJ: Wiley.

Fernandez-Stark, K., Bamber, P. and Gereffi, G., 2010. *Workforce Development in Chile's Offshore Services Value Chain*. Center on Globalization, Governance and Competitiveness. Durham, NC: Duke University.

Fernandez-Stark, K., Hernández, R.A., Mulder, N. and Sauvé, P., 2014. Introduction. In: R. A. Hernández, N. Mulder, K. Fernandez-Stark, P. Sauvé, D. López Giral and F. Muñoz Navia, (eds). *Latin America's Emergence in Global Services. A new driver of structural change in the region?* Santiago, Chile: United Nations publication, 13–37.

Freeman, R., 2005. *Does Globalization of the Scientific/engineering Workforce Threaten US Economic Leadership?* NBER working paper 11457, June.

Fröbel, F., Heinrichs, J. and Kreye, O., 1980. *The New International Division of Labour.* Cambridge: Cambridge University Press.

Fuller, C.J. and Narasimhan, H., 2007. Information technology professionals and the new-rich middle class in Chennai Madras. *Modern Asian Studies,* 41 (1), 121–150.

Gereffi, G. and Fernandez-Stark, K., 2010. *The Offshore Services Global Value Chain.* North Carolina: CORFO-Report, Center on Globalization, Governance and Competitiveness. Durham, NC: Duke University.

Ghani, E. and O'Connell, S.D., 2014. *Can Service Be a Growth Escalator in Low Income Countries?* World Bank Policy Research Working Paper 6971, Washington, DC: World Bank.

Graham, M. and Mann, L., 2013. Imagining a silicon savannah? Technological and conceptual connectivity in Kenya's BPO and software development sectors. *The Electronic Journal of Information Systems in Developing Countries*, 56 (2), 1–19.

IBPAP (IT and Business Processing Association of the Philippines), 2012. *2012–2016 Philippine Information Technology and Business Process Management IT-BPM Roadmap*. Makati City: IT and Business Processing Association of the Philippines.

James, A. and Vira, B., 2012. Labour geographies of India's new service economy. *Journal of Economic Geography*, 12 (4), 841–875.

Kleibert, J.M., 2014. Strategic coupling in 'next-wave cities': Local institutional actors and the offshore service sector in the Philippines. *Singapore Journal of Tropical Geography*, 35 (2), 245–260.

Kleibert, J.M., 2015. Industry-academe linkages in the Philippines: Embedding foreign investors, capturing institutions? *Geoforum*, 59 (2), 109–118.

Kobayashi-Hillary, M. (ed.) 2008. *Building a Future with BRICs. The Next Decade for Offshoring*. Berlin: Springer.

Levy, F. and Murnane R.J., 2005. *The New Division of Labor: How Computers Are Creating the Next Job Market.* Princeton: Princeton University Press.

MacKinnon, D., 2012. Beyond strategic coupling: Reassessing the firm-region nexus in global production networks. *Journal of Economic Geography,* 12 (1), 227–245.

Massini, S. and Miozzo, M., 2012. Outsourcing and offshoring of business services: Challenges to theory, management and geography of innovation. *Regional Studies*, 46 (9), 1219–1242.

Metters, R. and Verma, R., 2008. The history of offshoring knowledge services. *Journal of Operations Management,* 26, 141–147.

Milberg, W. and Winkler, D., 2013. *Outsourcing Economics: Global Value Chains in Capitalist Development*. Cambridge: Cambridge University Press.

Murphy, J., 2011. Indian call centre workers: Vanguard of a global middle class? *Work, Employment and Society*, 25 (3), 417–433.

NASSCOM (National Association of Software and Services Companies), 2014. *The IT-BPM Sector in India, Strategic Review 2014*, New Delhi: NASSCOM.

Ofreneo, R.E., Ng, C. and Marasigan-Pasumbal, L., 2007. Voice for the voice workers: Addressing the IR concerns in the call center/BPO industry of Asia. *Indian Journal of Industrial Relations,* 42 (4), 534–557.

Rodrik, D., 2014. October 13. Are services the new manufactures? Online: www.project-syndicate.org/commentary/are-services-the-new-manufactures-by-dani-rodrik-2014-10

Rubalcaba, L., 2007. *The New Service Economy: Challenges and Policy Implications for Europe*. Cheltenham: Edward Elgar.

Taylor, P. and Bain, P., 2005. India calling to the far away towns. *Work, Employment and Society*, 19, 261–282.

Tholons, 2014. *2014 Tholons Top 100 Outsourcing Destinations: Regional Overview*. Online: www.tholons.com/TholonsTop100/pdf/Tholons_Top_100_2014_Rankings_and_Report_Overview.pdf

UNCTAD (United Nations Conference on Trade and Development), 2005. *World investment Report: The shift Towards Services*. New York: United Nations Conference on Trade and Development.

UNESCAP (United Nations Economic and Social Commission for Asia and the Pacific), 2011. *Asia-Pacific Trade and Investment Report 2011. Post-crisis trade and investment opportunities*. New York: United Nations Economic and Social Commission for Asia and the Pacific.

World Bank, 2007. *Global Economic Prospects: Managing the Next Wave in Globalization*. Washington, DC: The World Bank

World Bank, 2009. *World Development Report 2009: Reshaping Economic Geography*. Washington, DC: The World Bank.

World Bank, 2011. *Global Development Horizons 2011. Multipolarity: The New Global Economy*. Washington, DC: The World Bank.

World Bank, 2012. *Exporting Services: A Developing Country Perspective*. Washington, DC: The World Bank.

World Bank, 2013. *Philippine Economic Update: Accelerating Reforms to Meet the Job Challenge*. World Bank: Poverty Reduction and Economic Management Unit East Asia and Pacific Region. Online: www.worldbank.org/content/dam/Worldbank/document/EAP/Philippines/Philippine_Economic_Update_May2013.pdf.

Part I

The latest wave in globalization

Long-term and comparative perspectives

2 Service-sector driven economic development from a historical perspective

Robert C. Kloosterman, Niels Beerepoot and Bart Lambregts

Introduction

The people working in the financial services in London, Singapore, Hong Kong and other global cities; the software specialists in Silicon Valley, Bangalore and Taipei; the designers in Milan, Seoul, Taipei and Eindhoven; but also the workers in the call centres and back offices in Mumbai and Manila staring at their screens and talking to customers in another continent and a different time zone: they all are part of a brave new, interconnected world of service activities. Services have become increasingly digitised, commodified and tradable due to advances in ICT (Eichengreen and Gupta 2011). They also are increasingly *unbundled*: carved up into separate operations, which can, in principle, take place in different locations. These locations are obviously not limited to the developed countries and a whole array of globally competitive service activities – from call centres to accounting and from bookkeeping to x-ray reading – can now be found in what used to be called developing countries. Even more striking is the fact that these export-oriented service activities have evolved rather independently from manufacturing activities. This in itself can be considered as a break with documented historical developmental trajectories (Elfring 1988, Kuznets 1973), where significant growth of these services only occurred after industrialisation had run its course from low-skilled (e.g. textiles, garment) to higher-skilled types of manufacturing (e.g. cars, electronics).

Are we, then, witnessing a more fundamental departure from established models of economic development that are based on a sectoral sequence in time: from a dominance of agriculture to manufacturing, and, eventually, to services as the largest employer? Do services offer a new promising avenue of sustained economic growth for developing countries? Are we, in other words, able to, more or less, skip the manufacturing phase and move straight from an economy dominated by agriculture to one by service activities? These questions have already been looked at by several scholars and they have come up with quite different answers (Dossani and Kenney 2007, Eichengreen and Gupta 2011, Ghani and O'Connell 2014, Rodrik 2014, Kleibert 2015).

The aim of this chapter is to put the service-led developmental trajectories into a broader historical perspective and, subsequently, identify some of the key issues at stake. First, a more general view of the current phase of global capitalism is offered. We then go back in time and have closer look at historical trajectories of development based on industrialisation. After that, we turn to the offshoring of services to developing countries. Finally, we discuss services as a possible course of economic development in the current phase of global capitalism.

A new phase in global capitalism

According to Allen Scott (2008, 2012), we have entered a new phase of capitalism. This new phase of what he calls *cognitive-cultural capitalism* can be characterised by looking at two key dimensions. First, we can observe a fundamental shift in the production system of advanced economies towards cognitive-cultural activities that depend on the input of highly skilled labour. These activities comprise high-tech (e.g. software, life sciences), high-control/coordination (e.g. headquarters of transnational corporations and business and financial services) and high-concept (e.g. cultural and creative industries) activities (Scott 2008, 2012). Related to this shift is the move away from standardised mass production and the emergence of an ever-more varied landscape of products (goods and services) that do not just compete on price but also on features such as aesthetic qualities and, for instance, (after-sales) service. Engaging in these kinds of production requires ever-more service activities to provide specialised knowledge, finance, insurance, advertising, logistics and information. The growth of employment in these so-called *transactional activities* has, accordingly, outstripped that in manufacturing or *transformational activities* in advanced economies in the past decades (Kay 2004: 361).

The second change concerns the changes in the global division of labour. The high-end cognitive-cultural activities are certainly not limited to advanced economies in North-America, Europe and the Southern hemisphere – we can nowadays also find them in China, India, Latin America and parts of Africa. The core-periphery pattern – which emerged in the sixteenth century (Frank 1978, Wallerstein 1979) and characterised by core countries (at first countries as Spain, Portugal and later the Dutch Republic, France and especially England and later on, in the twentieth century, the United States) engaged in high-value added production and peripheral countries providing raw materials and foodstuffs (Kay 2004: 275) – has transformed into a much wider and more complex 'global mosaic' of large metropolitan regions (Scott 2012: 60). These so-called global city-regions, home to the leading sectors of the emerging cognitive-cultural economy, also constitute strategic nodes in global networks, interconnected through flows of goods, services, money, knowledge and, of course, people (Taylor *et al.* 2014). A whole array of different (global) city rankings exist, whatever their differences they tend to agree on the top-dogs (New York, London, Tokyo, Hong Kong, Singapore, Shanghai) as well as on the growing importance of especially Asian cities as global players (www.globalsherpa.org/world-rankings).

It is obviously hard to disentangle the web of causal factors behind this sea change in the world economy, but two interrelated factors can be singled out, namely technological change – notably in information and communication technology (ICT) – and neoliberal policies of deregulation opening up hitherto more or less closed economies to the wider world (Baldwin 2011, Dicken 2011, Frieden 2006, Scott 2012). Because of digitisation, large batches of information can be stored, processed, manipulated and also transmitted across the globe almost instantly (Dicken 2011: 80). The ICT revolution has fundamentally changed the production system by making new ways of production as well as new products possible. The shift to cognitive-cultural economy with its emphasis on knowledge-intensive activities and ditto products and its vertically disintegrated production processes would not have been possible without ICT. The same can be said with respect to the unbundling of production. In the phase of the *first unbundling*, the value chain of transformational activities was split up into the extraction of raw materials, production and consumption. This process accelerated during the Industrial Revolution when the introduction of railroads and steamships made an ever-wider spatial separation of these phases possible (Baldwin 2011). After 1995, the phase of the *second unbundling* started as ICT made it not just increasingly economical to geographically separate manufacturing stages (Baldwin 2011: 8), but also enabled to carve up transactional activities or services into separate operations (Eichengreen and Gupta 2011).

The advances in ICT on their own, however, were not sufficient 'to confront entrenched ideologies, political positions and interests' (Frieden 2006: 397). What was needed as well was a breaking down of all kinds of barriers that hampered international economic integration. The neoliberal wave, which first swept the United States and the United Kingdom in the 1980s, eventually became a more or less global phenomenon as many governments both in the developed and in the developing countries – out of their own free will or forced under the Washington Consensus embarked on programmes of liberalisation, deregulation and privatisation. In many developing countries (mostly in Asia and to a lesser extent in Central America (Dicken 2011: 193), the neoliberal turn was spatially confined to export processing zones or special economic zones to attract foreign direct investment by offering spaces with low taxes, relatively lax regulation regarding labour and the environment (Dicken 2011). These spaces come in a different number of forms: coastal zones, seaports, commercial zones close to cities (Dicken 2011: 193), and even 'service-based special economic zones (SEZs) in the central business districts of Metro Manila', which form 'islands of globalisation' within the metropolis and combine global production with consumption features' (Kleibert 2015: 45).

Whatever the spatial expression of the various neoliberal policies pursued after 1980, together with the spread of ICT, the opening up of potential production locations in developed and developing countries across the globe created the conditions for the emergence of a fine-grained spatial division of labour as part of a complex mosaic of global city-regions (Scott 2012: 60). The evolving global mosaic in its turn encouraged both further advances in ICT and new rounds of liberalisation. To an increasing extent, firms, wherever located, are confronted with opportunities as well as competitors across the globe. This is in marked contrast to the first phase of industrialisation at the end of the eighteenth century, when English manufacturing firms were essentially without real competitors.

The Industrial Revolution

The causes of the Industrial Revolution in Britain are still being hotly debated (Acemoglu and Robinson 2012, Clark 2007, 2012, Landes 1998, Vries 2003). According to the historian Gregory Clark (2007: 231), 'the seemingly abrupt escape of this tiny island nation, within less than one generation, from millennia of pitifully slow economic progress-is one of history's great mysteries'. More recently, the debate on the causes has been framed in a rather different way as comparisons with China in the eighteenth century (and now also with India and the Ottoman Empire) – which did not industrialise at that time – has forced a reconsideration of a whole array of explanations (Jacques 2012, Landes 1998, Pomeranz 2009, Vries 2013). What still stands out is the state of technology and science in Britain, an openness towards innovations and innovators, the pre-eminence of individual identity over group identity, mercantilist policies benefiting traders and manufacturers, a refined fabric of financial institutions (a national bank, chartered companies) and a particular geographical endowment (accessible coal resources), whereas more Smithian arguments that stress the importance of large free markets have lost much of their appeal, as China appears to have had larger markets which were at least as free as in Britain (Clark 2007, Vries 2003: 57–63).

Whatever were the causes of Britain's Industrial Revolution, there is a broad consensus of its essential features. To start with, there was a cluster of interrelated technological changes with the substitution of machines for human skill, the substitution of inanimate for animate sources of power (i.e. the steam engine) and the use of new, abundant raw materials such as coal (Landes 1998: 186). These technological changes in the production system yielded not just a steep rise in productivity, but also laid the basis for sustained growth (Landes 1998). After Britain, other European countries followed suit: first, Belgium, benefiting from its rich coal resources and British entrepreneurs such as Cockerill (Landes 1998), France and subsequently Germany. With each new round, followers faced a different configuration with more competitors and they had adjust their policies and strategies to deal with these established competitors. Germany, for instance, protected its infant industries behind high trade barriers and created a comprehensive educational system that fostered scientific advances enabling firms to compete more on the basis of innovation.

The United States, the first non-European country to industrialise, initially relied on British technology and knowledge, but quite soon found its own path of development based on standardisation and mass production as it had faced a rather different situation with a huge domestic market and a scarcity of skilled labour (Landes 1998). This culminated in the Fordist production system of the twentieth century. Just as in Germany, American firms were protected by high tariff walls. The only non-Western country experiencing an industrial revolution in the nineteenth century was Japan. After the Meiji Restoration in 1868, the Japanese embarked on conscious policy of industrialisation. According to Martin Jacques (2012: 65) 'Japan was the world's first example of reactive modernisation: a modernity necessitated by Western power and pre-eminence'. The German example of creating a solid scientific base was followed and Japan closed the gap to the technological frontier very rapidly (Landes 1998).

At the beginning of the twentieth century, there were a few countries who had become industrial societies. The fundamental breakthrough of sustained economic growth created not just a whole new type of society with industrial capitalists and a working class, but also changed the balance of power on a global scale. The global division of labour between core countries exporting manufacturing products and peripheral countries supplying raw materials was significantly strengthened as first Britain and subsequently other European countries industrialised. This was not just a matter of comparative advantage, but also of conscious policies on behalf of the core countries – some of them strong colonial powers – to prevent peripheral parts of the world to follow the model pioneered by Britain (Jacques 2012: 48). As a result, other parts of the world were left far behind in terms of economic growth, share of the global economy and political and military power, thereby contributing to a further strengthening of the core–periphery model.

Given this configuration, 'spontaneous industrialisation' became ever less likely and governments outside the core had to intervene to industrialise. An extreme example of state intervention was the Soviet Union with its top-down detailed five-year plans to launch a forced autarkic industrialisation. Not just tariff walls but state-led enormous investments in industry, to a large part funded by (also in a literal sense) starving the agricultural sector, to create an industrial society. At first, the Soviet model seemed a 'stunning success' in sheer quantitative output terms and the country industrialised very rapidly in about a decade between 1928 and 1937 (Frieden 2006: 219). The human and environmental costs, however, were also staggering with millions starved to death or executed. Notwithstanding these huge costs, the Soviet model with its five-year plans proved to be attractive to many developing countries.

After the Second World War and its wake a global wave of decolonisation, many developing countries, partly inspired by the Soviet model, 'closed themselves to foreign trade and pursued rapid industrialisation' (Frieden 2006: 302, Scott 2012: 53). Adopting *dirigiste* policies of import-substituting industrialisation or ISI started in Latin America and were later on followed by many Asian countries including Taiwan, South Korea, India, Thailand, Indonesia and Malaysia. ISI was aimed at building comprehensive domestic supply chains, as it was assumed that a broad and deep industrial base was needed to become globally competitive (Baldwin 2011: 4). ISI was usually backed by a coalition of industrialists, industrial labour, government employees, the army and left-wing oriented intellectuals who emphasised the anti-imperialist element (Frieden 2006: 302). ISI consisted of high barriers to trade, subsidies and incentives to the domestic industry, manipulation of the exchange rate to provide cheap money to manufacturers, foreign loans and nationalisation of much of the infrastructure.

The results of ISI were at first impressive, as many countries experienced a rapid expansion of their manufacturing sector and, hence, strong economic growth (Frieden 2006: 317). They indeed 'jump-started' economic development (Dicken 2011: 190). In the 1970s, however, ISI ran into difficulties. Typically, firms, protected high barriers and an overvalued currency and the limited size of the domestic market, were not able to compete on world markets (Scott 2012). Countries faced problems in paying for the loans to fund continual capital investment, the imports of raw materials, machinery and spare parts through exports (Frieden 2006: 351). They were then 'caught in a vicious circle of balance of payments deficits, inflation, and recession' (Frieden 2006: 352). Still, ISI turned out to be quite tenacious as it was supported by political coalitions consisting of the army, government officials, local capitalists and trade unions (Dicken 2011, Frieden 2006: 318–319).

Smaller Asian countries – notably Singapore, Taiwan and South Korea – abandoned ISI policies and changed tack and instead started to adopt export-oriented industrialisation or EOI (Dicken 2011, Frieden 2006, Scott 2012). The basis for this policy was, obviously, a cheap, adaptable and docile labour force to be able to compete on world markets. The introduction of EOI was, however, also related to more fundamental changes in the global economy (Dicken 2011: 191). The already mentioned liberalisation of world trade after 1980, and the shrinkage of geographical distance through ICT and the introduction of the container ushered in the phase of the *second unbundling*, which meant that TNC could carve up supply chains in many separate parts and locate the production of these parts in new industrial spaces (often export processing zones) with low wages and low levels of regulation (Scott 2012). As Baldwin (2011: 4) states 'Today, nations can industrialise by joining a supply chain – there is no need to build a supply chain'. Joining an existing supply chain has turned out to be much easier and has boosted economic growth notably in Asian countries, but also in Latin America and former communist countries. Increasingly, it is not just manufacturing activities that are (re-)located to developing countries, but also an array of service activities. In *A World in Emergence*, an overarching analysis of the contemporary global economy and its building blocks, Allen Scott (2012: 58–59) paints a clear picture of linkages that are characteristic of the *second unbundling* phase:

> Today, an enormous diversity of products at different levels of design and performance complexity … move through subcontracting relations embedded in global production networks. Even service firms in the Global North increasingly subcontract-out batches of work, including software programming, to firms in the Global South … Other examples are the subcontracting of business services from Western Europe to producers in Eastern and Central Europe … and (at the lower end of the skills spectrum) call center operations to the Caribbean, India, the Philippines, and other part of the world periphery.

Services as distinctive path to economic development

The offshoring of services is, compared to that in manufacturing, a rather recent phenomenon. Initially, many took the view that services could only expand in so-called mature economies, which means after manufacturing had fully developed

(Elfring 1988, Ghani and O'Connell 2014). It seemed as if a positive correlation existed between gross domestic product (GDP) per capita and the relative size of the service sector (Eichengreen and Gupta 2011). In addition, it was assumed that services displayed only limited degrees of freedom with respect to their location. Not just personal services, say hairdressing or house cleaning, which can only take place in proximity to the customer, but also business services were seen as activities that could only take place close to their customers. In the latter case, the exchange of information was either through face-to-face meetings or on paper. The digitisation, splitting-up and subsequent commodification, however, have made relocation and even offshoring of a wide variety of service tasks hallmarks of the second unbundling phase. Especially, the so-called 'second wave of modern (financial, communication, computer, technical, legal, advertising and business) services that are receptive to the application of information technologies' can be offshored (Eichengreen and Gupta 2009: 5).

In the more traditional view services were not just seen as largely untradeable, it was also taken for granted that the growth of labour productivity in services would be too low (Baumol's cost disease) to allow for significant economic development. The focus, then, was on manufacturing in which sustained significant productivity gains were possible. Economic development, which hinges on the sustained growth of labour productivity, could, hence, only come from manufacturing – at least in the earlier stages of economic development (Ghani and O'Connell 2014). Services may be not so much as parasitic as dependent on and subsequent to manufacturing. The logical consequence of this view is, of course, that only industrialisation can provide an economic take-off and offer a solid base for further economic growth.

Already before the proper introduction of ICT, doubts were raised with respect to the validity of Baumol's cost disease for at least some (business) service activities (cf. Elfring 1988). Digitisation, however, fundamentally changed the picture by greatly enhancing the scope for productivity growth in services (Eichengreen and Gupta 2011, Wölfl 2005). This does not hold for more traditional services, such as personal services, restaurants and hotels, which are rather resistant to digitisation and show only modest growth of productivity (if at all). The *second-wave services* of financial, communication, computer, technical, legal, advertising and business services, however, are very much at the heart of processes of digitisation and have displayed 'growth rates comparable to those of some high-growth industries within manufacturing' (Ghani and O'Connell 2014: 5).

In their report for the World Bank, *Can Service be a Growth Escalator in Low Income Countries?*, Ejaz Ghani and Stephen O'Connell (2014) present an empirical analysis of the role of services in less-developed or low-income countries. Their findings are clearly at odds with the long-held view of services. First, they found that services are the fastest growing component of world trade. Second, the average growth of service exports from developing countries has exceeded that of advanced countries in last two decades. Third, services contribute more to GDP growth than manufacturing in many developing countries. Fourth, labour productivity growth in services in developing countries has not just accelerated but also outstripped productivity growth in the industrial sector.

We can thus observe the actual expansion of the service sector in countries with not just relatively low levels of GDP, but which also have a relatively small manufacturing sector (Dossani and Kenney 2007). It seems, then, that a particular segment of the service sector – the second wave activities – do indeed offer a distinct path to sustained economic growth for less-developed countries. Apparently, conditions for sustained productivity growth in services are present and, in addition, barriers to entry, join or to set up export-oriented service activities as part of global supply chain have been greatly lowered. Services, then, do already constitute at least a partial avenue of economic development in a sectoral (only a part of the service sector, Eichengreen and Gupta 2009, 2011), spatial (highly concentrated, partly in specific economic zones, Kleibert 2015, and see the contribution of Xu Zhang in this volume) and social sense (only a particular segment of the population is directly involved, Beerepoot and Hendriks 2013, and see Leian Marasigan, Randhir Kumar, Sandhya Krishnan and Jana Kleibert in this volume).

Not everyone is convinced though. Dani Rodrik (2014) is much more sceptical regarding the escalator function of services when explicitly discussing the findings of Ghani and O'Connell (2014). He concedes the point that '[b]anking, finance, insurance, and other business services, along with information and communications technology (ICT), are all high-productivity activities that pay high wages' (Rodrik, 2014: 2). Such activities, however, require high-skilled labour and this tends to be scarce in many developing economies that typically have predominantly low-skilled labour forces: 'In such economies, tradable services cannot absorb more than a fraction of the labour supply'. Rodrik (2014: 2) also points at what he sees as the limited demand for services: 'in services, where market size is limited by domestic demand, continued success requires complementary and simultaneous gains in productivity in the rest of the economy'.

These objections, however, have to be nuanced. First, the average level of educational qualifications is on the rise in low-income countries. It has risen from 2.1 in 1950 to 7.1 years in 2010 (Barro and Lee 2010). Second, Eichengreen and Gupta (2009) found that the mix of skilled and unskilled labour in manufacturing and services in India is increasingly similar. Manufacturing itself has become more skill-intensive and technological advances have decreased the demand for workers. Third, transactional activities are becoming more important as both products and the production system become more complex, thereby boosting the demand for services such as ICT-related services, research, accounting, financial, legal, design, engineering and medical services. In contrast to the high income elasticity of services, consumers and households in developed countries tend to spend less on manufactured goods when incomes rise (Ghani and O'Connell 2014: 4).

The so-called second-wave services, then, do provide opportunities for less-developed countries and they even offer a perspective of sustained growth of the sector itself. Not all less-developed countries, however, are able to attract these services as they are dependent on certain conditions. The first condition that has to be met is, obviously, the presence of a labour pool of high-skilled workers who are proficient in a foreign language (mostly English). A second condition is that of an efficient and reliable ICT infrastructure to support the export-oriented services.

Third, an openness towards the world and other cultures and also to transnational corporations. A fourth condition that has to be fulfilled is that of a wider institutional context, which is seen as fostering and protecting their businesses, which refrains from excessive taxation and regulation, which is also capable of maintaining and improving the infrastructure, and which can guarantee safe spaces for the workers (many of them are women). According to Eichengreen and Gupta (2011: 8) 'the greater importance of the second wave in medium-to-high-income countries is most evident in democracies, in countries that are close to major financial centers, and in economies that are relatively open to trade', in other words, in countries that can provide a skilled workforce, a suitable infrastructure and that are open, more tolerant and more acquainted with foreign contacts.

If these conditions are fulfilled and export-oriented service industries have taken root in a developing country, how can their potential to generate sustained economic growth be tapped? We will turn to this strategic question below, after we have positioned service-sector driven development in a brief historical perspective of stages of developmental paths.

Conclusion

Spontaneous industrialisation as a path to sustained economic development was very much a one-off. After Britain industrialised, it became ever more difficult for newcomers to follow that same path. State intervention, fencing off the home market by protective walls to protect the infant industries, was necessary to industrialise and in addition industrialised countries often pursued conscious policies to prevent industrialisation of other (peripheral) less-developed countries. After the Second World War, import substitution policies were launched by many these developing countries and, for while, this seemed quite successful as in many cases they were able to build more or less comprehensive supply chains from basic to consumer industries – often almost from scratch – in a short span of time. In the 1980s, this path of development became more of a dead end as these industries could not compete on world markets, making it difficult if not impossible to pay for imports and loans.

Even before this, in the 1960s, a few Asian countries (Singapore, Taiwan and Korea) had abandoned import substitution and opted for encouraging exports. Keeping wages low, their goal was to conquer market shares through low prices. They focused at first on selected low-skill manufacturing activities such as textiles, toys and later on electronics. These policies turned out to be highly successful, both in the sense that they indeed were able to gain large market shares and, moreover, also in the long-term as these activities constituted the basis for the upgrading of their manufacturing base to high-value added high-tech activities requiring highly skilled workers. Still, these countries are among the few examples of countries that were able to overcome the middle-income trap and join the ranks of high-income countries.

From the 1980s onward, these export-oriented strategies became *the* model for economic development. The phase of the second unbundling had set in, helped by advances in ICT and successive rounds of trade liberalisation, in which transnational corporations created complex global production networks by seeking the most efficient locations for the components of their supply chains (Coe 2011, Fernandez-Stark *et al.* 2011). Typically, specific areas with low levels of regulation, i.e. export processing zones, were designated to accommodate these activities. The opening up of China in 1978 under Deng Xiaoping roughly coincided with these shifts and, after that, can be seen as important driver itself of the unbundling of supply chains. China has become so successful in, at first, attracting manufacturing activities offshored by transnational corporations and subsequently setting up its own firms, that its dominance of large segments of global markets in manufacturing products is now blocking the way for other developing countries. As *The Economist* (2015: 13) in its leader puts it: 'China and its neighbours may have been the last countries to be able to climb the ladder of development simply by recruiting lots of unskilled people to make things cheaply'. Pressured by the competition of Chinese firms, some developing countries are already deindustrialising before they have developed a mature manufacturing sector, a process described by Rodrik (2014) as premature deindustrialization. Up to a certain extent, then, these other developing countries are *forced* to look for alternative ways of economic development. The second unbundling, however, also offers new opportunities as services can be offshored. How can this potential be utilised?

The first issue, evidently, is that of relative size. To make a difference, a substantial number of workers have to be employed in these export-oriented services. Again to quote the leader of *The Economist* (2015: 13) 'India's IT-service sector shows what can be achieved, but is high-skilled and barely taps into the country's vast ocean labour'. It would be hard to envisage a majority of Indian labour moving out of agriculture straight into export-oriented services anyway, but sustained growth of the sector is an obvious necessary condition to generate sustained overall growth. This depends not just on existing demand, but also on the ability of the service providers to broaden their product lines and even to come up with new products. Second, the impact of spillovers through backward and forward linkages should be exploited and where possible promoted. The biggest effect on the local and perhaps even on the national economy of export-oriented services in developing countries is, arguably, through the backward linkages with the educational system. As these services need highly skilled workers, the local and national educational systems have to supply them. This upgrading of the educational system does not just entail tertiary but also secondary and primary schooling. The effects of this could (and even should) transcend the needs of the service sector and benefit larger society. Improving the infrastructure is also a positive spillover effect. The service sector thereby contributes to the accumulation of economy-wide capabilities in the form of human capital and institutions. Forward linkages through expenditures by workers in the services will have an impact on the wider economy as well, not just in a direct sense, but also in projecting a particular, more cosmopolitan lifestyle (see the contributions by Sandhya Krishnan and Beerepoot and Vogelzang in this volume). A third factor determining the contribution of export-oriented is the power relationships within the supply chains: who captures the value created? If the export-oriented services are predominantly owned by foreign transnational corporations, the effect will be considerably smaller than if they are owned by domestic entrepreneurs. With respect to the latter, spin-offs, i.e. workers leaving an established firm to set up their own businesses, tend to be a crucial link in local innovation processes and in capturing locally created value and in increasing the contribution of the export-service sector on a long term basis.

To take advantage of the growth potential of the service sector, active state intervention is needed to improve the educational system and infrastructure, and to foster entrepreneurship. This is very much in line with a string of successful cases of post-war economic developments – from Singapore to China. The second unbundling is often framed within a neoliberal discourse of liberalisation, deregulation and privatisation, but this tends to overlook the crucial role of the state. Not every developing country has the governance capacity to deal with these issues and the service sector is evidently not a one-size-fits-all path to economic development. Even in countries that are successful in accommodating an expanding service sector, it may still make sense to broaden the portfolio and look for opportunities to join supply chains in specific agricultural and manufacturing activities. The homegrown business service sector could play a crucial role in that as well.

References

Acemoglu, D. and J.A. Robinson (2012), *Why Nations Fail: The origins of power, prosperity and poverty* (Vol. 4). New York: Crown Business.

Baldwin, R. (2011), *Trade and Industrialisation After Globalisation's 2nd Unbundling: How building and joining a supply chain are different and why it matters* (No. w17716). Washington DC: National Bureau of Economic Research.

Barro, R.J. and J.-W. Lee (2010), *A New Data Set of Educational Attainment in the World, 1950-2010*. NBER Working Paper No. 15902 (www.nber.org/papers/w15902)

Beerepoot, N. and M. Hendriks (2013), 'Employability of offshore service sector workers in the Philippines: opportunities for upward labour mobility or dead-end jobs?', *Work, Employment and Society*, 27(5): 823–841.

Clark, G. (2007), *A Farewell to Alms. A Brief History of the World*. Princeton, N.J.: Princeton University Press.

Clark, G. (2012), 'Review essay: The enlightened economy. An economic history of Britain, 1700–1850 by Joel Mokyr', *Journal of Economic Literature*, 50(1): 85–95

Coe, N.M. (2011), 'Unpacking globalization: Changing geographies of the global economy'. In A. Leyshon, R. Lee, L. McDowell and P. Sunley, *The SAGE Handbook of Economic Geography*. London: Sage: 89–101.

Dicken, P. (2011), *Global Shift, Mapping the Changing Contours of the World Economy* (6th Edition). Los Angeles/London/New Delhi/Singapore/Washington DC: Sage.

Dossani, R. and M. Kenney (2007), 'The next wave of globalization: Relocating service provision to India', *World Development*, 35(5): 772–791.

Economist, The (2015), 'Made in China', *The Economist*, 14 March: 13.

Eichengreen, B. and P. Gupta (2009), *The Two Waves of Service Sector Growth*. Working Paper No. 14968. Cambridge, MA: National Bureau of Economic Research.

Eichengreen, B. and P. Gupta (2011), *The Service Sector as India's Road to Economic Growth* (No. w16757). Washington DC: National Bureau of Economic Research.
Eichengreen, B. and P. Gupta (2013), 'The two waves of service-sector growth', *Oxford Economic Papers*, 65(1): 96–123.
Elfring, T. (1988), 'Service employment in advanced economies, a comparatibe analysis of its implications for economic growth'. Groningen: Dissertation Universiteit Groningen.
Fernandez-Stark, K., P. Bamber and G. Gereffi (2011), 'The offshore services value chain: Upgrading trajectories in developing countries'. *International Journal of Technological Learning, Innovation and Development*, 4 (1–3): 206–234.
Frank, A.G. (1978), *Dependent Accumulation and Underdevelopment*. London: Macmillan.
Frieden, J. (2006), *Global Capitalism, Its Fall and Rise in the Twentieth Century*. New York/London: W.W. Norton and Company.
Ghani, E. and O'Connell S.D. (2014), *Can Service be a Growth Escalator in Low Income Countries?* Policy Research Working Paper 6971. Washington, DC: World Bank.
Jaques, M. (2012), *When China Rules the World*. London: Penguin Books.
Kay, J. (2004), *The Truth About Markets: Why some nations are rich but most remain poor.* London: Penguin Books.
Kleibert, J.M. (2015), *'Expanding Global Production Networks, The emergence, evolution and the developmental impact of the offshore service sector in the Philippines'.* Amsterdam: Dissertation Universiteit van Amsterdam.
Kuznets, S. (1973), *Modern Economic Growth, Rate, Structure, and Spread*. New Haven/London: Yale University Press.
Landes, D.S. (1998), *The Wealth and Poverty of Nations, Why Some Are So Rich and Some So Poor*. London: Little, Brown and Company.
Mokyr, J. (2009), *The Enlightened Economy: An Economic History of Britain 1700–1850*. New Haven/London: Yale University Press.
O'Rourke, K.H. and J.G. Williamson (1999), *Globalization and History, The Evolution of a Nineteenth-Century Atlantic Economy.* Cambridge, MA/London: The MIT Press.
Pomeranz, K. (2009), *The Great Divergence: China, Europe, and the Making of the Modern World Economy*. Princeton, NJ: Princeton University Press.
Rodrik, D. (2014), 'Are services the new manufactures?', (www.project-syndicate.org/commentary/are-services-the-new-manufactures-by-dani-rodrik-2014-10)
Scott, A.J. (2008), *Social Economy of the Metropolis: Cognitive-Cultural Capitalism and the Global Resurgence of Cities*. Oxford: Oxford University Press.
Scott, A.J. (2012), *A World in Emergence, Cities and Regions in the 21st Century*. Cheltenham, UK/Northampton, MA: Edward Elgar.
Taylor P.J., B. Derudder, J. Faulconbridge, M. Hoyler and P. Ni (2014), 'Advanced producer service firms as strategic networks, global cities as strategic places', *Economic Geography*, 90(3): 267–291.
Vries, P. (2003), *Via Peking back to Manchester: Britain, the Industrial Revolution, and China*. Leiden: CNWS Publications/Leiden University.
Vries, P. (2013), *Escaping Poverty. The Origins of Modern Economic Growth*. Vienna and Göttingen: Vandenhoeck und Ruprecht.
Wallerstein, I. (1979), *The Capitalist World-Economy*. Cambridge: Cambridge University Press.
Wölfl, A. (2005), *The Service Economy in OECD Countries*. OECD/Centre d'études prospectives et d'informations internationales (CEPII), OECD Science, Technology and Industry Working Papers, 2005/03, OECD Publishing, (http://dx.doi.org/10.1787/212257000720).

3 Services-led economic development

Comparing the emergence of the offshore service sector in India and the Philippines

Jana Maria Kleibert

Introduction

The offshoring of services has created opportunities for developing countries to generate revenue and employment by delivering services to the Global North (Dossani and Kenney 2007, Ghani 2010: 3). Changes in information and communications technology (ICT) have led to a 'tradability revolution' (UNCTAD 2004), allowing international trade in so-called 'modern services'. This enabled the spatial reorganisation of service value chains and global service production networks (GSPNs). So far, most interest has arisen from a Western perspective on the potential and actual threats of offshoring for developed economies. The impact on receiving countries, however, has been less explored. Bryson claims that the 'offshoring literature tended to over-emphasise potential or actual negative impacts being experienced by developed market economies and to neglect impacts on foreign service providers' (Bryson 2007: 41). Arguably, the growth of exports of IT-enabled services has created new opportunities for developing countries to leapfrog industrialisation and to achieve services-led economic development (Dossani and Kenney 2007, Gereffi and Fernandez-Stark 2010: 6).

This chapter addresses a gap in current research looking deeper into the experiences of developing countries and the newly emerging division of labour in offshore service delivery.[1] It presents a comparative historical analysis of the emergence of an offshore service sector in India and the Philippines. The similarities and differences of the emergence of the sector in both countries are analysed and the causal factors for divergent trajectories are distilled. So far, little comparative research on this topic has been done and 'much of the emerging conventional wisdom is based on an extrapolation of the Indian experience as a potential development alternative available to other developing countries' (Majluf 2007: 148). Milberg and Winkler (2013: 13) argue that India's IT sector may have 'suffered from a selection bias of successful cases', especially since the increasing sophistication of work conducted out of India has received much scholarly attention (Dossani and Kenney 2007, 2009: 99–100).

India is by far the largest provider of IT and business process outsourcing (IT-BPO) services globally, holding a global market share of 58 per cent (NASSCOM

2012: 7). The Philippines has emerged more recently as a participant in the offshore service sector, but has already overtaken India in one subsector, namely call-centre operations (IBM 2010, *Economist* 2012). India and the Philippines are among the world's largest providers of global offshore services and the top eight offshoring cities are located in either of the two countries (Tholons 2013: 2). This chapter investigates the interplay of factors that gave rise to offshore service delivery from India and the Philippines and the role of diverse actors in the 'strategic coupling' of regions with offshore service networks, as discussed in the global production network (GPN) framework (Henderson *et al.* 2002, Coe *et al.* 2004, 2008).

Analysing the similarities and differences between two countries, both of which have been successful in integrating into GSPNs and delivering services to developed countries, is a first step in a critical discussion of services-led development strategies. The rise of the offshore service sector is a relatively recent and very dynamic phenomenon. Therefore, it is important to look not only at the current configuration of GSPNs but also at their evolution:

> It is clear that the evolution of offshoring cannot be understood as an isolated event, but … result[s] from the interplay and interaction of multilevel agenda and endogenous and exogenous factors, demand and supply or push and pull factors which interplay and affect one another to result in emerging dynamics.
> (Massini and Miozzo 2012: 1238)

The relevance of this study lies in understanding the underlying mechanisms of current processes of globalisation and the offshoring of services in a comparative perspective. Using several variables, this comparative case study argues that key differences have led to diverging processes of integration into GSPNs in India and the Philippines. Moreover, it explains *how* and *why* both countries follow different trajectories and discusses potential future pathways. For this research, 40 interviews were conducted with key stakeholders, including representatives of business associations, managers of shared services and call centres, special economic zone (SEZ) authorities, and sector experts in India (Mumbai) and the Philippines (Metro Manila). In addition, secondary sources, including academic articles, business reports, (online) newspaper articles and popular biographies (and hagiographies) of IT-firm founders, were reviewed. The majority of secondary sources available focused on the Indian case, as apart from non-academic business reports, publications on the emergence of the IT-BPO sector in the Philippines are still a scarce commodity.

Several limitations and challenges need to be mentioned for this comparative sector study. First, the use of different, not clearly defined and overlapping terminologies exists in the field of offshore services. This limits the ability to compare data (Sass and Fifekova 2011). Second, individual, country-specific data on the sector are estimates by business associations, which admit in interviews to not always having access to accurate data themselves. Recently, both the Indian business association NASSCOM and the Business Processing Association of the Philippines (BPAP) have changed the way they calculate data,[2] which makes even tracking the development of a single case over time difficult. Third, cross-country international trade figures available for offshore services are inherently flawed. One problem is that non-outsourced activities usually occur between a head office and cost centres as intra-firm trade, creating possibilities for transfer pricing. Another problem is that trade data do not consider value-added (Milberg and Winkler 2013: 41). Therefore, this chapter concentrates on the more qualitative aspects of the integration of India and the Philippines into GSPNs.

In order to achieve its aims, this chapter first develops a theoretical understanding of the prerequisites for the local emergence of a (viable) offshore services sector. Next, similarities and differences are identified between the development trajectories of the offshore services sectors in India and the Philippines. The differences are then explained, after which the implications for the debate on service-led economic development are considered and suggestions formulated for further research.

Prerequisites for integration into global service production networks

Several globalisation forces combined have led to the creation and expansion of GPNs, namely economic liberalisation policies, increased global competition, and the spread and pervasive use of ICTs (Henderson *et al.* 2002: 443). The same three processes have played a role in the offshoring of services. The establishment of service provision centres in developing countries has taken place due to increased competition of service providers and in order to reap cost-benefits, as well as potential economies of scale (due to centralised service provision), access to skilled labour and new markets. Though service production and consumption was believed to be spatially inseparable, today, reliable and cheap high-speed communication technologies allow back-office and call centre activities to be provided across large distances. In fact, all services that do not require face-to-face interaction, that can be transmitted via modern telecommunications infrastructure, have a considerable wage difference across space and do not require extensive networking, can be offshored (UNCTAD 2004).

The offshore service sector is a heterogeneous category, including various services and activities, located at different points of the value chain (Gereffi and Fernandez-Stark 2010). The acronym BPO encompasses among others: customer services (voice-based services conducted in call centres; or non-voice-based services delivered via email and chat programmes), back-office services (e.g. data processing), engineering services, transcription services and creative services (e.g. animation). These vary vastly in terms of routine, codability, and skill level required, on a scale from simple to complex work. High-end services, such as legal services, financial analytics and engineering design require domain expertise and specific skills, whereas the lower-end functions found in call centres are scripted, routine functions.

The financial services sector has been a driver of offshore services. The majority of global financial corporations have relocated part of their activities to India or the Philippines. Increasingly, firms are opting for service delivery from both countries simultaneously (also in an effort to hedge country-specific risks), creating increasingly complex GSPNs. The network metaphor employed by the GPN framework, instead of a linear conceptualisation of a value 'chain', is useful to illustrate the complex forms of organisation of contemporary service production. In contrast to earlier approaches (e.g. the global commodity chain), the GPN framework is more inclusive in terms of the types of actors, who are understood to shape and influence the networks. These include firms, labour and institutions, which hold asymmetric powers and operate at various scales (Coe *et al.* 2008).

A main contribution of the GPN approach is the conceptualisation of regional development as the outcome of attracting investments and becoming integrated into GPNs through a process of 'strategic coupling'. This notion refers to the actions of regional actors to link, or couple, the strategic assets of a given region with the demands of a GPN (Coe *et al.* 2004). Existing regional assets are therefore crucial for the ability for developing countries to 'couple' their regions with the offshore service sector.

English language skills are an important strategic asset and, in fact, a precondition for exporting services to the largest offshore service market: the United States (US). Since labour arbitrage is the main rationale for sourcing tasks from developing countries, a key asset required for the participation in the offshore service sector is a low-cost, but sufficiently skilled, workforce. This skill level (and especially language abilities) of workers is the main difference from earlier relocation of manufacturing activities from the Global North to lower-cost destinations around the globe. By focusing on their skilled workers, countries, which have been unable to gain from this earlier offshoring of manufacturing due to uncompetitive business environments, are now able to participate in GPNs:

> countries such as India and the Philippines are doing well in cross-border exports of skill-intensive services but are lagging in labour-intensive manufacturing exports, not because of their absolute advantage in services – they remain relatively abundant in unskilled labour – but because of their comparative disadvantage in manufacturing.
>
> (Goswami *et al.* 2012: 8)

In contrast to manufacturing, offshore services generally require relatively little infrastructure investment, except for communications infrastructure. Reliable and cost-efficient internet connectivity to transfer large volumes of data are key requirements for offshore service delivery. The liberalisation of the telecommunications sector has been pivotal to increase competition, reduce costs and raise investment in the sector (Goswami *et al.* 2012). However, only business hubs need to be equipped with telecommunications infrastructure; the overall share of households with internet connection is not decisive.

Both India and the Philippines are characterised by globally uncompetitive business environments and deficient physical infrastructure. In a ranking of 'ease of doing business' India and the Philippines occupy positions 132 and 138 respectively, out of a total of 183 countries (World Bank and IFC 2013: 3). In order to attract investments in an uncompetitive business environment, government policies and special incentives are required by national governments to facilitate the emergence of an offshore service sector. To sum up, three crucial factors for the attraction of offshore service investments are: (1) a lower-cost labour force with widespread English-language skills, (2) the liberalisation of the telecommunications sector, and (3) government incentives for services exports.

Comparing the offshore service sector in India and the Philippines: similarities

All three requirements for offshore service sector development are fulfilled by India and the Philippines, which constitute the main similarities of both countries' integration into GSPNs. First, and most importantly, both India and the Philippines have been under the rule of English-speaking colonisers and both are developing countries with skilled, but under-utilised, workers.

Second, the telecommunications sector in both countries has been liberalised. Panagariya (2008) defines the Indian telecommunications sector reform as one of few successful policies introduced by the technocratic government in the mid-1990s. Despite generating the opportunity for companies operating in business hubs to link up to the internet, it is noteworthy that India's national internet penetration is only 2 per cent (Nilekani 2008: 371). In the Philippines, the privatisation and liberalisation of the telecommunications sector under the Ramos presidency drastically reduced end-user rates. Introducing competition for long-distance communications in 1995 provided a further increase in competitiveness (Fink *et al.* 2001).

Third, the government in both countries has facilitated the rise of the offshore service sector through a range of policies. In India, private sector representatives argued frequently during interviews that the offshore service sector grew 'despite the government' and did not receive any special attention for facilitation by the government. The sector, however, formed an exception to government-enforced general restrictions to foreign investment, which initially led to more advantageous conditions for offshore service firms compared to other sectors (Karnik 2012).

A closer look also reveals that in both India and the Philippines the offshore service sector benefited from a range of investment incentives and received substantial state support in forms of the creation of SEZs for offshore services. In India, the Software Technology Parks of India (STPI) were founded in 1991. The establishment of these parks has been a critical national state policy, offering tax incentives and subsidised infrastructure (Upadhya 2011: 179). Though the STPI regime was terminated in 2011, a new SEZ scheme, which offers fairly similar incentives, has taken its place.

In the Philippines the offshore service sector was recognised as an investment priority area, thereby qualifying for tax incentives and exemption from foreign ownership restrictions by the Board of Investments and the Philippines Economic Zone Authority (PEZA). PEZA was privatised in 1995 and the minimum space requirements for SEZs were reduced. This helped the offshore service sector, since individual floors of prime office buildings in central business districts became eligible for tax incentives. IT parks and centres mushroomed from zero in 1999 to 168 in 2013, according to PEZA data.

Aside from tax incentives, the SEZs fulfil two important roles: first, they provide enclaves of good business environments, in terms of infrastructure and internet connectivity, in countries that generally lack these (Engman 2010: 234). Second, the formation of one-stop shop professional organisations for foreign investors cuts red-tape and decreases opportunities for corruption and bureaucratic delay (Yi 2012: 141). The national and state governments have played a role in supporting the growth of the offshore service sector through these policies. In addition, the Philippine government has also provided more direct financial support to the sector through funding of its business association and educational programmes, which are directed at increasing the supply of a suitable workforce for the sector.

Comparing the offshore service sector in India and the Philippines: differences

Sector composition

The offshore service sectors in India and in the Philippines differ in many ways, as Table 3.1 shows. India's total offshore service sector is much larger than that of the Philippines, employing almost three times the number of employees and receiving close to five times more revenue for its exports. Labour productivity for IT-BPO services (measured as revenue per employee), is almost double in India compared to the Philippines, demonstrating that higher value-added service provision is taking place in India. This is also related to the different revenue generating opportunities in different subsectors. Moreover, different types of foreign investors have invested in India and the Philippines, and the business associations have performed different roles, as explained in more detail below.

Figure 3.1 uses export revenue to depict the composition of the offshore service sectors in India and the Philippines. In the Philippines, call centres (voice BPO) make up 66 per cent of the total export revenue earned; the voice and non-voice BPO sectors combined account for 85 per cent. In contrast, less than 23 per cent of revenue stem from BPO services in India. Instead its share of IT services is dominant with 58 per cent, the corresponding figure of the Philippines is only 9 per cent. High value-added engineering and research and development (R&D) work contributes 19 per cent in India. In the Philippines, health services (including transcription work), engineering services, animation and game development in total contribute 6 per cent of offshore service sector export revenues.

Foreign investors

Foreign investors have been a fundamental driver of the offshore service sector. In India, domestic-industry protectionism under the License Raj led IBM in 1978 (then still largely a producer of computer hardware) to leave the country. IBM

Table 3.1 Offshore service delivery in India and the Philippines in 2012

Year 2012	*India*	*Philippines*
Full-time employees (FTE	2,175,000	772,000
Annual export revenue ($US)	69 billion	13 billion
Annual revenue per FTE ($US)	31,700	16,800
Rationale of companies	Cost and availability of IT skills, benefits of scale	Cost and availability of English-language, customer-service ability
Type of services	Predominantly IT related, back-office, decreasing voice-services	Mainly voice-based services, transcription, back-office, animation and creative services
Foreign investors	Third-party providers and in-house shared-service IT centres, changing interrelationships with domestic companies	Large third-party providers (many US-owned call centres), MNC shared-service back-offices on the rise
Business associations	NASSCOM: strong body, independent funding, focus on services selling	BPAP: government-funded, focus on investment attraction

Source: NASSCOM.in; BPAP.org; author's analysis

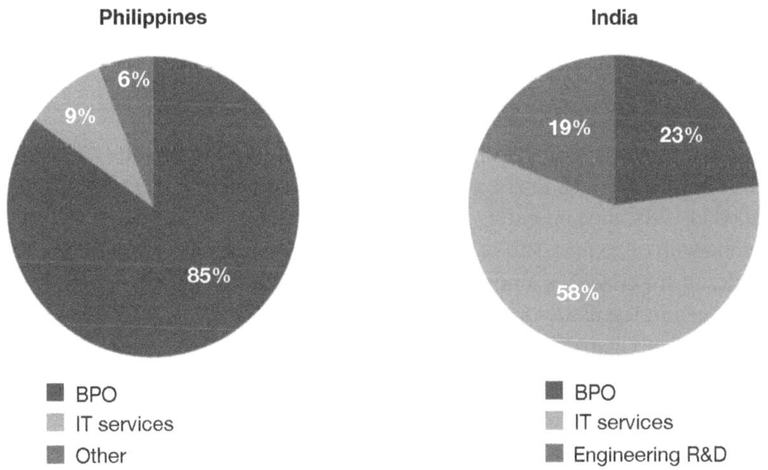

Figure 3.1 Comparison of export revenue: India and the Philippines by subsector

Source: Based on data provided by the Information Technology and Business Process Association of the Philippines (IBPAP) through personal communication in 2012, NASSCOM (2012)

re-entered India through a joint-venture only after gradual liberalisation of the economy after 1991 (Das 2002). The softening of foreign-ownership restrictions led to increased foreign direct investment flows into India. Many foreign investors started services offshoring on a small scale through existing subsidiaries of multinational corporations (MNCs), which were catering to the local market. When firm managers discovered to opportunity for labour arbitrage in service provision, they started setting up separate service operations for their companies.

Many of these businesses operated 'under the radar' at first, as their cost savings were considered an advantage over competitors, and therefore kept secret. Several early movers set up their dedicated in-house offices in India in the early 1990s. These included firms such as General Electric, financial service providers and outsourcing companies, such as IBM and Accenture. Some of these subsidiaries of foreign-owned companies for service delivery from India were later taken over by Indian-owned companies: General Electric's in-house centre started servicing other clients and became an independent third-party supplier (Genpact); a British Airways shared-services centre, in a similar fashion, became WNS.

One of the earliest foreign investors to provide offshore services from the Philippines was AOL, which started in 1997 to cater to US clients from Subic Freeport Zone. In the following years, mainly foreign-owned BPO companies such as Convergys and Sykes, mostly with previous offshoring experience in India, set up additional offices in the Philippines. Later, MNCs started to relocate their back-office operations to Metro Manila. These stem primarily from the financial sector, but also include other industries such as manufacturing, logistics and publishing. Compared to India, an inverse process of changing ownership can be witnessed: foreign-owned companies buy out Filipino-owned companies, which cannot compete with the larger international third-party suppliers. As a result, the Philippine offshore service sector is primarily foreign-owned, with foreign equity participation in the sector standing above 90 per cent (Yi 2012).

Business associations for offshore service delivery

Business associations can be important drivers of the advancement of a sector. The Indian National Association of Software and Services Companies (NASSCOM) was founded in 1988, then operating out of a small apartment in Delhi, and has grown to a membership of about 1,350 companies. This professional organisation has become the lodestar for countries aiming at replicating India's IT sector success, which can also be seen in the names given to these associations (e.g. BRASSCOM in Brazil, GASSCOM in Ghana). NASSCOM is privately funded through membership fees and the majority of its members are Indian-owned companies.

The Business Processing Association of the Philippines (BPAP)[3] was founded in 2004 and is much smaller than its Indian counterpart. The majority of its 210 industry members are foreign-owned companies but its board of directors consists exclusively of Filipinos. Of the five sub-organisations, the contact centre association (CCAP) is by far the most powerful one, representing the largest share of activities. Apart from membership fees, a considerable amount of funding is obtained from the government and from Filipino-owned support organisations profiting from the offshore service sector, such as telecommunication providers and commercial real estate developers (see also Raquiza in this volume). Their role in supporting the sector is also apparent in the fact that they fill three board positions (of the non-industry board) in addition to the five head strong industry board.

In terms of their core work, both proactive agencies follow relatively similar policies. The Philippines acknowledges replicating some of NASSCOM's strategies, especially in terms of organising the training and testing of the potential workforce for employment in the sector, engaging in government lobbying for incentives, and in terms of marketing and branding efforts. Due to the dominance of foreign-owned companies in the Philippines' BPO sector, the umbrella organisation has mainly engaged in foreign investment promotion through road shows and campaigns. A difference in power, size and its forerunner position, means that NASSCOM has been forced to deal with a US backlash against offshoring of services, lobbying the US government abroad and representing the interests of Indian IT companies globally (Karnik 2012). BPAP has had less reason to engage in this, since most companies delivering offshore work from the Philippines are US-owned MNCs that are better positioned to lobby their own government rather than working through BPAP.

Causal factors for different trajectories of offshore service sector development in India and the Philippines

The main reasons why India and the Philippines differ in the positions they occupy within global offshore service networks are summarised in Table 3.2. They are discussed in detail below.

Timing of integration into global service production networks

Comparing India's service-led development with China's manufacturing success, Ghani (2010: 95) argues that both were shaped by 'their relative strength in education and infrastructure, and the timing of the globalization of services'. The point in time at which a country integrates into global production networks matters, as historic windows of opportunity can be open or closed. As a forerunner in the sector, India started providing services to the US under very different conditions from the Philippines, which entered the IT-BPO sector almost 15 years later. Already during the 1980s India engaged in the practice of short-term labour migration (or 'body-shopping') of software programmers to client's offices in the Global North (Parthasarathy 2013: 380–381).

During that time, service delivery focused on IT services, since the telecommunication infrastructure was still too rudimentary for voice-based services. The dotcom bubble had a preferential impact on the development of offshore service delivery from India in two ways: during the boom, over-investment in optic fibre cables reduced connectivity costs globally, while the bust led to cost pressures for companies, and therefore, offshoring to India. The Y2K bug, in the run-up to the

Table 3.2 Variables explaining differences in offshore service sector emergence

	India	*Philippines*
Timing	Forerunner (1980s onwards), body-shopping, dotcom bubble, Y2K	Later entrant (starting 2000s) after Asian financial crisis, liberalisation of telecommunication
Labour pool	Former British colony, education system with high technical and management training for small percentage	Former American colony, 'cultural affinity' and English-language skills, high literacy but lower quality
Domestic-owned firms	Domestic-owned firms drove growth of sector; now large actors in the global industry	No active role by domestic-owned firms in initial sector; now mainly small, uncompetitive actors
Returnee migrants	Important 'brain circulation', established business contacts and networks	Less important role, large labour migration is mainly unskilled/ non-BPO related

year 2000, was another decisive moment for Indian IT companies to prove their capabilities (Dossani and Kenney 2009: 81, Dossani 2013). Gaining a foothold early in the sector has been an important advantage for India, as Milberg and Winkler note that 'GPNs have a cumulative and herd-like character … as one firm in an industry has success, others have tended to follow' (2013: 33).

The Philippines entered the offshore service sector on a large scale only after the year 2000. The Asian financial crisis brought down commercial property prices in Metro Manila, which reduced the cost of office space for foreign investors in prime locations. By then, advances in communications technology allowed low-cost voice-based services, and exports in this field mushroomed. More recently, the rise of social media use and advanced mobile phone technology has created opportunities for marketing and customer service via social network sites, which are being delivered out of customer service centres in the Philippines. The difference in timing can therefore partially explain a difference in orientation towards particular sub-sectors; however, the main explanatory variable are regional assets in the form of a large, skilled labour force.

Size and skill sets of the labour force

While both countries have a large number of English speakers, their respective educated labour pools differ. The difference of population in size of the two countries should be kept in mind, since economies of scale are important in the offshore service sector. Early on, India developed high-standard technical education through the renowned Indian Institutes of Technology (IITs), elitist public schools, which were the result of Nehru's education policy in the 1950s. At 16 per cent India has a relatively low percentage of tertiary education enrolment (World Bank 2013), but with 220,000 students at IITs and Indian Institutes of Management combined, the total number of highly skilled individuals is still considerable (Brown *et al.* 2011: 33).

Due to the opening of the education sector to private providers, who received subsidies by selected states in India, a dramatic increase in the supply of engineers in these states resulted – leading to a concentration of offshore service activities in Andhra Pradesh, Karnataka, Maharashtra and Tamil Nadu (Nilekani 2008: 346, Dossani 2013: 162–163). With a focus on top tertiary education for a few, primary education has been neglected in India. This has led to low literacy rates, especially among women, almost half of whom are illiterate (UNESCO 2006).

This contrasts with a literacy rate above 95 per cent for both genders in the Philippines (UNESCO 2008). Moreover, tertiary education enrolment is high with 28 per cent in 2009 (World Bank 2013), as a result of an implementation of the US-style college system. The quality of tertiary education however suffers from the fact that 90 per cent of all higher education institutes are privately owned (and largely non-accredited), and less than 10 per cent of academic staff hold PhDs (Welch 2011). Overall, research capabilities are limited, and some universities and colleges offer low-quality degrees (Tullao 2003).

Only ten school years are required for students entering university, two years less than in most countries. As a result, an often-mentioned problem by offshore service companies located in the Philippines are the limited general skills of graduates (including English-language skills), leading to hiring rates of less than 10 per cent in voice-based services. This problem has been recognised by the government and current reform efforts in the Philippines include the introduction of a 12-year curriculum (K+12) to increase the competitiveness of Filipino graduates.

Although English is widely spoken in India and the Philippines as a result of colonisation, there are differences between both countries as a result of their colonial histories. US colonisation of the Philippines (1898–1946) introduced institutions according to the American model and the interaction led to what is often labelled 'cultural affinity' of the Philippines with the US (Rodolfo 2005: 35). Especially work that involves direct customer interaction with American clients over the phone values the 'neutral' accent of Filipinos.

Services offshoring in both cases has been driven by cost reductions, leading to 'efficiency-seeking vertical investments' (Hardy *et al.* 2011), but the difference in existing labour pools in both countries means that the sourcing strategies of foreign investors have differed. In the case of India, technical, and to a lesser extent, managerial skills have been sought after. The Philippines strongest asset has been English-language skills. This, in combination with cultural affinity with the main offshore market – the US – has led firms to source voice-based services from the Philippines.

Domestic-owned companies and the role of domestic entrepreneurs

The most striking difference between the sector in India and the Philippines is the role of domestic-owned companies. While India boasts a considerable amount of homegrown companies that have acquired the status of MNCs today, (notably Tata

Consultancy Services [TCS], Infosys, and Wipro), there are few sizable Filipino-owned offshore services. Also in absolute numbers the offshore service sector in the Philippines is dominated by foreign-owned firms, whereas in India, the majority of firms are domestic owned. The reasons for this divergence are yet to be better understood.

Interviewees in both countries use cultural arguments to attribute an 'entrepreneurial mindset' to Indians and an 'employee mindset' to Filipinos. However, a strong entrepreneurial spirit among Filipinos can be seen when it comes to small companies and self-employment, for instance organised through international job websites such as *oDesk*, where a significant percentage of all completed tasks and assignments is conducted from the Philippines (Beerepoot and Lambregts 2015). It is also noteworthy that some successful Filipino-grown companies were acquired by foreign companies when they entered the market, leading to a decreasing number of Filipino-owned companies.

In India, the offshore service sector has grown due to domestic entrepreneurs and the availability of engineering and managerial talent. Oftentimes companies emanated from old conglomerates, such as Tata Steel in the case of TCS. The six largest Indian IT firms were founded between 1968 and 1986 (Dossani 2013: 157). The early founders of offshore service companies and today's IT tycoons are admired individuals and their stories have been well documented (e.g. Ramadorai 2011). Several of them had undergone engineering training at universities in the US before returning to India and setting up their firms (Dossani 2013). Indian entrepreneurs have played a central role in upgrading into higher-end functions due to the accumulation of technical expertise (Parthasarathy and Aoyama 2006).

In the Philippines, existing conglomerates with enough financial and manpower to set up offshore service firms have been reluctant to do so. Diversification from real estate and retailing business has mainly been directed at telecommunications and utilities sectors (Gutierrez and Rodriguez 2013). These can be considered more traditional rent-seeking activities (see also Raquiza in this volume). The only conglomerate to experiment with voice-based service delivery to foreign clients has been Ayala Corporation, which created the BPO-investment arm LiveIT Investments and acquired the US-based contact centre Stream.

Diaspora networks, returnee migrants and brain-circulation

Development studies scholars and practitioners have long discussed the negative implications of a brain-drain from developing countries towards the Global North. More recently, the idea of a 'brain-circulation' has taken hold, in which highly educated professionals return to their home countries and bring crucial experience and networks with them (Saxenian 2002, Majluf 2007). Both India and the Philippines exhibit a large outward labour migration. Close to 10 million overseas Filipino workers (OFWs) are employed as contract workers abroad, contributing more than US$21 billion (in 2012) in remittances to the Philippine economy (NSO 2013). The majority of their work is in unskilled or low-skilled service jobs, or unrelated to (potential) offshore services. Only 1 per cent of OFWs occupy administrative/managerial or technical professions in the US (Yi 2012: 130). So far, the impact of returnee migrants on the Filipino offshore service sector has therefore been low.

Although India has seen much low-skilled labour migration as well, a considerable number of highly skilled professionals and researchers have migrated to the US. These diaspora networks have been crucial for the rise India's IT sector (Engman 2010: 225). The US is the most attractive destination for Indian PhD students and Indians encompass the largest group of foreign students in engineering and sciences in the US, namely 68,000 students in 2009 (van Riemsdijk 2013).

Recently, many US-educated and trained professionals have returned to India due to increased economic opportunities in their home country, as well as due to personal, cultural and lifestyle reasons (Wadhwa *et al.* 2011). Several of these returned non-resident Indians (RNRIs) set up own successful offshore service businesses in India with the help of their experience and networks from abroad (Chacko 2007). Brain-circulation has been an important component of India's integration into the global economy and it remains to be seen if the Philippines is able to benefit from returning outward migration in the future.

Conclusions: emerging specialisations in the international division of labour

This chapter has shown how varied the integration into GSPNs in India and the Philippines has been. Though foreign investors and clients started to source services from both countries based on the idea of labour arbitrage, strategic coupling took place on the basis of different regional assets. In the Indian case, this was based on technical and management capabilities of the Indian elite, whereas in the Philippines, English-language advantages of the Filipino labour force were the main regional asset. This constitutes the single most important difference in regional assets and has important implications for the types of services produced. The differences in human capital, not limited to the local workforce but also in the existence of successful entrepreneurs and technically skilled returnee migrants with crucial networks in the service recipient home markets, distinguish the Indian case markedly from the Philippines.

These findings provide a first starting point for further discussions of a services-led model of economic development, since they show how diverse the trajectories of both countries' integration into GSPNs has been and how strategic coupling of regions with the sector has taken place in very different ways. So far, the maturing of the offshore service industry has led to an emerging specialisation of the roles India and the Philippines occupy in the international division of labour. Though the different entry points into the offshore service sector play a role, they do not fully explain the differences in the type and quality of services provided, which depend on the availability of regional assets. With the maturing of the offshore service sector these differences have become more pronounced over time, for example due to the relocation of voice-based activities from India to the Philippines. Both countries have not been acting independent of each other, but their offshore delivery networks have become increasingly connected. MNCs have hedged their investment by opting for advanced models of offshore service delivery, including offshore service centres operating out of several countries simultaneously.

More recently, Indian companies have started to invest in the Philippines, mainly establishing subsidiaries offering voice-based services to clients in the Global North. This increasing specialisation in call centre work, which is considered to be at the lower-end of the value chain, places the Philippines at a lower-end spectrum of services provision. By retaining management and control functions, as well as higher value-added services in India, these companies orchestrate the formation of a deeper international division of labour. At the same time, both countries pursue strategies for moving up the services value chain and upgrading opportunities may exist for the Philippines into higher value-added non-voice based services. If upgrading strategies in the Philippines prove successful, more direct competition for similar types of services between both countries might arise.

To what extent the relatively low-end service provision from the Philippines will be beneficial for economic development in the long run remains to be seen. This chapter has focused on the emergence of the sector, discussing strategic coupling on a state level of two countries. Future research could continue the enquiry at a different scale: how does the process of strategic coupling occur in specific cities and regions, and which (local) actors are involved in enabling and facilitating investment attraction and offshore service delivery? Also, more research is needed on the evolution of GSPNs. To what extent is upgrading into higher value-added services occurring and how can this be facilitated in both India and the Philippines? Finally, more research on local outcomes of services-led economic development is required for understanding the opportunities and implications arising from this form of contemporary globalisation for local economic development.

Notes

1 The term 'offshoring' refers to a change of location of a tasks, independent of whether simultaneous outsourcing (the transfer of ownerships of the tasks) is occurring, and can be defined 'the transnational relocation or dispersion of service related activities that had previously been performed in the home country' (Bunyaratavej *et al.* 2011: 71).

2 Domestic services have been included in the calculation (though offshoring is usually export oriented) and more recently even hardware production (both for domestic consumption and exports) has been added (e.g. NASSCOM 2012) to augment total numbers.

3 BPAP was renamed in 2013 Information Technology Business Processing Association of the Philippines (IBPAP) to signify a move away from simple processing to IT.

References

Beerepoot, N. and B. Lambregts (2015) Competition in online job marketplaces: towards a global labour market for service outsourcing? *Global Networks*, 15 (2): 236–255.

Brown, P., H. Lauder and D. Ashton (2011) *The Global Auction: The Broken Promises of Education, Jobs, and Incomes*. Oxford University Press: Oxford

Bryson, J.R. (2007) The second global shift: The offshoring or global sourcing of corporate services and the rise of distanciated emotional labour. *Geografiska Annaler: Series B, Human Geography*, 89 (S1): 31–43.

Bunyaratavej, K., J. Doh, E.D. Hahn, A.Y. Lewin and S. Massini (2011) Conceptual issues in services offshoring research: A multidisciplinary review. *Group and Organization Management*, 36 (1): 70 –102.

Chacko, E. (2007) From brain drain to brain gain: Reverse migration to Bangalore and Hyderabad, India's globalizing high tech cities. *GeoJournal*, 68 (2–3): 131–140.

Coe N.M., M. Hess, H.W.C. Yeung, P. Dicken and J. Henderson (2004) 'Globalizing' regional development: A global production networks perspective. *Transactions of the Institute of British Geographers*, 29 (4): 468–484.

Coe N.M., P. Dicken and M. Hess (2008) Global production networks: Realizing the potential. *Journal of Economic Geography*, 8 (3): 271–295.

Das, G. (2002) *India Unbound. From Independence to the Global Information Age*. Penguin Books: New Delhi.

Dossani, R. (2013) A Decade after the Y2K problem: Has Indian IT emerged? In: Breznitz D. and J. Zysman, (eds). *The Third Globalization,* pp. 158–177. Oxford University Press: New York and London.

Dossani, R and M. Kenney (2007) The next wave of globalization: Relocating service provision to India. *World Development*, 35: 772–791.

Dossani, R and M. Kenney (2009) Service provision for the global economy: The evolving Indian experience. *Review of Policy Research*, 26 (1–2): 77–104.

Economist, The (2012) At the Front of the Back Office. How the Philippines beat India in Call Centres. 23 June. www.economist.com/node/21557350. Accessed on 9 September, 2013.

Engman, M. (2010) Exporting information technology services: In the footsteps of India. In: Cattaneo, O., M. Engman, S. Saez and R.M. Stern, (eds). *International Trade in Services: New Trends and Opportunities for Developing Countries*, pp. 219–262. World Bank: Washington, DC.

Fink, C., A. Mattoo and R. Rathindran (2001) *Liberalizing Basic Telecommunications: The Asian Experience*. Policy Research Working Paper 2718, World Bank: Washington, DC.

Gereffi, G. and K. Fernandez-Stark (2010) *The Offshore Services Global Value Chain*. CORFO-Report, March. Center on Globalization, Governance and Competitiveness, Duke University, North Carolina.

Ghani, E. (2010) *The Service Revolution in South Asia*. Oxford University Press: Oxford

Goswami, A.G., A. Mattoo and S. Saez (2012) *Exporting Services: A Developing Country Perspective*. World Bank: Washington DC.

Gutierrez, B.P.B. and R.A. Rodriguez (2013) Diversification strategies of large business groups in the Philippines. *Philippine Management Review*, 20: 65–82.

Hardy, J., M. Sass and M.P. Fifekova (2011) Impacts of horizontal and vertical foreign investment in business services: the experience of Hungary, Slovakia and the Czech Republic. *European Urban and Regional Studies*, 18 (4): 427–443.

Henderson, J., P. Dicken, M. Hess, N.M. Coe and H.W.C. Yeung (2002) Global production networks and the analysis of economic development. *Review of International Political Economy*, 9(3): 436–464.

IBM (Global Business Services) (2010) *Global Location Trends Annual Report*. IBM Corporation: Somers, NY.

Karnik, K. (2012) *Coalition of Competitors. The Story of NASSCOM and the IT Industry.* HarperCollins Publishers: Noida.

Majluf, L.A. (2007) Offshore outsourcing of services: Trends and challenges for developing countries. In: Paus, E. (ed.). *Global Capitalism Unbound: Winners and Losers from Offshore Outsourcing*, pp. 147–161. Palgrave MacMillan: New York.

Massini, S. and M. Miozzo (2012) Outsourcing and offshoring of business services: Challenges to theory, management and geography of innovation. *Regional Studies*, 46 (9): 1219–1242.

Milberg, W. and D. Winkler (2013) *Outsourcing Economics. Global Value Chains in Capitalist Development.* Cambridge University Press: Cambridge.

NASSCOM (2012) *The IT-BPO Sector in India. Strategic Review 2012.* Executive Summary. www.nasscom.in/sites/default/files/researchreports/SR_2012_Executive_Summary.pd. Accessed on 20 September 2013.

Nilekani, N. (2008) *Imagining India. Ideas for the New Century.* Allen Lane, Penguin Group: New Delhi.

NSO (National Statistics Office) (2013) Total number of OFWs is estimated at 2.2 Million. www.census.gov.ph/content/total-number-ofws-estimated-22-million-results-2012-survey-overseas-filipinos. Accessed on 9 September 2013.

Panagariya, A. (2008) *India the Emerging Giant*, Oxford University Press: New York.

Parthasarathy, B. (2013) The changing character of Indian offshore ICT services provision, 1985–2010. In: Bardhan, A., D.M. Jaffee and C.A. Kroll, (eds). *The Oxford Handbook of Offshoring and Global Employment,* pp. 380–404. Oxford University Press: Oxford.

Parthasarathy, B. and Y. Aoyama (2006) From software Services to RandD services: Local entrepreneurship in the software industry in Bangalore, India. *Environment and Planning A*, 38 (7): 1269–1285.

Ramadorai, S. (2011) *The TCS Story ... and Beyond.* Portfolio, Penguin Group: New Delhi.

Rodolfo, C.S. (2005) *Sustaining Philippine Advantage in Business Process Outsourcing.* Discussion Paper Series No. 28. Philippine Institute for Development Studies.

Sass, M. and M. Fifekova (2011) Offshoring and outsourcing business services to Central and Eastern Europe: Some empirical and conceptual considerations, *European Planning Studies*, 19 (9): 1593–1609.

Saxenian, A. (2002) Transnational communities and the evolution of global production networks: The cases of Taiwan, China and India. *Industry and Innovation*, 9 (3): 183–202.

Tholons (2013) *2013 Top 100 Outsourcing Destinations. Rankings and Report Overview.* www.tholons.com/TholonsTop100/pdf/Tholons%20Top%20100%202013_Rankings%20and%20Report%20Overview.pdf.

Tullao, T.S. (2003) *Globalization and Education.* Philippines APEC Study Center Network and Philippines Institute for Development Studies: Makati City.

UNCTAD (United Nations Conference on Trade and Development) (2004) *World Investment Report 2004: The Shift Towards Services.* United Nations Conference on Trade and Development: New York and Geneva.

UNESCO (United Nations Educational, Scientific and Cultural Organization) (2006) *General Profile – India.* Institute for Statistics. http://stats.uis.unesco.org/unesco/TableViewer/document.aspx?ReportId=124andIF_Language=engandBR_Country=3560andBR_Region=40535. Accessed on 10 August 2013.

UNESCO (2008) *General Profile – Philippines.* Institute for Statistics. http://stats.uis.unesco.org/unesco/TableViewer/document.aspx?ReportId=124andIF_Language=engandBR_Country=6080andBR_Region=40515. Accessed on 10 August 2013.

Upadhya, C. (2011) Software and the 'new' middle class in the 'New India'. In: Baviskar, A. and R. Ray, (eds). *Elite and Everyman: The Cultural Politics of the Indian Middle Classes*, pp. 167–192. Routledge: New Delhi.

van Riemsdijk, M. (2013) Talent acquisition in the IT industry in Bangalore: A multi-level study. *Tijdschrift voor Economische en Sociale Geografie*, 104 (4): 478–490.

Wadhwa, V., S. Jain, A. Saxenian, G.A. Gereffi and H. Wang (2011) *The Grass is Indeed Greener in India and China for Returnee Entrepreneurs*, Part IV. Kauffman Foundation: Kansas City, Missouri.

Welch, A. (2011) *Higher Education in Southeast Asia. Blurring Borders, Changing Balance.* Routledge: New York.

World Bank (2013) *Data: Tertiary School Enrolment.* http://data.worldbank.org/indicator/SE.TER.ENRR. Accessed on 8 September 2013.

World Bank and IFC (International Finance Corporation) (2013) *Doing Business 2013.* www.doingbusiness.org/~/media/GIAWB/Doing%20Business/Documents/Annual-Reports/English/DB13-full-report.pdf. Accessed on 6 September 2013.

Yi, S. (2012) Reaching the world through private sector initiative: Service exports from the Philippines. In: Goswami, A. G., A. Mattoo and S. Saez, (eds). *Exporting Services: A Developing Country Perspective*, pp. 121–159. World Bank: Washington, DC.

4 The BPO industry and the Philippine trade in services

Boon or bane?

Antoinette R. Raquiza

Introduction

In recent years, the Philippines has distinguished itself as having one of the fastest growing economies in Southeast Asia – a record that would have been unthinkable a decade ago when the country was struggling to keep pace with its industrializing neighbors (Bello 2000; Medalla *et al.* 1995; Tecson 2003). With its gross domestic product registering 7.2 per cent growth in 2013 and an annual growth average of 5.9 per cent for 2011–2013 (Navarro and Llanto 2014: 1), the country seems to have broken from its past of low productivity, policy misfires and corruption and be on track to becoming the region's next rising star. And partly the reason for its exceptional performance has been the booming business process outsourcing (BPO) services industry.

The rise of the BPO services industry in the country, in fact, has been nothing less than spectacular. Earning only about US$350 million in 2001 (Satumba 2008: 14), it has grown into a multi-billion dollar industry in record time. For the year 2012, the Bangko Sentral ng Pilipinas (2014) put the industry's earnings at $13.5 billion and workforce at 769,932. The industry is today among the biggest employers of the country's skilled labor. Equally important, the BPO industry has indirectly fuelled growth in other businesses – notably, retail, banking, telecommunications, and electricity (see also Beerepoot and Vogelzang, this volume). According to the Information Technology and Business Process Association of the Philippines (IBPAP), for every BPO job, about 2.5 jobs are created in support industries.[1]

Surveying BPO establishments in the country, but especially in Metro Manila, one would get a sense of how the industry is changing the urban landscape and domestic economy. Mixed-use commercial complexes – with residential units, hotels, shops, restaurants, and convenience stores – have sprung around high-rise call centers catering to the 24/7 BPO community. One such place, for instance, is Eastwood Cyberpark in Pasig City, Metro Manila: it boasts of having 59 companies, including some of the country's biggest call centers, that reportedly employ a total workforce of 60,000 (Lee and Sayson 2014). In this light, the success of the BPO industry has been cited as the harbinger of better days for the region's erstwhile economic laggard.

The Philippine pattern of economic growth, however, deserves careful scrutiny. The economy's apparent good fortune has been propelled by the dramatic growth of the country's trade in services. Long an exporter of labor, the Philippines has recently added tourism, gaming, and the BPO industry as its top dollar earners. The country today is not only the world's third biggest recipient of overseas workers' remittances, it is also among the choice destinations of BPO foreign investors. In effect, the country's economic take-off has come largely on the back of a surging services sector that caters to the needs of foreign markets.

At the core of the Philippine pattern of trade in services is a paradox. The country has been able to distinguish itself as among the top services outsourcing destinations in the world, and its comparative advantage over other developing countries is its labor force (Shiraishi 2014). The Philippines places high in BPO investors' preferred locations largely due to its English-speaking, skilled workers, many of whom have a 'cultural affinity' with the west (Alava 2006). Yet, these same factors that bring in foreign investors (or locators), looking for a cost-competitive, service-oriented workforce that can relate with their international clientele, have since the 1970s promoted the outmigration of the country's best and brightest in search of better-paying jobs abroad (see, for instance, Gonzalez 2008) – thus producing contradictory currents in the domestic labor market. In fact, however, no explanation can rely entirely on the character of the Philippine workforce – rather, how the skills and capacities of that workforce are mobilized into either BPO work in the country or overseas employment depends on an underlying structure of those political and economic forces that structure how labor resources are deployed.

The present chapter links the explosion of export labor to the country's political economy: the merging of political and business interests in state institutions means that the change in political leadership has also occasioned changes in policy constituencies – an institutional setting that has worked against the development of strategic industries that could absorb highly skilled labor. Limited sectoral development, in turn, has greatly contributed to labor migration (Ruiz 2014). The chapter also suggests that the tug and pull in the country's trade in services could eventually become a drag on the country's climb up the BPO value chain unless the country broadens and diversifies the base of the real economy.

The chapter begins by presenting an overview of the Philippine BPO industry toward identifying factors that explain its success and the challenges to its continued growth. I then situate this discussion within an analysis of the Philippine economy, including structural constraints that have previously stumped the country's growth and prompted more and more Filipinos to seek work abroad. I therefore stress an approach that links the BPO industry's fate to that of the country's political economy.

The rise of the Philippine BPO industry

The Philippine BPO services industry has three distinct features.[2] First, it specializes and is, in fact, the global leader in contact or call centers. Voice-based services account for much of the industry's growth. In 2012, contact centers contributed about 56 and 63 per cent to the industry's total revenues and employment, respectively; they also accounted for $7.1 billion or 56.5 per cent of the industry's export receipts (Bangko Sental ng Pilipinas 2014). While much has been said about the country now moving toward high-value, non-voice services, available government figures show mixed results. On the one hand, the breakdown of total employment figures in Table 4.1 shows that the number of people working in contact centers is on the decline, while those in the separate categories of transcription services and 'other BPO' services (e.g., human resources, accounting, and finance) are rising. On the other hand, as per Table 4.2, the call center industry continues to rake in more than half of the total BPO revenues; between 2005 and 2012, the revenue share of transcription services went up from 0.4 per cent to 1.5 per cent while that of services under the residual category of 'other BPOs' actually went down from about 29 per cent to 20 per cent.

Second, the industry is dominated by multinational enterprises (MNEs). Over the years, the participation of foreign businesses increased, from 66.9 per cent (or $0.3 billion) in 2005 to 95 per cent (or about $7 billion) of the total equity capital investments in 2012. Conversely, the number of Filipino-owned BPO companies declined, with not a few selling or turning over control of their businesses to MNEs – definitely an added draw to foreign capital looking to gain a foothold or expand market power in the domestic industry. For instance, in January 2014, the Ayala Corporation sold its 29 per cent share in Stream Global Services, Inc. to US-based Convergys (Loyola 2014). Both Stream Global Services and Convergys specialize in customer management services globally, including in the Philippines. A year earlier, the giant Philippine Long Distance Telephone Company (PLDT) sold its BPO subsidiary, SPi Global, to Asia Outsourcing Gamma Limited (AOGL), which is controlled by a global private equity firm, Capital Partners (Lowe 2013).[3] In both cases, the MNEs gained majority control over the BPO companies in order to increase their market power in the Philippines and globally. That said, the Philippine conglomerates in these cases maintained some involvement in the BPO services industry but at a drastically limited scale. Third, primarily because of the nature of its leading subsector and the dominance of MNEs, the BPO services industry's main contribution to economic growth falls in the realm of trade in

Table 4.1 Employment by IT-BPO category, Philippines, 2005 and 2012

	2005		*2012*	
	No. of Workers	*%*	*No. of Workers*	*%*
Contact center	96,246	69.7	487,757	63.3
Transcription	1,785	1.3	16,997	2.2
Animation	1,864	1.4	4,164	0.5
Software development	17,829	12.9	64,922	8.4
Other BPOs	20,278	14.7	196,092	25.5
Total industry	**138,002**	**100**	**769,932**	**100**

Source: Bangko Sentral ng Pilipinas (www.bsp.gov.ph/statistics/keystat/ict/itbpo_4.htm)

Table 4.2 Revenue by IT-BPO category, Philippines, 2005 and 2012

	2005		*2012*	
	No. of Workers	*%*	*No. of Workers*	*%*
Contact center	986	49.4	7,587	56.4
Transcription	8	0.4	198	1.5
Animation	17	0.9	80	0.6
Software development	399	20.0	2,848	21.2
Other BPOs	585	29.3	2,736	20.3
Total industry	**1,996**	**100**	**13,450**	**100**

Source: Bangko Sentral ng Pilipinas (www.bsp.gov.ph/statistics/keystat/ict/itbpo_1.htm)

services. More than 90 per cent (or $12.5 billion) of the entire industry earnings in 2012 came from export receipts (see Table 4.3).

Global character

As suggested by its specific configuration, the BPO services industry is largely a product of a globalizing economy. While the industry has been in the Philippines since the 1980s when pagers hit it big in the domestic market, its potential as a driver of domestic economic growth became clear only in the 1990s. By then, the reorganization of production, distribution, and consumption global networks due to technological advances, competitive pressures, and further economic liberalization had facilitated the offshoring and outsourcing (OandO) activities of MNEs. For knowledge-based businesses, advances in information and communication technology (codification and digitization of information, real-time monitoring, etc.) meant an explosion of the OandO of services at a global scale (Bartels and Lederer 2009).

Table 4.3 Revenue of and foreign direct investment in IT-BPO Services, Philippines, various years

	2005	*2006*	*2007*	*2008*	*2009*	*2010*	*2011*	*2012*
Sales revenue[a] (in US$M)	1,996	2,906	4,368	6,325	8,258	10,058	12,074	13,450
Export revenue[b] (in US$M)	1,388	2,288	3,490	5,288	7,717	9,470	11,160	12,503
Foreign direct investment[c] (In US$M)	329	376	821	1,825	2,376	4,288	5,355	6,959
Foreign-to-total equity ratio[c] (per cent)	66.9	60.4	87.9	93.3	91.8	97.6	93.2	95

Source: Bangko Sentral ng Pilipinas: [a] www.bsp.gov.ph/statistics/keystat/ict/itbpo_1.htm; [b] www.bsp.gov.ph/statistics/keystat/ict/itbpo_2.1.htm; [c] www.bsp.gov.ph/statistics/keystat/ict/itbpo_3.1.htm

This trend, allowing for the fragmentation and dispersal of global services provision, proved a boon to the Philippines. The country that had struggled to match the amount of foreign investments that its industrializing neighbors enjoyed[4] began cashing in on the BPO services industry. This link between the global economy and the domestic BPO services industry, in fact, could be gleaned in the second half of 2000s when the 2007–2008 global financial and economic crises saw many more MNEs relocating their front or back office services to offshore in-house centers or contracting these functions out to third-party service providers. As Table 4.3 shows, from 2006 to 2012, foreign investments in the IT-BPO sector rose from a mere $376 million to around $6.96 billion while foreign-to-total equity ratio went up from about 60 to 95 per cent.

A key factor for the country landing among the MNEs' preferred offshoring sites for services is the distinct nature of its labor force. The country boasts of of a low-cost, yet, skilled working population that, due to the country's colonial past, is also culturally attuned to northern populations and global markets. Largely left untapped before the surge of the BPO services industry, millions of college graduates and professionals were able to find work and thrive abroad. Today, the BPO services industry is providing new graduates a viable work alternative to going overseas (Beerepoot and Hendriks 2013). According to the World Bank (2013), during the past decade, 200,000 college graduates yearly left to work abroad while 52,000 of the 240,000 who found employment in the country's domestic formal sector went to work for the BPO industry.

The global BPO services industry, therefore, found a ready talent pool that appealed to an international clientele. Batt *et al.* (2009), noting that MNE call centers are generally located in former colonies, argue that cultural affinity between the host country and the foreign clientele is much more important in the services industry than it is to manufacturing, where direct access to raw materials and product markets are primary considerations (pp. 464–465). The Philippine experience would bear out this pattern. In Asia, the country stands out for being dominantly Catholic, a legacy of 300-year Spanish rule. More importantly, almost half a century under American colonial rule had laid down the foundation of electoral democracy and set the English language as the dominant medium of instruction and for policy-making. The Philippines takes pride in being the world's third largest English-speaking country.[5] To this day, an American-style educational system produces as many as 300,000 to 500,000 college graduates every year. Such 'westernized' cultural and institutional features make the country a relatively easy pick for foreign investors, notably Americans and Europeans, locating their customer care services abroad. Finally, labor cost in the Philippines is relatively low: one estimate pegged it at only 16 per cent of what a company would pay for the same kind of work in the United States (Satumba 2008: 13).

The other proximate factor for the BPO services industry's rapid expansion in the country is the existence of a robust domestic entrepreneurial class. In fact, it was the private sector, notably those in the real estate business, that first took notice of the BPO services industry's potential and sought government action to more effectively attract foreign MNEs to invest in the Philippines. In 1997, with the

Asian financial crisis wreaking havoc on the property sector, the idea of transforming empty skyscrapers, originally intended as residential and office spaces, into IT centers or parks came upon Megaworld's Andrew Tan.[6] Tan campaigned to have Eastwood City get accreditation under the Philippine Economic Zone Authority (PEZA) program and thus qualify for ecozone fiscal and non-fiscal incentives. As part of working out the program, PEZA sent a team that included Megaworld business executives to Bangalore to study that city's successful promotion of the BPO export services industry. Inputs from the study visit went to amending the Special Economic Zone Act of 1995 to provide incentives to BPO services providers who set up office in PEZA-registered IT parks and centers or buildings, *and* to BPO *facilities* providers, or those who build, own, and lease out these so-called cyberzones. In 1999, Eastwood became the first PEZA-registered IT center.

Since the late 1990s, government has become the third pillar of the domestic BPO services industry. In 2000, the Board of Investments included the BPO and IT-related industries in its annual Investment Priorities Plan (De Vera and Lee U 2003: 171), entitling BOI-registered IT and BPO business activities to incentives under the Omnibus Investment Act of 1987. The industry has also earned a place in the Medium-Term Philippine Development Plan (2005–2010, and 2011–2016). As for PEZA, by August 2014, it had launched and administered incentives to 306 operating ecozones, 201 of which are IT parks and centers (Magkilat 2014).

Government incentives, therefore, sought to draw in BPO services MNEs. Yet, these incentives have also directly and indirectly fuelled real estate and property development. In so doing, the policy incentivizes two sets of industry players, cementing a partnership between them: Filipino property developers who provide BPO operators, usually MNEs, with state-of-the-art facilities and prime real estate, and BPO operators that are located in PEZA-accredited in these PEZA-accredited IT parks and centers and thus get incentives as well. The biggest BPO companies lease office space in several buildings, spread out across the metropolis and in other regions and owned by the country's largest property developers.

The country's richest have been quick to take advantage of the opportunities presented by these foreign investors. From retail giant Henry Sy's SM Prime Holdings to beer and tobacco maker Lucio Tan's Eton Properties and real estate magnet Andrew Gotianun's Filinvest – all have since joined Andrew Tan in building and renting out high-rise call center and IT-enabled facilities for BPO MNEs (Raquiza 2014). At least two family conglomerates – the Ayalas and Gokongweis – have set up some IT businesses but are more vested in providing BPO facilities through their real estate and property development companies, Ayala Land and Robinson Land, respectively.

There are also a few big companies whose main business is to construct and provide top-of-the-line building and telecommunication facilities – the so-called IT enablers. A prime example is the Diversified Technology Solutions International Inc. (DTSI) Group that has partnered with the biggest MNEs in the business (e.g., leading IT-BPO operators Accenture and Convergys as well as JP Morgan's global in-house service center). According to its corporate website, DTSI has set up 60 per cent of call center seats in the Philippines (including 12,000 that it directly manages) and leases out 100,000 square meters of office space. Founded in 1997, DTSI entered into a strategic partnership with Nippon Telephone and Telegraph (NTT) Communications Corporation in 2012, when the Japanese telecommunication giant bought a 50.1 per cent stake in DTSI's holding company (Dumlao 2014).

As may be gleaned from the discussion thus far, the rapid growth of the global BPO industry has largely benefited Philippine conglomerates – those who are highly liquid and thus can, with relative ease, shift investments in response to changing demands of the global economy (Raquiza 2014). The existence of a strong domestic commercial class has provided MNEs a domestic platform on which to build their BPO services businesses. Philippine A-list corporations presented themselves or their subsidiaries as attractive partners of these MNEs – either as minority stakeholders in multinational BPO services enterprises or as providers of BPO facilities. They have also driven policy to make such partnerships highly profitable.

The robust growth of the sector may be gleaned from the high-profile role played by the Information Technology and Business Process Association of the Philippines (IBPAP). IBPAP was established in 2004 and is composed of the major industry players, both multinational and top domestic corporations. In 2011, the industry, with government support, produced the IT-BPO Road Map 2012–2016[7] that projects the generation of 1.3 million industry jobs and $25 billion in export receipts by 2016 – a figure that, as industry leaders highlight, would match the amount of remittances sent home by some 10 million Filipino permanent, temporary, and irregular (or undocumented) migrants (Veniles 2013).

Structural constraints

In order to fully understand the success and the prospects of the country's BPO services industry, there is a need to examine the economy on which it is grafted. In important ways, the BPO services industry reflects the best and most troubling aspects of the Philippine economy. The industry has been able to tap into the country's skilled labor force – a resource that, it can be argued, had mostly been best utilized abroad. Because of the BPO industry's growing contribution to the economy, it has become possible for government and the corporate sector to think of a future in which economic success lies in the country keeping its best talents at home. Perhaps referring to the country's growth strategy that had in years past relied heavily on export labor, an IBPAP official said: 'The difference is that our 1.3 million workers will be here with their families, and they spend all their money here.'[8]

The current configuration of the country's BPO services industry, however, also speaks of its present constraints. That the industry is dominated by MNEs that hire Filipinos to staff its Philippine front and back offices servicing foreign markets suggests that the industry has shallow roots in the country's economy. This outward orientation of the BPO industry can partly be explained by the economy having experienced limited structural transformation. Agriculture and manufacturing suffer from low productivity, while the services sector, which contributes more than 50 per cent of the country's growth, specializes in low-value, low-skilled activities (World Bank 2013: 2). Even as modern high-rises have begun to crowd the country's skyline, about 92 per cent of all registered businesses are micro enterprises, each employing no more than one to nine people (Aldaba 2012). In fact, one study suggests that the limited demand for skilled labor in other industries has contributed to lowering labor costs in the BPO services industry (Mitra 2011).

It is also noteworthy that the BPO services industry has few forward linkages with other domestic sectors and industries. A 2008 study noted that the country's BPO industry was more of a consumer of inputs from, rather than a supplier of inputs to, other sectors. It availed of the services of banking, telecommunication, electricity, and 37 other industries, but itself provided services to only three other industries: tourism, whole and retail trade, and banking (Magtibay-Ramos *et al.* 2008: 6). As such, it can be argued that the biggest contribution of the BPO services industry to the country's economy is in job generation that, in turn, has contributed to the expansion of the middle class and fuelled the country's consumption-led economy. This trend lines up with the Philippines's other big economic story: the phenomenal growth over the past two decades of Filipino overseas workers' remittances, with the amount totalling $25 billion in 2013. At present, the country deploys 1 million temporary workers to overseas destinations every year, most of whom are, however, rehires (Orbeta 2014).

Equally noteworthy is the limited participation of Filipino entrepreneurs in BPO service delivery. To be sure, Filipino BPO owners and operations have kept up a presence in the industry. There is the Philippine Call Center Alliance that represents the interests of small and medium enterprises in the sector. Yet, the main form of participation of Philippine big business in the industry is as builders and landlords of BPO facilities (see also Kleibert in this volume). Simply put, the main players in the Philippine side have been real estate and property developers and the so-called IT enablers – a fact that may be gleaned from their inclusion in government missions abroad aimed at drawing in foreign locators.

What would account for this pattern of growth? In another work, I suggest that the rise of the services sector may be rooted in the institutional settings of Filipino elites (Raquiza 2012). Since the establishment of the first all-Filipino colonial state in 1935, this institutional setting has characterized the interaction of politics and economic policy-making in the country. Political leaders get into public office based on their personal wealth and social networks, while most of the country's top economic managers are appointed based on their personal ties with the incumbent rather than membership in the state bureaucracy. Because there is very little institutional differentiation between public policy-making authority and private economic power, political competition presents a risk to contending politicians' economic allies. Accordingly, regime changes have often displaced the top management of economic agencies – and so have been disruptive to long-term public and private investments. Contrast this institutional setting, for instance, with that of Thailand: due to a history of state-building dating back to the nineteenth century, the technocracy is a much stronger policy actor than elected national politicians, who first flexed their muscles in the 1970s.[9] In Thailand, even as national political leaders come and go, the technocrats are able to shepherd programs and policies through political transitions. Hence, despite the numerous coups that pepper Thai history, domestic businesses have been able to grow, partly because state elites have been able to maintain policy continuity (Raquiza 2012).

There are myriad consequences of the Philippine political arrangement, which I have called the proprietary polity because of the close connection between political control and economic power. For the present purposes, however, two consequences deserve particular attention. One, in the context of weak state institutions (i.e., when public authority merges with private interests), incumbents have tended to hold on to power by going after the economic concerns of potential rivals and their business allies. Two, policy-makers tend to have short-time horizons partly in anticipation of political turnovers (even those that follow from scheduled elections). In the country's history, two transitions stand out as turning points in the country's sectoral development: the imposition of martial law in 1972 when President Ferdinand Marcos did away with the traditional opposition, many members of which had allies or families that benefited from the country's import substitution industrialization policy; and, the restoration of electoral democracy in 1986 when the Corazon Aquino presidency summarily dismantled industrial programs and projects that were identified with Marcos and his cronies (Raquiza 2012). These two regime changes occasioned massive government reorganization and dramatic economic policy swings.

In this light, political transitions have been disruptive to the economy and, more specifically, to long-term capital accumulation. Rather, the incentive structure of a proprietary polity favors fast-moving commercial transactions rather than long-gestating, slow-maturing investments. It is noteworthy that, among the Association of Southeast Asian Nations (ASEAN) emerging markets (i.e., Thailand, Malaysia, and Indonesia), only the Philippines has seen a steady, long-term decline of its manufacturing sector since the 1980s. To illustrate, Philippine manufacturing's contribution to gross domestic product decreased from 26 per cent in 1980 to 21 per cent in 2012, while that of Thailand went up from 22 per cent in 1980 to 33 per cent in 2013 (World Bank n.d.).

While this link between state settings and industrialization requires further investigation, the Philippine experience suggests that long-maturing investments and sunk capital costs of industrial development were harder to sustain in the volatile environment of the proprietary polity. In contrast, commercial interests, which thrive on quick turnovers, are better able to survive political disruptions. That the global BPO industry has found fertile ground in the Philippines is partly a testament to the market power and resilience of the country's commercial elites – a virtual who's who in *Forbes* magazine's richest Filipinos (Raquiza 2014).

Challenges

The Philippines presents a case of how trade in services has enabled the country to break from a history of low growth and into the elite circle of emerging economies. The presence of a competitive workforce has positioned the Philippines to partake in the promise of globalization, in which the changing organization of capitalist production has allowed for new and more flexible working arrangements. The Philippines, in fact, is able to meet the demands of the diversifying global market: it not only exports labor, largely but not exclusively to meet the demand for low-skilled work in advanced capitalist countries, but also now provides skilled labor for MNEs' offshore services outsourcing activities. In these areas, the Philippines has been able to respond to external demand for labor but with limited spillover effects on domestic production.

This chapter questions whether trading in human resources, as currently configured in the Philippines, is a sustainable path to development. The BPO industry and export labor pull in different directions: while climbing the BPO value chain requires increasing the ranks of highly skilled workers in the country, the dominant trend continues to be for such workers to seek employment abroad (Gonzalez 2008). One study attributes the outflow of professionals to the underdevelopment of the Philippine economy and, therefore, the low demand for highly skilled labor (Ruiz 2014). According to the Science Education Institute, there were some 16,000 professionals with science training who left the country between 2000 and 2012 in search of higher-paying jobs; from 1990 to 2009, the number of such highly skilled professionals with work contracts went up 148 per cent to 24,502 (Icamina 2012). More noteworthy, there has also been a trend of BPO workers actually leaving to work for higher-paying call centers abroad (Cahiles-Magkilat 2012).

In this connection, two specific questions arise: first, will the BPO industry expand and diversify enough to absorb and, in fact, entice the country's highly mobile, high-skilled professionals to stay given the wage differential between similar work here and abroad? Second, will the country's educational system produce enough talents to make up for lost human resources?

In order to ensure a steady to ensure a steady supply of skilled labor to meet the growing IT-BPO industry's needs, government and the private sector have begun to invest in education and supplemental trainings. One major initiative is the Service Management Program (SMP). Developed by IBPAP and the Commission on Higher Education (CHED), the SMP is a 21-unit specialized course to be run by partner universities aimed at developing business administration, management, or information technology students' skills to correspond to the qualifications for a BPO entry-level position.[10] Yet, urgent and necessary as this response is, it cannot adequately address the need for a comprehensive and long-term approach to raising the IT-BPO industry's competitiveness.

For the domestic BPO services industry to climb to the intermediate and even high end of the BPO value chain requires situating the industry within a robust industrializing economy. In this connection, one study stresses the importance for developing countries to see services offshore outsourcing and manufacturing offshore outsourcing as both integral to the growth process, suggesting that one feeds into the other as they generate and deepen knowledge and skills needed by the other (Bartels and Lederer 2009).

In fact, it can be argued that the Philippines is the exception that proves the rule: it is ranked with rapidly industrializing India, China, and Malaysia as among the top BPO destinations but it is the only country among the four whose main participation in the BPO global network is – at least for now – largely through the delivery of relatively low-end voice-based services. In contrast, an analysis of India's informatics reveals that the attempt at manufacturing hardware, albeit with relatively middling success, has given rise to a robust software industry (Evans 1995) – a development that, in turn, can partly explain the leading role played by India's National Association of Software and Services Companies (NASSCOM) in its country's IT-BPO industry (Karnik 2012). A comparison between India and the Philippine BPO industries also reveals that, in 2005, while software and IT services contributed 70 per cent of the total revenues in India, they contributed only 13 per cent in the Philippines (Magtibay-Ramos *et al.* 2008: 4).

The full potential of global offshore outsourcing industry is still unfolding, producing different results in differently configured domestic political economies. The BPO services industry touches on the broader question on whether the perennially changing patterns of production, distribution, and consumption represent a qualitative break in an international political economy marked by the core–periphery power asymmetries. Bartels and Lederer (2009), for instance, assert that the offshore outsourcing industry is shifting the focus of multinational enterprises in labor markets, from blue-collar, factory to white-collar office workers. Nevertheless, decentralization and fragmentation of office functions generally follow the spatial distribution of the traditional international division of labor with high-value research and development functions centralized in advanced industrialized countries and low-value functions concentrated in developing countries.

The Philippine case seems to indicate that the more things change, the more they stay the same. While the country has increased its profile in the global economy, its participation in the global services industry closely follows the traditional international division of labor. The Philippine economy has greatly benefited from the rise of the offshore services outsourcing, but its greatest contribution remains clustered in relatively low value-added services. Unless it integrates its trade in services into a comprehensive development strategy, it may be overtaken by others willing to do the hard work to build their economies from the ground up.

Notes

1 The Information Technology and Business Process Association Philippines chair Danilo Reyes, for instance, noted: 'Think of all the additional jeepney and taxi drivers, Starbucks baristas, and convenience store staff that were added to support the 24x7 lifestyle of our industry!' (IBPAP 2014).

2 Unless otherwise stated, figures in this paragraph are based on Bangko Sentral ng Pilipinas (2014). The Philippine government defines BPO as the delegation of one or more IT-intensive business processes to a third party. Besides call centers, other BPO activities include: software development, animation/creative services, data transcription (for the legal or health professions); back-office processes (related to finance, accounting, and human resource administration); and, engineering design. See 'Understanding the Business Process Outsourcing (BPO) Industry in the Philippines, www.nscb.gov.ph/factsheet/pdf07/FS-200711-ES2-01_BPO.asp (accessed on 5 November 2014).

3 In the PLDT case, it invested some of the proceeds from the sale in AOGL, thus gaining 20 per cent share of the company (Lowe 2013).
4 For 2012, foreign direct investment flows to the Philippines were the lowest among Southeast Asia's emerging markets: with the Philippines estimated to have received only $1.5 billion, as against Thailand's $8.1 billion and Indonesia's $19.2 billion (UNCTAD 2013: 6).
5 See, for instance, the Philippine Department of Tourism's press release at www.tourism.gov.ph/sitepages/history.aspx.
6 The events relayed here based on an interview with Gigi Virata, then a senior officer of the IBPAP on 4 April 2014 in Metro Manila as well as news reports (See 2014; Mangawang 2014).
7 The IT-BPO Road Map 2012–2016 was produced by the Everest Group and Outsource2Philippines with the active participation of the Business Association of the Philippines (later renamed IBPAP) and funding from the Commission on Information and Communications Technology (IBPAP n.d.).
8 IBPAP Chief Executive Officer Jose Mari Mercado, quoted in Lee and Sayson (2014).
9 For a fuller discussion on the relationship between the Thai state and elected politicians, see Anek (1992), Hewison (1989), and Pasuk and Baker (2002).
10 Interview with Virata on 4 April 2014. See also Team Asia (2013) press release.

References

Alava, Aileen S. 2006. 'Industry report: the problem of sustainable competitive advantage in Philippine call centers,' *Philippine Management Review* 13: 1–20.

Aldaba, Rafaelita M. 2012. 'Small and medium enterprises' (SMEs) access to finance: Philippines,' *PIDS Discussion Paper Series* No. 2012 05. Philippine Institute for Development Studies.

Anek Laothamatas. 1992. *Business Associations and the New Political Economy of Thailand: From Bureaucratic Polity to Liberal Corporatism.* Boulder: Westview Press; Singapore: Institute of Southeast Asian Studies.

Bangko Sentral ng Pilipinas. 2014. 'Philippine IT-BPO Services Industry Sustains Double-Digit Growth in 2012.' www.bsp.gov.ph/publications/media.asp?id–3432. Accessed 15 October 2014.

Bangko Sentral ng Pilipinas. n.d. 'Overseas Filipinos (OF) Remittances.' www.bsp.gov.ph/statistics/keystat/ofw.htm. Accessed 15 October 2014.

Bartels, Frank and Suman Lederer. 2009. *Outsourcing Markets in Services: International Business Trends, Patterns and Emerging Issues, and the Role of China and India.* Vienna: United Nations Industrial Development Organization.

Batt, Rosemarie, David Holman and Ursula Holtgrewe. 2009. 'The globalization of service work: comparative institutional perspectives on call centers,' *Industrial and Labor Relations Review* 62 (4): 453–488.

Beerepoot, Niels and Mitch Hendriks. 2013. 'Employability of offshore service workers in the Philippines: opportunities for upward labour mobility or dead-end jobs?' *Work, Employment and Society*, 27 (5): 823–841.

Bello, Walden (2000) 'The Philippines: the making of a neo-classical tragedy,' in Richard Robison, Mark Beeson, Kanishka Jayasuriya and Hyuk-Rae Kim (eds) *Politics and Markets in the Wake of the Asian Crisis.* London and New York: Routledge.

Cahiles-Magkilat, Bernie. 2012. 'Call centers oppose wage hike,' *Manila Bulletin* 3 April.

De Vera, Roberto and Peter Lee U. 2003. 'Information technology and e-commerce in Philippine economy,' in Seiichi Masuyama and Donna Vandenbrink (eds) *Towards a Knowledge-based Economy. East Asia's Changing Industrial Geography*. Tokyo, Nomura Research Institute and Singapore, Institute of Southeast Asian Studies.

Diversified Technology Systems Inc. (n.d.) 'Home page.' www.dtsigroup.com/. Accessed on 2 December 2014.

Dumlao, Doris C. 2014. 'Japanese firm invests in leading BPO enabler,' *Philippine Daily Inquirer* 24 May.

Evans, Peter. 1995. *Embedded Autonomy: States and Industrial Transformation*. Princeton, NJ: Princeton University Press.

Gonzalez, Adelaida P. 2008. 'Heroes or losers: Retention of highly skilled professionals in the Philippines.' Master's thesis, Institute for Social Sciences Graduate School of Development Studies, The Hague, The Netherlands.

Hewison, Kevin. 1989. *Bankers and Bureaucrats: Capital and the Role of the State in Thailand*. New Haven, CT: Yale University Southeast Asia Studies.

IBPAP (IT-Business Process Association Philippines). 2014. 'Speech of IBPAP Chairman Danilo Reyes at 6th IIS.' www.ibpap.org/media-room/ibpap-news/880-speech-of-ibpap-chairman-danilo-reyes. Accessed on 5 November 2014.

IBPAP. n.d. 'IT – BPO Road Map 2011–2016.' www.ibpap.org/about-us/it-bpo-road-map-2011-2016. Accessed on 5 October 2014.

Icamina, Paul. 2012. 'Science-minded Pinoys leave RP,' *Malaya Business* 15 March.

Karnik, Kiran. 2012. *The Coalition of Competitors: The Story of Nasscom and the IT Industry*. Noida, Uttar Pradesh: HarperCollins Publishers India.

Lee, Yoolim and Ian Sayson. 2014. 'Philippines' rise as call-center nation lures expats home,' Bloomberg Businessweek. www.businessweek.com/news/2014-09-23/philippines-rise-as-call-center-nation-lures-expats-home#p2. Accessed 30 November 2014.

Lowe, Aya. 2013. 'PLDT gives up control of largest Filipino-owned BPO,' Rappler 7 February. www.rappler.com/business/21102-pldt-to-sell-its-bpo-businesses. Accessed 25 November 2014.

Loyola, James. 2014. 'Ayala sells BPO stake to Convergys,' *Manila Bulletin* 7 January.

Magkilat, Bernie. 2014. 'PEZA investments up 31% in 7 months: Total P127.45 billion,' *Manila Bulletin* 1 August.

Magtibay-Ramos, Nedelyn, Gemma Estrada and Jesus Felipe. 2008. 'An input–output analysis of the Philippine BPO industry,' *Asian-Pacific Economic Literature* 22 (1): 41–56.

Mangawang, Cesar D. 2014. 'Tan pioneers BPO office dev't in a township setting,' *Philippine Daily Inquirer* 25 October.

Medalla, Erlinda, Gwendolyn Tecson, Romeo Bautista, and John Power. 1995. *Philippine Trade and Industrial Policies: Catching up with Asia's Tigers*. Manila: Philippine Institute for Development Studies.

Mitra, Raja M. 2011. 'BPO sector growth and inclusive development in the Philippines.' www-wds.worldbank.org/external/default/WDSContentServer/WDSP/IB/2011/12/22/000333037_20111222002222/Rendered/PDF/660930WP0P122100B0BPO0Sector0Growth.pdf. Accessed 25 October 2014.

Navarro, Adoracion M. and Gilberto M. Llanto. 2014. 'The Philippine economy in 2013 and prospects for 2014,' *PIDS Development Research News* XXXII (1): 1–21.

Orbeta, Aniceto. 2014. 'Remittance and household behavior (consumption/investment),' presentation at the 'Finance in development' workshop, Philippine-Japan Workshop on economic policies (Series 6), Makati City, 12 December.

Pasuk Phongpaichit and Christopher J. Baker. 2002. *Thailand: Economy and Politics*, 2nd ed. Oxford, New York: Oxford University Press.

Raquiza, Antoinette R. 2012. *State Structure, Policy Formation, and Economic Development in Southeast Asia: the political economy of Thailand and the Philippines*. London: Routledge.

Raquiza, Antoinette R. 2014. 'Changing configuration of Philippine capitalism,' *Philippine Political Science Journal* 35 (2): 225–250.

Ruiz, Neil G. 2014. 'Made for export: labor migration, state power, and higher education in a developing Philippine economy.' PhD dissertation, Department of Political Science, Massachusetts Institute of Technology.

Satumba, Ahmma Charisma L. 2008. 'Business process outsourcing in financial and banking services in the Philippines,' Working Paper Series 2008, Institute for Labor Studies.

See, Dexter A. 2014. 'BPOs leaving Metro Manila,' *Manila Standard Today* 19 November.

Shiraishi, Takashi. 2014. 'Changing fortunes: comparing state-building and economic development' in Indonesia, the Philippines, Thailand, and Malaysia,' in Keijiro Otsuka and Takashi Shiraishi (eds) *State Building and Development*. Abingdon, Oxon: Routledge.

Team Asia. 2013. 'BPAP, CHED sign agreement to integrate Service Management Program into SUC curricula.' 2 March. www.teamasia.com/newsroom/read-client-news.aspx?id=434:bpap-ched-sign-agreement-to-integrate-service-management-program-into-suc-curricula. Accessed on 2 December 2014.

Tecson, Gwendolyn. 2003. 'Confronting regionalism in Asia: a view from the Philippines,' in Ryōkichi Hirono (ed.) *Regional Co-operation in Asia*. Singapore: Institute of Southeast Asian Studies.

UNCTAD (United Nations Conference on Trade and Development). 2013. 'Global Investment Trends Monitor,' No. 11, 23 January, UNCTAD.

Veniles, Cherry Joy. 2013. 'Immigrants outnumber OFWs,' *Philippine Daily Inquirer* 17 March.

World Bank. 2012. *Philippine Economic Update: Accelerating Reforms to Sustain Growth*. Metro Manila: World Bank Philippine Office.

World Bank. 2013. *Philippine Development Report: Creating More and Better Jobs*. Metro Manila: World Bank Philippine Office.

World Bank. n.d. 'Manufacturing, value added (percentage of GDP).' http://data.worldbank.org/indicator/NV.IND.MANF.ZS. Accessed 26 November 2014.

5 Inter-organizational linkages, global value chains and national innovation systems

Disconnected realities in the Philippines[1]

Chie Iguchi

Introduction

The purpose of this chapter is to gain a better insight in the factors affecting the shifting technological level of local suppliers within a national innovation system (NIS), focusing on multinational enterprise (MNE) subsidiaries' governance structures in sectors producing for global markets, structures we refer to as global value chains (GVC). This chapter examines how MNE subsidiaries and potential inter-organizational linkages within the GVC can enhance the NIS framework by focusing on the case of Japanese subsidiaries located in the Philippines and their linkages with local Filipino firms.

The Philippines' economy has experienced economic growth through increases in foreign direct investments (FDI) in manufacturing from the late 1980s. However, the growth of the industrial sector has slowed in recent years (see Scott 2005, McKay 2006, Beerepoot and Hernandez-Agramonte 2009, Ofreneo this volume). Between 2010 and 2012, the growth rate of the primary sector was 2.8 per cent, of the secondary sector 6.8 per cent, and the tertiary sector grew 7.6 per cent (NSCB, 2014).

Despite significant investments of Japanese MNEs in the Philippines (see NSCB 2014), several studies have identified weaknesses in inter-organizational relationships between Japanese MNE subsidiaries and local Filipino suppliers (see e.g. Beerepoot and van Westen 2001). Using interview data collected in the Philippines focusing on organizational linkages between Japanese MNE subsidiaries and local firms, this chapter explores the inter-organizational linkages between MNE subsidiaries and local suppliers. One factor affecting MNEs' motivation for utilizing inter-organizational linkages is local suppliers' technological capabilities. When the supplier's technological capability meets the subsidiaries' demands it contributes to the development of strong inter-organizational linkages between subsidiaries and local firms. With the rapid global technological advances and the ongoing process of globalization, local firms must be more technologically capable if they aim at participating in global value chains, as MNEs can easily find other suppliers, even in other countries.

Inter-organizational linkages are the main organizational interactions within the NIS context. Strong interaction between key actors in a NIS contribute to flows of new technology between firms, and can thus contribute to a higher level of innovation in local firms. Connecting the NIS and GVC literatures in this chapter will be helpful in reconsidering the roles of MNE subsidiaries and the effectiveness of each actor in a NIS. This chapter is organized as follows. The following provides the theoretical overview on the technological innovative capabilities and the NIS literature, followed by discussing inter-organizational linkages within the NIS framework, and an introduction to the global value chain literature. We then introduce MNEs' global approach to research and development (R&D) as one of the vertical integrating activities in a host country, followed by discussion of the data from the Philippines and the importance of MNE–subsidiary roles for inter-organizational linkages in a host country. Finally, we present the concluding remarks.

Systems of innovation

Technological innovation is considered to be either product innovation or process innovation, and is a narrower definition of innovation. Firms do not normally innovate in isolation, but in collaboration and interdependence with other organizations, such as other firms (suppliers or buyers), universities, research institutes and government organizations (Fagerberg and Godinho 2004). Innovations always emerge in such 'systems of innovation'. Edquist (2004) argues that systems of innovation have a function to pursue innovation processes, i.e. to develop, diffuse, and use innovations. The activities by main actors in systems of innovation are the same as the determinants of the main function, and thus influence the development, diffusion, and use of innovation. Industrial development and technological absorptive capacity must thus be seen from a systems view (Bell and Marin 2004, Lorentzen and Barnes 2004, Mytelka and Barclay 2004, Rasiah 2004). While learning and knowledge absorption take place at the firm level, the success or failure of individual firms occurs within a system (Lall and Narula 2004), which can be referred to as an 'innovative system' (Lundvall 1992, Edquist 1997) or 'learning system' (Lall 1992, Viotti 2002).

The NIS is defined by Freeman (1987: 1) as 'the network of institutions in the public and private sectors whose activities and interactions initiate, import and diffuse new technologies'. Two major studies are by Lundvall (1992) and Nelson (1993). Nelson (1993) emphasizes empirical case studies and narrowly focuses on national R&D systems. Lundvall (1992: 1) seeks to develop an alternative to the neoclassical tradition in economics by placing interactive learning, user–producer interaction and innovation at the center of analysis. Both Lundvall (1992) and Nelson (1993) define NIS in terms of determinants of, or factors influencing, innovation processes, but they use different determinants in their definition, reflecting what they believe to be the most important determinants of innovation (Edquist, 2004).

Important constituents of a NIS include components, inter-relationships, functions, and activities. Organizations and institutions are considered the main components of systems of innovation (see Figure 5.1). Organizations are defined as entities within the system, such as firms, universities, or public agencies responsible for innovation policy and competition policy, and are formal structures that are consciously created and have an explicit purpose (Edquist and Johnson 1997: 46–47). Adopting this definition, institutions include patent laws as well as rules and norms influencing relations between firms and universities. North (1990) describes institutions as 'the rules of the game', and organizations as 'the players' in a 'game' such as innovation systems. Functions and activities were not addressed in the original literature; however, as Liu and White (2001: 1093) focus on 'activities' being related to 'the creation, diffusion and exploitation of technological innovation within a system', we stress activities and functions within a NIS as important factors affecting vertical linkages.

The global value chain approach

Recent trends in the globalization of production have driven industrial capabilities in developing host countries and the vertical disintegration of MNE activities has grown rapidly. MNEs are redefining their core competencies by focusing on innovative activities, product development, marketing, and aim at the highest value-added segments of manufacturing and services, while reducing their direct ownership of remaining functions, such as mass production. This leads to new opportunities for local firms in developing countries to take over such activities and benefit from linkages with MNEs. The GVC framework allows us to understand how global industries are organized by examining the structure and dynamics of

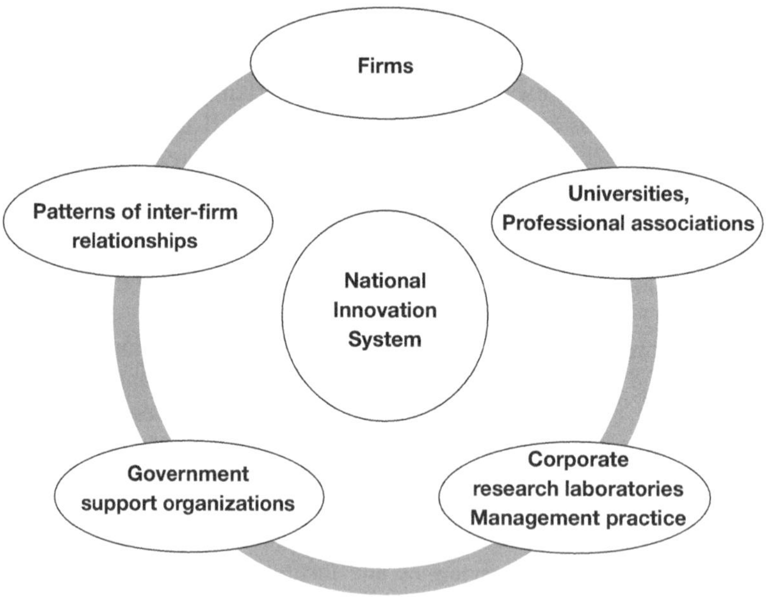

Figure 5.1 Main actors in a national innovation system

different actors involved in a given industry (Gereffi *et al.* 2005, Gereffi and Fernandez-Stark 2011). The GVC framework gives a better understanding of the shifting patterns of global production, linkages between geographically dispersed activities and actors in a single industry, and determines the roles they play in developed and developing countries. When we analyze a GVC within a single industry, it provides the job descriptions, technology level, products, processes, and markets in specific industries and countries, providing a view of global industries both from the top down and the bottom up (Gereffi and Fernandez-Stark 2011: 2). Therefore, it offers a detailed understanding of the activities that are part of local (NIS) and global (GVC) networks. GVCs are typically coordinated by MNEs with cross-border networks of subsidiaries, contractual partners, and arm's-length suppliers, creating organizational linkages between these actors.

The GVC analysis provides both conceptual and methodological tools for looking at the global economy from different vertical perspectives. The top-down view focuses on lead firms and inter-firm networks, using varied typologies of industrial 'governance'. The bottom-up view focuses on countries and regions, which are analyzed in terms of various trajectories of economic and social 'upgrading' or 'downgrading' (Gereffi and Fernandez-Stark 2011). According to Gereffi *et al.* (2005: 171), economic upgrading is defined as firms, countries, or regions moving to higher value-added activities in GVCs in order to increase the benefits (e.g. security, profits, value-added, capabilities) of participating in global production.

Cantwell and Iguchi (2005) argue that inter-organizational linkages in a host country (e.g. backward linkages) are critical for local firms to upgrade their technological level to meet lead firms' (MNE subsidiaries) demands in a host country. Figure 5.2 illustrates the inter-organizational relationship between lead firms and local suppliers, based on five GVC governance types by Gereffi *et al.* (2005: 89). Table 5.1 provides key implications for local suppliers and for key GVC developments, based on the framework of the five GVC governance types.

According to Gereffi and Fernandez-Stark (2011: 9), modular governance occurs when complex transactions are relatively easy to codify. Typically, suppliers in modular chains make products to a customer's specifications and take full responsibility for process technology using generic machinery. This keeps switching costs low and limits transaction-specific investments, even though buyer–supplier interactions can be very complex. Therefore, we can expect inter-organizational linkages to be more substantial than in simple market transactions due to the high volume of information flows across the inter-organizational linkages. Information technology and standards for exchanging information are both key to the functioning of modular governance. Key implications for local suppliers in modular governance networks are lower dependence on lead firms (as suppliers tend to operate in more than one GVC) and limited transaction-specific investments (e.g. generic machinery that can be used for more than one client). Key development implications are the substantial scope for linkages and relatively high volume of information flow across firm linkages (Gereffi *et al.* 2005, UNCTAD 2013: 144).

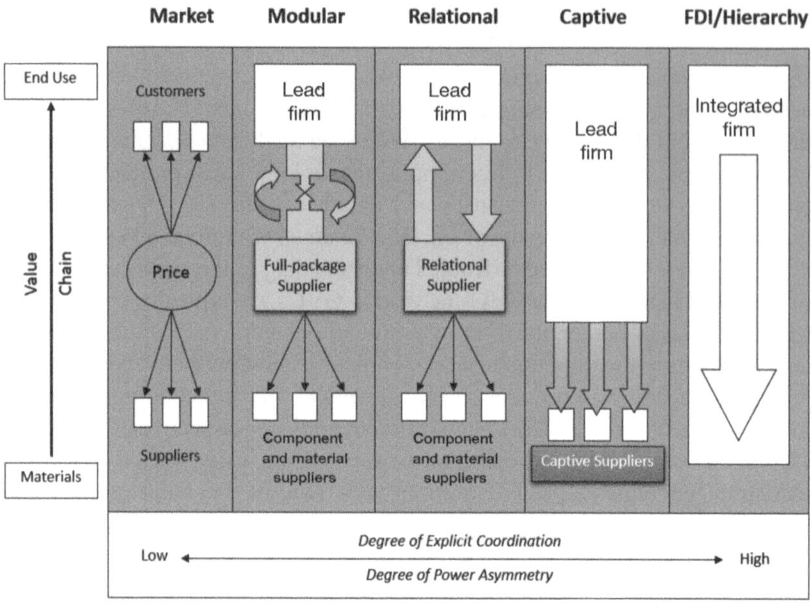

Figure 5.2 Inter-organizational linkages within five GVC governance types

Source: Gereffi *et al.* (2005): 89.

According to Gereffi and Fernandez-Stark (2011: 9), relational governance occurs when buyers and sellers rely on complex information that is not easily transmitted or learned. This results in frequent interactions and knowledge-sharing between parties. Such inter-organizational linkages require trust and generate mutual reliance, which are regulated through reputation, social and spatial proximity, family and ethnic ties, and the like. Despite mutual dependence, lead firms still specify what is needed, and thus have the ability to exert some level of control over suppliers. Producers in relational chains are more likely to supply differentiated products based on quality, geographic origin, or other unique characteristics. Relational linkages take time to build, so the costs and difficulties required to switch to a new partner tend to be high. Key implications for local suppliers of relational governance are that a degree of mutual dependence and frequent interactions and knowledge exchange between partners can be expected, and suppliers are more likely to produce differentiated products; key development implications are that knowledge transfer and learning are likely to be relatively high and demand more stable, due to higher switching costs for lead firms (Gereffi *et al.* 2005, UNCTAD 2013, p.144).

Accumulating or learning the technological capabilities to generate technological changes is necessary for competitiveness in developing countries (Bell and Pavitt 1995). For instance, Kokko *et al.* (2001) highlight the role of a country's past

Table 5.1 Types of GVC governance: supplier perspective

Governance types	*Key implications for suppliers*	*Key GVC development implications*
Market	No formal cooperation between partners Low switching costs for customers	Full exposure to market forces Learning options limited to trade channels
Modular	Lower degree of dependence on lead firms; suppliers tend to operate in more than one GVC Limited transaction-specific investments (e.g. generic machinery that can be used for more than one client)	Substantial scope for linkages Relatively high volume of information flowing across firm linkages
Relational	Degree of mutual dependence between partners Frequent interactions and knowledge exchange between partners Supplier more likely to produce differentiated products	Degree of knowledge transfer and learning relatively high More stable demand due to higher switching costs for lead firms
Captive	Relatively small suppliers; high degree of power asymmetry High degree of monitoring and control by lead firm Knowledge-sharing focuses on efficiency gains	Can generate relatively high degree of dependency on few MNEs that may have low switching costs Knowledge transfer occurs (due to mutual benefits), but limited in scope
FDI	Supplier is fully vertically integrated and under full managerial control	Fastest and often only approach to gaining ownership advantages required for GVC access Business linkages required to widen the scope of technology and knowledge transfer

Source: UNCTAD (2013: 144), Gereffi *et al.* (2005).

industrialization experience as a precondition for technology transfer. The absence of such experience results in lack of local absorptive capacity (Radosevic 1999), thus firms in such countries cannot generate technological changes. Lall and Narula (2004) suggest that the development of capacities and capabilities is a key to both attracting FDI and increasing technological spillovers from MNEs. When local technological capacities and capabilities are weak, industrialization has to be more dependent on the activity of MNEs; however, MNEs cannot drive industrial growth without local technological capabilities (Lall and Narula 2004). A subsidiary in a host country creates vertical linkages, both backward and forward among a supply chain within a MNE group. Backward linkages refer to all the relations established with supplier firms and that exist when MNE subsidiaries acquire goods or services from local suppliers, whereas forward linkages involve the relations established with customers in the host country or in the global market. For Filipino local firms, having backward linkages with MNE subsidiaries is critical, since the backward linkages are a channel by which MNE subsidiaries transfer technology and knowledge, and create spillovers so that local suppliers can acquire modern technologies as well as new management or organizational practices (Iguchi 2008).

Global research and development by MNEs

R&D by MNE subsidiaries is one of the vertical disintegration features of MNE activities discussed above. Of various different activities by MNEs, we focus on R&D activities by MNE subsidiaries in a host country. Developing countries have promoted inward FDI in order to link host countries' technology or firms with global technology and innovation networks through MNE subsidiaries (UNCTAD 2005). Through the competence-creating roles of MNE subsidiaries, host countries can be provided with important knowledge, and thus can create new technology and diffuse it internationally. These firms are able to create unique capabilities that are described as repositories of knowledge. Since their capabilities are fostered through firm-specific social learning processes, they are easier to transfer within the MNE group than across organizations, and constitute the true ownership advantages of the MNE as a group (Cantwell 1989, 1991, 1994, Kogut and Zander 1993, 1995). Promoting FDI and welcoming MNE subsidiaries alone, however, are not enough. In order to utilize new technologies efficiently, host countries are required to create additional absorptive capacities and make efforts to keep up with technical change (UNCTAD 2005, Narula and Dunning 2010). Transferring knowledge or technology from MNE subsidiaries to other actors in a NIS is not easy, even though flows or links between MNE subsidiaries and other actors are prominent (Niosi *et al.* 1993). Such flows include technological, scientific and information flows, which form a key element of a NIS (Dosi *et al.* 1990, 1994), as discussed in the previous section.

As much of the existing literature on the globalization and decentralization of R&D suggests, MNEs have been trying to innovate through knowledge creation, utilizing subsidiaries' R&D resources and laboratories in a host country. Hymer (1976) also emphasizes that global R&D provides MNEs with competitive advantages that are unavailable in single-country centralized R&D (Penner-Hahn 1998, Brouthers *et al.* 2001). The literature also suggests that such competitive advantage is based on how efficiently knowledge is shared between the company's headquarters and subsidiaries in host countries (Gupta and Govindarajan 2000, Doz *et al.* 2001). Figure 5.3 illustrates potential knowledge flows between MNE headquarters and a subsidiary, a subsidiary and other actors in a host country, and innovative output by subsidiaries and local firms and the MNE headquarters. We can also expect to see knowledge flows between a host country's innovation system and the MNE group as a whole.

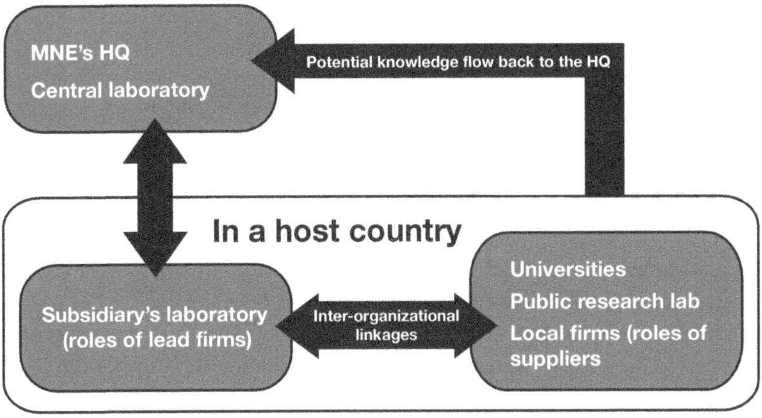

Figure 5.3 Potential inter-organizational linkages and knowledge flows in and from host countries

Source: Illustrated by the author based on Gupta and Govindarajan (2000) and Doz *et al.* (2001).

Although R&D has been considered the least globalized function of MNE groups (UNCTAD 2005), the more global the company, the more it is pressured to employ its R&D human resources strategically. Traditionally, R&D decentralization occurred from a developed home country to a developed host country, typically in the USA or Europe. When MNEs undertook R&D in developing countries, the R&D function was to adapt products and processes to local conditions. The production process, however, is in many cases no longer driven only by the need for local adaptation; R&D is required to respond to increased competition, to access foreign pools of research-appropriate human resources, to reduce R&D costs, and to speed up technology development (UNCTAD 2005). A subsidiary is defined as a value-adding entity for a parent MNE, located in a host country. This definition allows an MNE group to have several subsidiaries in any given host country or in different countries, and they may be independent in their roles. A subsidiary can perform a single activity (e.g. manufacturing) or an entire value chain of activities. In focusing on the activities of MNE subsidiaries in a host country, subsidiary performance needs to be considered in relation to the parent MNE's strategy and the host country's environmental perspectives. The parent MNE's corporate strategy is one factor behind the relocation of a subsidiary's production facilities, through the transfer to a subsidiary in a host country of technology and knowledge that the parent MNE possesses. The role of a subsidiary from its formation is to meet the demands of the parent MNE through activities that are guided and controlled by that parent company.

The literature focusing on MNE group networks considers that ownership-specific advantages do not have to be tied to the home country (Rugman and

Verbeke 1992), but can instead be acquired or developed by the subsidiary itself. MNE groups are sometimes modelled as an 'inter-organizational network' (Bartlett and Ghoshal 1991) of loosely coupled entities, rather than a singular hierarchy, which gives the subsidiary the necessary freedom to develop and shift its own unique resource profile, including human and technological resources, within the host country. This view provides a valuable perspective on the emergence of competence-creating subsidiaries, because it can lead that subsidiaries have specialised capabilities not possessed by other subsidiaries in the MNE group. The 'autonomous behaviour' defined by Burgelman (1983) in a subsidiary can occur in the absence of top management levels of the MNE group, and sometimes in ways not actively encouraged by the group's top management. For MNE subsidiaries, the concept of autonomous behavior is important, because it suggests a process of internal growth that is rarely controlled by parent MNEs, thus with the possibility of enhancing the subsidiary's autonomy level. This approach attaches importance to the role of the subsidiary's capabilities and emphasizes that the subsidiary is part of a network (Birkinshaw and Hood 1998). In the case of Japanese MNE subsidiaries in Malaysia, activities traditionally carried out within firms have been outsourced to local suppliers as Japanese subsidiaries have gained greater autonomy (see Iguchi 2008). Long experiences in doing business in the host country gave the Japanese MNE subsidiaries the autonomy to find local suppliers and to establish inter-organizational linkages.

Research questions, methodology, and presentation of data

Interviews were conducted in the Philippines on different occasions between March 2010 and March 2013, targeting Japanese MNEs operating in this country. In order to identify the roles of Japanese as opposed to non-Japanese MNEs, we also conducted interviews with local firms and non-Japanese MNEs. We obtained data from 41 firms (17 Japanese MNEs, six non-Japanese MNEs, and 18 local Philippine firms), but focus in this chapter on the data from the 17 Japanese MNE subsidiaries. We employed structured interview methods and our questionnaire included questions on whether a subsidiary has: a factory; R&D functions; collaborative research; types of inter-organizational linkages with local firms in the Philippines; and collaborative projects with local universities and local research institutes. Results from the 17 Japanese MNE subsidiaries are summarized in Table 5.2.

Since the Philippines is slightly different from other Southeast Asian host countries in terms of government supports, industrial structures, and level of technological development, we also use interview data from Malaysia, Thailand, Singapore, and India to compare with the Philippines case. Interviews with Japanese MNEs' subsidiaries were conducted in these countries between March 2010 and March 2013. We obtained data from six subsidiaries in Malaysia, six subsidiaries in Thailand, three subsidiaries in Singapore, and two subsidiaries in India. Results from these 17 Japanese MNE subsidiaries are summarized in Table 5.3.

Table 5.2 Summary of characteristics of firms interviewed in the Philippines

	Industry categorization	*Entered host country*	*R&D functions for new product development*	*R&D functions for new product development through collaboration with headquarters*	*R&D functions for new product development through collaboration with local universities or local research institutes*	*Any collaboration with local firms (suppliers)*
Philippines 1	Manufacturing	1940s	✓		✓	
Philippines 2	Manufacturing	1950s	✓		✓	
Philippines 3	Manufacturing	1960s	✓	✓	✓	
Philippines 4	Manufacturing	1960s				
Philippines 5	Manufacturing	1970s				
Philippines 6	Manufacturing	1970s			✓	✓
Philippines 7	Manufacturing	1970s				✓
Philippines 8	Sales & Marketing	1970s				
Philippines 9	Manufacturing	1980s				
Philippines 10	Manufacturing	1990s	✓			✓
Philippines 11	Manufacturing	1990s				
Philippines 12	Manufacturing	1990s				
Philippines 13	Manufacturing	1990s				
Philippines 14	Manufacturing	1990s				
Philippines 15	Manufacturing	1990s				✓
Philippines 16	Service industry	1990s				
Philippines 17	Manufacturing	2000s				

Source: Obtained and summarised by the Author.

Table 5.3 Summary of characteristics of firms interviewed outside of the Philippines

	Industry categorization	*Entered host country*	*R&D functions for new product development*	*R&D functions for new product development through collaboration with headquarters*	*R&D functions for new product development through collaboration with local universities or local research institutes*	*Any collaboration with local firms (suppliers)*
Malaysia 1	Electronics	1960s	✓			
Malaysia 2	Electronics	1960s	✓			
Malaysia 3	Electronics	1960s				
Malaysia 4	Electronics	1960s				✓
Malaysia 5	Electronics	1990s	✓			
Malaysia 6	Electronics	1980s	✓			
Singapore 1	Electronics	1990s	✓			✓
Singapore 2	Food and beverages	1980s	✓			✓
Singapore 3	Electronics	1970s	✓			
Thailand 1	Electronics	1980s	✓			
Thailand 2	Automobile	1960s	✓			
Thailand 3	Automobile	1990s	✓			
Thailand 4	Automobile	2000s	✓			
Thailand 5	Food and beverages	1960s	✓			✓
Thailand 6	Food and beverages	2000s	✓			
India 1	Electronics	1990s	✓	✓		
India 2	Electronics	2000s	✓		✓	✓

Source: Obtained and summarised by the Author.

Local linkage formation in the Philippines

As summarised in Table 5.2, of the 17 Japanese MNE subsidiaries, 14 are manufacturing, and 4 have R&D functions. Three of the 17 companies are actively engaged in exchanges with universities (such as factory tours and offering guest speakers) in order to have access to future employees, and two companies are offering technology or know-how for manufacturing related technology to local universities. Most of these 17 Japanese MNE subsidiaries have experiences operating in other Association of Southeast Asian Nations (ASEAN) member countries, where they have made efforts to establish inter-organizational linkages with local firms. In the Philippines, most of the interviewed Japanese MNE subsidiaries did similar efforts but the results turned to be different from other ASEAN countries. Regarding responses to the questions on inter-organizational linkages, we can summarize the following four points. First, it is very difficult to find local Filipino suppliers, because the parts industries are not well developed. Second, it is hard to find local suppliers when a subsidiary requires specific technology, which, as a result, forces a subsidiary to import parts or products from Thailand or China. Third, even when a subsidiary looks for a local supplier of packaging material, for which high technical specifications are not required, it is very hard to source locally due to high import dependence, and fourth a subsidiary sometimes has local suppliers whose main role is to import from neighboring countries as a trader with Japanese capital. Attempts were made by Japanese MNEs in the Philippines to enhance their local backward linkages, but local suppliers' technological level failed to develop, despite MNEs conducting technology transfer and technology-related training through contracts between local suppliers and MNEs in the 1990s.

Unlike in Thailand and Malaysia, parts and components-related suppliers in the Philippines did not grow during the 1990s (see also Beerepoot and van Westen 2001). In these countries Japanese MNEs were aggressively focusing on the development of local suppliers' technology. This was the result of government policies in both countries which included support to the creation of a higher intensity of backward linkages (Iguchi 2008). It led to a higher technological development of local suppliers, which contributed to industrial growth and economic development. When comparing the actors of the NIS of Malaysia and Thailand with the Philippines, roles of government are significantly different. Industrial policy in Malaysia and Thailand stipulated local contents ratios for manufacturing industries, which led Japanese MNE subsidiaries to engage in inter-organizational linkages with local suppliers who supply parts or components. No similar policies have been formulated in the Philippines since industrial policies by the government had much less emphasis on technological development of local suppliers through inter-organizational linkages.

When Japanese MNE subsidiaries tried to integrate local Filipino firms in their GVC they were confronted with various problems. Japanese MNE subsidiaries tried to construct inter-organizational linkages with local suppliers but they tended not to see incentives for cost reduction in raising local-content ratio through increasing the technological capabilities of suppliers with low technological skills.

The form of governance in Japanese MNEs in the Philippines is market or modular. Survey results suggest that Japanese subsidiaries in the Philippines form GVCs that include neighboring countries, e.g. Thailand, Indonesia, and China, through imports from these countries, and do not develop inter-organizational linkages with local suppliers in the Philippines. Even when Japanese MNEs would like to manufacture differentiated products, it might be difficult to form a relational value chain in the Philippines since technological level and capabilities do not meet the requirements of lead firms.

R&D activities by MNE subsidiaries can be considered a vertical disintegration of MNE activities. We can also consider R&D activities by an MNE subsidiary and their collaborative research activities with local partners as inter-organizational linkages characterized by either modular or relational linkages. Within the NIS in a host country, R&D activities by MNE subsidiaries have various effects for host countries and governments in the Southeast Asian countries such as Thailand and Malaysia (Iguchi 2012). From host countries' points of view, inward R&D-intensive FDI works as a powerful mechanism for international technology transfer and can enable host countries to integrate into the GVC (Carlsson 2006). In addition, the driving forces and characteristics of their R&D functions and motivation for collaboration have been influenced by the parent MNE in the home country and the capabilities of local partners.

When we consider the Philippine NIS compared by other ASEAN countries, namely Malaysia and Thailand (Iguchi 2008, 2012), initiatives of actors in the NIS are underdeveloped in the Philippines. For example, Malaysian and Thai government institutions (such as Malaysian Investment Development Authority, Penang Development Corporation for Malaysia, and the Board of Investment of Thailand) act as facilitators for activities of actors within NIS. However, we were not able to find any roles similar to them in the Philippines. Roles of facilitators acting as linking between Japanese MNE subsidiaries and local suppliers have had huge impacts on technological development through spillover effects and inter-organizational linkages in Malaysia and Thailand. Without inter-organizational linkages with MNE subsidiaries, local Filipino firms will not develop absorptive capacities through them. As a result, the Filipino firms will have less opportunity to engage in GVCs by MNEs compared to other ASEAN firms. However, Japanese MNE subsidiaries still find some advantages in locating parts of their value chain in the Philippines, mainly due to lower labour costs and easier training (as most Filipinos are capable of receiving training in English). However, some Japanese MNE subsidiaries have interests in relocating their business activities from the Philippines to other ASEAN host countries where it is easier for subsidiaries to source parts or components locally.

Conclusion

This chapter aimed to provide a better understanding of the factors affecting the shifting technological level of local suppliers, focusing on MNE subsidiaries' inter-organizational linkages within a GVC. In the context of a NIS, the crucial actors in this study are MNE subsidiaries and local suppliers for technological innovative activity. For local partners in host countries, collaboration with MNE subsidiaries works as a powerful mechanism for knowledge flow from MNEs to local partners, which helps local partners to integrate into global value chains. For MNEs, the positive influences of inter-organizational linkages in a host country are that geographically diversified innovation and knowledge-creation activities can be enabled and MNEs can source potential knowledge dispersed in different host countries. However, our results find that Japanese MNE subsidiaries in the Philippines have weak inter-organizational linkages with local firms and did not form the critical technology-related inter-organizational linkages that have been possible in other Southeast Asian countries. The main reason why we cannot find effective inter-organizational linkages is that the role of the government as a facilitator to bond subsidiaries and local suppliers is underdeveloped.

Intensifying inter-organizational linkages within the GVC framework is crucial not only for upgrading local suppliers' technological levels, but also for improving national innovative and competitive performance and intensifying a host country's NIS. Government policies supporting higher-intensity of inter-organizational linkages are critical in order to intensify a NIS, which can thus lead to higher levels of technological development in local suppliers, contributing to industrial growth and economic development. The higher the technological level of local suppliers, the more attractive a host country becomes as a location for FDI by MNEs. Therefore, inducing inter-organizational linkages should be a priority for the Philippines government.

Note

1 The initial ideas for this paper were published in the *Mita Shougaku Kenkyu*, 56 (6), 33–46 in Japanese and modified to this version.

References

Bartlett, C.A. and Ghoshal, S. (1991). The multinational corporation as an inter-organisational network. *Academy of Management Review*, 15, 603–625.

Beerepoot, N. and Hernandez-Agramonte, J. (2009). Post MFA-adjustment of the Philippine garments sector: Women's cooperatives amidst manufacturing decline. *European Journal of Development Research*, 21 (3), 362–376.

Beerepoot, N. and van Westen, A.C.M. (2001). The Mactan export processing zone in comparative perspective. *Philippine Quarterly of Culture and Society*, 29 (3/4), 226–251.

Bell, M. and Marin, A. (2004). Where do foreign direct investment-related technology spillovers come from in emerging economics? An exploration in Argentina in the 1990s. *The European Journal of Development Research*, 16 (3), 653–684.

Bell, M. and Pavitt, K. (1995). Technological accumulation and industrial growth: contrast between developed and developing countries. *Industrial and Corporate Change*, 2 (2), 157–210.

Birkinshaw, J. and Hood, N. (1998). Multinational subsidiary evolution: capability and charter change in foreign-owned subsidiary companies. *Academy of Management Review*, 23 (4), 773–795.

Brouthers, K., Brouthers, L. and Werner, S. (2001). R&D mode choice in Central and Eastern Europe. *Journal of Business Research*, 52, 83–91.

Burgelman, R.A. (1983). A process model of internal corporate venturing in the diversified major firm. *Administrative Science Quarterly*, 28, 223–244.

Cantwell, J.A. (1989). *Technological Innovation and the Multinational Corporation*. Oxford: Basil Blackwell.

Cantwell, J.A. (1991). The international agglomeration of R&D. *In*: M.C. Casson (ed.). *Global Research Strategy and International Competitiveness*. Oxford: Basil Blackwell, 104–132.

Cantwell, J.A. (1994). *The Theory of Technological Competence and Its Application to International Production*. London: Routledge.

Cantwell, J.A. and Iguchi, C. (2005). Multinationals and their relationships with local suppliers: effects on local suppliers' development path in the Malaysian electrical and electronics industry. *In*: A. Giroud, A. Mohr and D. Yang (eds). *Multinational and Asia: Organisational and Institutional Relationships*. London: Routledge, 54–71.

Cantwell, J.A. and Mudambi, R. (2005). TNC competence-creating subsidiary mandates. *Strategic Management Journal*, 26 (12), 1109–1128.

Carlsson, B. (2006), Internationalization of innovation systems: a survey of the literature. *Research Policy*, 35, 56–67.

Dosi, G., Freeman, C. and Fabiani, S. (1994). The process of economic development. Introducing some stylized facts and theories on technologies, firms and institutions. *Industrial and Corporate Change*, 3, 1–28.

Dosi, G., Pavitt, K. and Soete, L. (1990). *The Economics of Technological Changes and International Trade*. New York: New York University Press.

Doz, Y.L., Santos, J. and Williamson, P.J. (2001). *From Global to Metanational: How companies win in the knowledge economy*. Boston, MA/Great Britain: Harvard Business School Press.

Edquist, C. (1997). *Systems of Innovation: Technologies, Institutions and Organisations*. London: Pinter.

Edquist, C. (2004). Systems of innovation, perspectives and challenges. *In*: J. Fagerberg, D.C. Mowery and R. Nelson (eds). *Oxford Handbook of Innovation*. Oxford: Oxford University Press, 181–208.

Edquist, C. and Johnson, B. (1997). Institutions and organisations in systems of innovation. *In*: C. Edquist (ed.). *Systems of Innovation: Technologies, Institutions and Organisations*. London and Washington: Pinter, 41–63.

Fagerberg, J. and Godinho, M.M. (2004). Innovation and catching-up. *In*: J. Fagerberg, D.C. Mowery and F.D. Nelson, (eds). *Oxford Handbook of Innovation*. Oxford: Oxford University Press, 514–542.

Freeman, C. (1987). *Technology and Policy and Economic Performance: Lessons from Japan*. London: Pinter.

Gereffi, G. (1999). International trade and industrial upgrading in the apparel commodity chain. *Journal of International Economics*, 48 (1), 37–70.

Gereffi, G. and Fernandez-Stark, K. (2011). *Global Value Chain Analysis: A Primer*. Center on Globalization, Governance and Competitiveness (CGGC). Durham.

Gereffi, G., Humphrey, J. and Sturgeon, T.J. (2005). The governance of global value chains. *Review of International Political Economy*, 12 (1), 78–104.

Giroud, A. (2003). *Transnational Corporations, Technology and Economic Development: Backward Linkages and Knowledge Transfer in South East Asia*. Cheltenham: Edward Elgar.

Gupta, A.K. and Govindarajan, V. (2000). Knowledge flows within multinational corporations. *Strategic Management Journal*, 21, 473–496.
Hymer, S. (1976). *The International Operations of National Firms: A Study Of Direct Foreign Investments*. Cambridge, MA: MIT Press.
Iguchi, C. (2008). Determinants of backward linkages: the case of TNC subsidiaries in Malaysia. *Asian Business and Management*, 7 (1), 53–73.
Iguchi, C. (2012). Globalisation of R&D by TNC subsidiaries: the case of South-East Asian countries. *Asian Business and Management*, 11 (1), 79–100.
Johnson, A. and Jacobsson, S. (2003). The emergence of a growth industry: a comparative analysis of the German, Dutch and Swedish wind turbine industries. *In*: S. Metcalfe and U. Cantner (eds). *Transformation and Development: Schumpeterian Perspectives*. Heidelberg: Physica/Springer, 64–88.
Kim, L. (1997). *Imitation to Innovation: The Dynamics of Korea's Technological Learning*. Boston, MA: Harvard Business School Press.
Kogut, B. and Zander, U. (1993). Knowledge of the firm and the evolutionary theory of the multinational corporation. *Journal of International Business Studies*, 24(4), 625–645.
Kogut, B. and Zander, U. (1995). Knowledge and the speed of the transfer and imitation of organizational capabilities: an empirical test. *Organization Science*, 6(1), 76-91.
Kokko, A., Zejan, M. and Tansini, R. (2001). Trade regimes and spillover effects of FDI: evidence from Uruguay. *Welwirtschaftliches Archive*, 137, 124–149.
Lall, S. (1992). Technological capabilities and industrialisation. *World Development*, 20(2), 165–186.
Lall, S. and Narula, R. (2004). FDI and its role in economic development: do we need a new agenda? *The European Journal of Development Research*, 16 (3), 447–464.
Liu, X. and White, S. (2001). Comparing innovation systems: a framework and application to China's transitional context. *Research Policy*, 30, 1091–1114.
Lorentzen, J. and Barnes, J. (2004). Learning, upgrading, and innovation in the South African automotive industry. *The European Journal of Development Research*, 16 (3), 465.
Lundvall, B.A. (ed.) (1992). *National Systems of Innovation: Towards a Theory of Innovation and Interactive Learning*. London: Pinter.
McKay, S.C. (2006). *Satanic Mills or Silicon Islands? The Politics of High-Tech Production in the Philippines*. New York: Cornell University Press.
Mytelka, L.K. and Barclay, L.A. (2004). Using foreign investment strategically for innovation. *The European Journal of Development Research*, 16 (3), 531–560.
Narula, R. and Dunning, J.H. (2010). Multinational enterprises, development and global ization: some clarifications and a research agenda. *Oxford Development Studies*, 38 (3), 263–287.
Nelson, R., (ed.). (1993). *National Systems of Innovation*. Oxford: Oxford University Press.
Niosi, J., Saviotti, P., Bellon, B. and M.C. (1993). National systems of innovation: in search of a workable concept. *Technology in Society*, 15, 207–227.
North, D. (1990). *Institutions, Institutional Change and Economic Performance*. Cambridge: Cambridge University Press.
NSCB (National Statistical Coordination Board) (2014) Philippine economy grew by 6.1 percent in 2014; 6.9 percent in Q4 2014 (www.nscb.gov.ph/sna/default.asp).
Penner-Hahn, J. (1998). Firm and environmental influences on mode and sequence of foreign research and development activities. *Strategic Management Journal*, 19, 149–168.
Radosevic, S. (1999). *International Technology Transfer and Catch-up in Economic Development*. Cheltenham: Edward Elgar.

Rasiah, R. (1989). Competition and restructuring in the semiconductor industry: implication for technology transfer and its absorption in Penang. *Southeast Asian Journal of Social Sciences*, 17 (2), 41–57.

Rasiah, R. (2004). Exports and technological capabilities: a study of foreign and local firms in the electronics industry in Malaysia, the Philippines and Thailand. *The European Journal of Development Research*, 16 (3), 587–623.

Rugman, A. and Verbeke, A. (1992). A not on the transnational solution and the transaction cost theory of multinational strategic management. *Journal of International Business Studies*, 23, 761–772.

Scott, A.J. (2005). The shoe industry of Marikina City, Philippines, a developing-country cluster in crisis. *Kasarinlan: Philippine Journal of Third World Studies*, 20, 76–99.

UNCTAD (United Nations Conference on Trade and Development). (2001). *World Investment Report 2001: Promoting Linkages*. New York and Geneva: United Nations.

UNCTAD. (2005). *World Investment Report 2005: Transnational Corporations and the Internationalisation of R&D*. New York and Geneva: United Nations.

UNCTAD. (2013). *World Investment Report 2013: Global Value Chains, Investment and Trade for Development*. New York and Geneva: United Nations.

Viotti, E. (2002). National learning systems: a new approach on technological change in late industrializing economies and evidences from the cases of Brazil and South Korea. *Technological Forecasting and Social Change*, 69, 653–680.

Part II

Capitalizing on (offshore) services in the shadow of giants

A look beyond India and the Philippines

6 From the 'workshop of the world' to the 'office of the world'?

Rethinking service-led development in the Pearl River Delta

Xu Zhang

Introduction

In recent years, the service economy and service sector-led development have attracted increasing attention in both academic and policy circles in China. Rising production costs and stagnating external demand for manufactured products are affecting the country's industrial advantages and slowing down the pace of its economic expansion (*Economist* 2012). Simultaneously, the success story of emerging offshore business services hotspots, such as India and the Philippines, has opened up a new way to capture the 'next wave of globalization' (Dossani and Kenney 2007, see also Chapters 1 and 2 in this book) and achieve socioeconomic modernization through tapping into the booming global services economy (Ghani and Kharas 2010). Services, once considered as 'non-productive' and therefore overlooked by policy makers (Lin 2005), are now taking up the centre stage of many Chinese cities and regions' economic development plans (Yeh and Yang 2013). Service sector-led development is also advocated by many scholars as an effective way to restructure and upgrade the country's predominant (low-end) manufacturing-based growth model (cf. Lu 2008, *Economic Daily* 2011, Shen 2011).

In contrast to this widespread emphasis on the economic significance of services, there is little reflection on whether service sector-led development will be a viable choice for most cities in China. Similar to other East Asian economies (e.g. Japan and South Korea), China's great economic success in the past three decades is primarily built on its powerful, export-oriented manufacturing sector. High-speed industrialization has not only led to impressive economic growth in a large number of Chinese cities and regions, but also profoundly shaped their urban systems, labour market structures and institutional settings in a way that fits their manufacturing bases. However, given the differences that exist between services production, especially knowledge-intensive advanced business services, and manufacturing activities (see below), the transition from an industry-based to a service sector-led economy is not a smooth process. As the experience of South Korea shows, success in manufacturing does not necessarily translate into success in services (ADB 2012: 47). It has been pointed out that most Chinese cities may not be well structured to address the demand of advanced business service firms (Daniels 2013). Most cities also lack an appropriate strategy to direct the development of their service sectors (Yeh and Yang 2013). Therefore, more theoretical and empirical research work is needed for a better understanding of the characteristics of business services economies and more grounded evaluations of relevant policies in the Chinese context.

This chapter discusses whether advanced business services can provide a viable substitution to manufacturing as the leading sector of economic growth in Chinese cities. In addition, it explores what service sector development strategies could fit different cities in China. The focus in this chapter is on cities in the Pearl River Delta (PRD).[1] This region has led China's dramatic industrialization in the past three decades (Enright *et al.* 2005), but is now affected by a new wave of economic restructuring enabled by relatively more advanced service activities. The PRD therefore provides an ideal case to examine the role of services in a transitional industrial region.

The chapter proceeds as follows. The next section presents a typology of business services economies and compares their distinction in market orientation, modes of development, key resources needed and locational preferences. Based on this framework, the chapter then examines the patterns of service sector development in the PRD. It then provides an evaluation of the currently widespread business service focused development policies in the PRD and identifies their major problems. The following section discusses what business service development strategies will be appropriate for different kinds of cities in the PRD. The chapter ends with concluding remarks and suggestions for further research.

A typology of business services economies

Business (or producer) services (already excluding consumer and public services) encompass a great variety of activities and products. Such heterogeneity makes it difficult to unambiguously categorize them. Although various standard statistical classifications of economic activities, such as the International Standard Industrial Classification of All Economic Activities (ISIC), the North American Industry Classification System (NAICS) and the Statistical Classification of Economic Activities in the European Community (NACE), have included service sectors, they mainly aim to divide services into various domains according to the main or final products produced (e.g. finance, insurance, accountancy, legal services, advertising, etc.). These classifications are less sensitive to the functional differences between business services that this chapter concentrates on. Functional differences commonly referred to in the literature include those between front-office and back-office services (Metters and Vargas 2000), routine and knowledge-intensive business services (Wood 2009), and regular and advanced producer services (Daniels and Moulaert 1991, Taylor *et al.* 2014). These differences are instrumental in separating types of service activities/products and exploring the dynamics of their spatial distribution and agglomeration. Therefore, they provide useful building blocks for the development of a typology of business services economies.

In most advanced economies and increasingly in emerging economies, the average city or town is very likely to be home to a quite varied collection of business service firms that participate in various types of service activities and produce a multitude of service products. Each city's exact mix of business service firms is likely to be affected by the city's general economic profile and, to a certain degree, reflect this profile. This is because due to the nature of services production and delivery (which in many cases still requires more or less intensive face-to-face interactions between producers and clients), the bulk of producer service firms still need to co-locate with (a good part of) their major clients derived from the local economy to grow (cf. Daniels and Moulaert 1991, Illeris 1994, Bennett *et al.* 2000). As a result, we can observe that, for instance, in a city functioning as a transport hub there tends to be a concentration of logistics services providers. The same also goes for legal services providers in an administrative centre, and for financial services providers in a trade hub, etc. This describes the archetypical or regular urban business services economy: a varied collection of producer service activities (e.g., financial and insurance services, legal advice, logistics, advertising, IT and management consultancy, etc.) that mainly caters to the demand of the local economy and, in terms of specialization, to a certain degree reflects the general profile of the local economy. Such a business services economy applies to the vast majority of cities and towns across the world.

In addition to this regular business services economy, there are three major exceptional types that tend to develop only in a selective number of cities. The first one is the global, all-round higher-order business services hub: cities such as London, New York, Tokyo, Paris, Hong Kong and Singapore. These cities, often prefixed by 'global' or 'world' in the literature, have over time developed into the 'command and control' centres of the global economy and have, on top of their regular business services, grown a sizable concentration or cluster of top-notch, knowledge-intensive business service firms (cf. Sassen 2001, Wood 2009, Taylor *et al.* 2014). These advanced business service firms not only cater to the demand of local economic actors, but also, and importantly, provide services to large international companies located elsewhere through their worldwide office (or affiliation) networks.

The second one is the highly specialized business services centres. These are cities, small or large, that have grown (again in addition to their regular business services) substantial concentrations of specialized service providers that either cater to the needs of the highly specialized local economy (e.g. oil and energy production in Aberdeen; international organizations in Geneva) or find their raison d'être in a city's unique position in, for instance, specific international trade networks (e.g. Antwerp as a hub of global diamond trading) or cultural spheres (e.g. Teheran and Kuala Lumpur as centres for Islamic banking) (cf. Cumbers 2000, Bassens *et al.* 2010, AWDC 2013). A critical mass of specialized regional demand and competition may encourage local business service providers to specialize and thus compete in wider markets (Wood 2009: 42). Therefore, this type differs from the 'archetypal business services economy' as defined above in the sense that its degrees of specialization and export potential are more profound.

Third, there are centres that specialize in offshore services production. This is a more recent phenomenon made possible by advances in information and telecommunication technologies and related changes in the organization of the production of routine, particularly back-office, services. As a result, many firms in advanced economies have relocated certain service production activities to lower-cost locations around the world. Cities such as Bangalore, Mumbai, Manila, Cebu City, Dalian and Dublin, that offer the right mix of cost reducing potential, sufficiently qualified labour and adequate ICT infrastructure, have emerged as offshore services production centres specializing in, among others, IT services, customer services and related activities (c.f. Dossani and Kenney 2007, Tholons 2014, Kleibert this volume).

As such, we can distinguish four basic types of business services economies, of which one (the 'archetypal or regular business services economy') is very common, and three (the 'global advanced producer services hub', the 'specialized services economy' and the 'offshore production centre for back-office services') are less so. The differences between them are articulated in Table 6.1.

These four types of business services economies also differ from each other in terms of the mode (or dynamic) of development and the types of resources needed.

Table 6.1 A typology of business services economies

Types of business services economies	*Market orientation and types of clients*	*Mode of development*	*Human resources needed*
A) Regular local, all-round business services economies	Predominantly firms and other organizations making up the local economy (local economic actors)	Organic (fuelled by demand from local economic actors)	Generally well-educated labour force
B) Global advanced producer services hubs	Apart from local economic actors, large international firms located elsewhere	Organic (fuelled by demand from local economic actors and external demand)	Highly-educated labour force, international connectivity
C) Highly specialized business services economies	Local economic actors and possibly specialized international firms located elsewhere	Organic (initially fuelled by demand from local economic actors, later possibly also by external demand)	Generally well-educated labour force plus a good number of people with specialized knowledge
D) Offshore production centres for back-office services	Predominantly medium-sized and large international firms	Foreign or domestic direct investments	Low-cost but yet sufficiently well-educated labour force, decent ICT infrastructure

The development of the first three business services economies is more close to an organic process, which is fuelled either by the demand from local economic actors (the 'regular business services economy'), or by that plus the demand from large or specialized international companies (the 'global advanced producer services hub' and some of the 'highly specialized services economies'). In comparison, the 'offshore services production centres' are mostly formed through foreign or domestic direct investments to take advantage of the availability of specific human resources in these locations to respond to the external (often foreign) demand for particular (back-office) service tasks.

In terms of key resources, the formation and growth of all four types of business services economies, in general, rely on a well-educated labour force. Some services economies may also have additional requirements on the quality (the 'global advanced producer services hub'), the specialized knowledge (the 'highly specialized services economy') or the cost (the 'offshore production centre for back-office services') of the labour. In addition, to secure efficient communication between local service firms and their worldwide offices and clients, the 'global advanced producer services hub' also needs to maintain top-notch international connectivity, such as first-class international airports and bandwidth. Similarly, the formation of the 'offshore services production centres' also demands high-quality ICT infrastructure.

The boundaries between different types of business services economies are neither clear cut nor static. For instance, after accumulating sufficient levels of knowledge and skills (normally accompanied with the sophistication and globalization of the local economy), a 'regular business service economy' may start to export one or more types of services to the national or even international market and, accordingly, gradually upgrade into a more 'advanced' (type B) or 'specialized' (type C) business services economy. Likewise, an 'offshore production centre for back-office services' also has the potential to move to a higher value added position in global value chains. However, when a city losses its comparative advantage in its favourable economic sector(s) (e.g. through technological changes or the spatial reorganization of production), it may also downgrade from a 'highly specialized business services economy' back to a more 'regular business service economy', or from a 'global advanced services hub' to a mainly national (or even regional) services hub. But in general, this typology of business services economies gives a basic reference to examine and compare service sector developments in different places. It also provides a useful tool to evaluate the conditions for developing business services and the feasibility of government policies in a specific city or region. Based on this framework, the following section explores the process and patterns of service sector development in the PRD.

The development of services in the Pearl River Delta

The economic significance of services in the PRD has only become apparent since 1978 (Figure 6.1). During the centrally planned period (1949–1978), services were seriously constrained in China due to the pro-industry national development strategy (Lin 2005: 285) and the dominance of the state in organizing production and allocating resources/products (Yang and Yeh 2013). In the PRD, in contrast to the fast growth of industries, services' share in the regional economic production and regional employment declined from 27 per cent and 15 per cent to 24 per cent and 11 per cent respectively between 1949 and 1979 (Figure 6.1). Most service activities were concentrated in the trade and logistics domain, such as wholesale, retail, transportation, storage and post (Table 6.2), which meant that the role of services was confined to meeting the basic need for the operation of the regional economy during this period.

After 1978, China's market-oriented economic reform and opening-up led to dramatic growth and restructuring in the PRD and transformed it into the often cited 'workshop of the world'. Meanwhile, the region also witnessed a period of rapid development of services. High-speed industrialization (and urbanization) and the growth of local income in the PRD created a large demand for both producer and consumer services, which now needed to be provided through the market. With the growing employment pressure caused by massive rural–urban migration and a large number of lay-offs due to the reforms of state-owned enterprises, the Chinese political leaders also gradually recognized the positive role of services in creating jobs, and removed many restrictions on them (Lin 2005, Li *et al.* 2008). Fuelled by these two factors, between 1979 and 2000 the share of the service sector in the region's economy increased substantially from 24 per cent to 44 per cent, which was more remarkable than the growth of industry (which only increased slightly from 44 per cent to 47 per cent). The regional employment structure also underwent a similar transformation. As shown in Figure 6.1, from 1979 to 2000 employment in agriculture went down sharply (from 72 per cent to 40 per cent), the industrial sector saw a modest increase in employment (from 17 per cent to 28 per cent) and the service sector experienced a significant rise (from 11 per cent to 32 per cent).

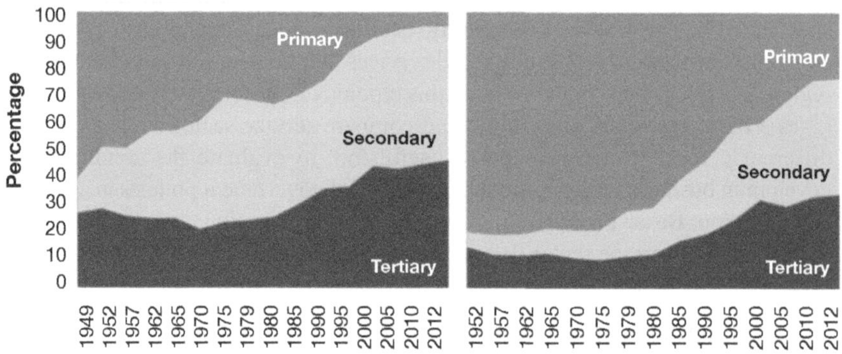

Figure 6.1 Changes of the structure of gross domestic product (left) and employment (right) in Guangdong after 1949

Source: GSB 1999, 2013.

Table 6.2 The composition of the service economy in Guangdong (per cent)

Sectors	*1979*	*2000*	*2012*
Transport and communication	22.0	23.9	15.0
Trade, catering and accommodation	46.5	26.0	28.8
Finance, insurance and real estate and business services	13.2	24.2	36.0
Public services	18.3	25.8	20.2

Source: calculated based on GSB 2001, 2013.

The service sector actually became the primary driver of both economic and employment growth in the PRD during this period. However, traditional types of services (e.g. transport, trade, catering, accommodation and public services) still largely dominated the sector (Table 6.2), reflecting the 'back factory' status of the PRD (Sit and Yang 1997) in the international division of labour at that time.

Since the 2000, service sector development in the PRD has entered a new stage. The pace of service growth has slowed down. As Figure 6.1 shows, the share of services in the regional economy and employment only increased slightly from 44 per cent and 32 per cent to 46 per cent and 34 per cent respectively between 2000 and 2012. However, in the meantime, finance, insurance and real estate (FIRE) and business services have quickly advanced and taken the lead in service sector growth in the region. These sectors only accounted for about 24 per cent of the regional gross services production in 2000, but soared to 36 per cent by 2012 (Table 6.2). This change reflects the increasing demand for higher-order business services in the PRD, spurred by the recent upgrading of the regional economy. With the region engaged in more advanced kinds of economic production and becoming more intensely tied up in the global economy, its demand for higher-order business services is also rising. Such services used to be provided by local manufacturing branch plants' parent companies, or by contractors or service suppliers that were located overseas, especially in Hong Kong, but now with improvements in the local infrastructure, skills and service quality, the PRD is developing its own business service sector (Yeh 2005).

The above review shows that, although constantly shaped by China's changing political agenda, service sector development in the PRD is primarily a response to the growing demand from the region's local economy, particularly that from the local industrial sector. Changes in the composition of the service sector also reflect the transformations of the local economic profile. In this sense, the service sector in the PRD can be classified as a 'regular business services economy' to use the typology of Table 6.1. Rather than emerging as a substitution to manufacturing, advanced (business) services contribute to the regional economy mainly through catering to the demand of the local industrial and other economic actors. To what extent they can develop an extra-regional orientation[2] (like type B and C in Table 6.1) and thus become an independent engine of regional economic growth remains to be seen.

Evaluating local policies for business services

Although still mainly playing a supporting role in the PRD's economy, services, especially advanced business services and international outsource services, have attracted a fair share of attention from local policy makers in recent years. The increasing pressures in the industrial sector (e.g. rising cost of land and labour, faltering global demand, intense competition from other low-wage countries as well as China's inland areas) means that both provincial and municipal governments in the PRD are eagerly searching for new sectors that can stimulate economic growth and enhance local competitiveness. High-order business services,[3] commonly recognized as a symbol of a modern economy and a beckoning prospect for future development, have become the focus of various regional and urban development plans. In the Plan for the Reform and Development of the Pearl River Delta (2008–2020) – one of the most important regional-scale policy guides in recent years – the goal for the PRD is defined as becoming 'a world-class base for advanced manufacturing and modern service industries'. To 'prioritize development of modern services' is highlighted (ahead of manufacturing) as the principal strategy to 'build a modern industrial system'. In the recent Twelfth Five Year Plan (2011–2015), all cities in the region promise to accelerate the development of a 'modern' or 'advanced' service industry to replace their low-end manufacturing sectors. Guangzhou and Shenzhen, the two leading cities in the region, both position themselves as a 'national service centre' with important international influences. Other cities have also set up ambitious targets and aim to become at least major service centres in the region.

Within China's political-economic context, policy makers' acknowledgement and commitment will become a strong incentive for the development of business services. However, examining their service development plans, it is not hard to observe 'a gap between the rhetoric and the knowledge' (Daniels 2013). In the PRD, most cities' service development priorities overlap with each other, which cover almost all typical sectors in the 'global advanced services hub' and 'offshore services production centre' types of business service economies (Table 6.1). These often include, for instance, 'finance', 'modern logistics', 'science-technology service', 'creative industry' and 'international outsource' etc. The stimulation efforts basically involve the physical construction of central business districts (CBDs) and various service dedicated zones, instead of sector-based and context-sensitive policy guides. It seems these cities' development targets, strategies and instruments for service sectors are largely copied from their former successful experience in attracting manufacturing activities (Yang and Yeh 2013). This indicates a poor understanding of the characteristics of business services economies as well as the specific local conditions of individual cities.

As discussed above, the development conditions and location preferences of business services firms are not only different from one type to another, but also quite distinct from that of manufacturing. Unlike low-end manufacturing activities, whose major concern is to minimize production and delivery costs, business services, especially higher-order ones, prefer locations that provide a large pool of well-educated (sometimes also specialized) service labour, a concentration of (large) corporate clients, as well as superior urban infrastructure and international connections (cf. Daniels 1985, Coffey and Polèse 1989, Coffey 2000). Both these resources and clients are unevenly distributed in the PRD. As Table 6.3 shows, only the provincial capital Guangzhou and the Special Economic Zone (SEZ) Shenzhen have accumulated a large pool of labour with a relatively higher level of education that can meet the general requirement of advanced business services. Most other cities' labour education level is not only far behind that of these two cities, but also below the national average. On the demand side, the largest companies in the PRD are also highly concentrated in Guangzhou and Shenzhen, reflecting their headquarter functions in the region. In comparison, other cities lack a strong cluster of large corporate clients which can generate adequate demand for higher-order business services (Table 6.3). Moreover, the region's major international airports and ports, high-speed railway stations and internet hubs are all located in Guangzhou and Shenzhen.

The labour, demand and infrastructure conditions of most lower-tier cities in the PRD are still deeply geared to their (low-end) manufacturing-dominated urban economy, which now become a constraint to the development of their business service sectors. As a result, advanced business services are concentrated in two regional core cities: Guangzhou and Shenzhen. In 2010, these two cities accounted for about 40 per cent of the gross regional employment and only 36 per cent of that in the secondary sector. However, they provided 56 per cent of the employment in services and 60 to 90 per cent of that in most advanced business service sectors,

Table 6.3 The labour and client conditions for business services in the Pearl River Delta and three Chinese leading cities

City	*Percentage of population with higher education (2010)**	*Number of companies in the Fortune China 500 list (2013)*
Guangzhou	19.6	10
Shenzhen	17.6	27
Zhuhai	18.5	1
Foshan	9.7	2
Huizhou	6.4	0
Dongguan	7.3	0
Zhongshan	8.0	0
Jiangmen	5.6	0
Zhaoqing	4.6	0
Beijing	31.5	77
Shanghai	22.0	42
Hong Kong	25.4	84
China	8.9	500

Source: GSB 2012, Fortune China 2013, HKCSD 2011, NBS 2011

Note: *Data of mainland China are calculated based on 'Population with junior college and above education per 100,000 persons'; data of Hong Kong are 'Population aged 15 and over with post-secondary educational attainment'.

including ICT, finance, business services, scientific-technical services and air transportation services (calculated based on GSB 2012, GSB and OPCGP 2012). All other cities in the region, except another SEZ, Zhuhai, provided much fewer jobs in business services than in manufacturing. Outsource services are even more concentrated. Over 95 per cent of such activities in Guangdong province are located in Guangzhou and Shenzhen (DCGP 2013).

This unequal pattern stands in stark contrast to the believe held by many second- and third-tier cities in the PRD that advanced business services can provide a remedy to their declining industrial competitiveness. Unlike manufacturing-led development, in which (smaller) cities were able to attract industrial investment once cheap land and tax exemptions were provided, the construction of massive office spaces and the provision of favourable policies may not guarantee the 'anticipated' growth of high-order business services in small and medium cities (Yang and Yeh 2013). The development of advanced business services is more difficult to be planned as the tradability of many such services remains at a rather low level, whereas the key conditions required for the production of them tend to concentrate only in a limited number of cities. This does not suggest that any regional policy emphasizing business services will be unsuccessful. However, to be effective, such a policy needs to be tailored according to the characteristics of individual areas (Coffey and Polèse 1989: 22).

Rethinking strategies for developing business services in the Pearl River Delta

It is quite clear now that a business service-led development model will not be the best choice for all cities. Arguably, a 'blanket approach' (Coffey and Polèse 1989: 24) that covers a comprehensive package of business service sectors is unlikely to generate similar success in every city. Instead, local policy makers need to carefully examine the conditions in their cities and, based on it, focus on a specific type(s) of business services economy (Table 6.1) and formulate more targeted strategies and policy directions. Given the differences in labour supply and market conditions between cities in the PRD, at least two business service development logics should be distinguished: one for regional core cities and another one for secondary cities.

The two core cities in the region, Guangzhou and Shenzhen, have the potential to transform into service sector-led economies and develop into business services centres that can cater to the demand across the entire region and even look transregional (i.e., similar to type B, but at a lower level). They also have a great chance to benefit from the fast-growing global offshore services market, especially in the ITES-BPO sector (see Tholons 2014). The main challenge for them is the intense competition from other leading cities in China. These two cities are lagging behind Beijing and Shanghai – the two largest business services centres in mainland China (Zhang forthcoming) – and Hong Kong – the adjacent global city – in terms of both labour and market conditions (see Table 6.3), which puts them at a disadvantage in top-level business service sectors. Meanwhile, the relatively higher labour and living costs compared to China's inland cities (e.g. Chengdu, Wuhan and Xian etc.) are also detrimental to their competitiveness in attracting some lower- and medium-order business services (e.g. BPO activities). Whether Guangzhou and Shenzhen can continuously attract a sufficient amount of highly skilled labour through targeted policy design will be crucial for their success in the service sector-led economic transition. This may not be an easy task since the region no longer enjoys a special policy support from the Chinese central government.

As two cities with similar economic development levels and regional status, Guangzhou and Shenzhen also have to deal with the problem of 'division of labour' between each other (and, to some extent, with Hong Kong) in business services economies. It is unlikely that two (or more) advanced business services centres (type B) with similar sector focus can co-develop within a same region. Based on their respective comparative advantages, a more rational choice would be for Shenzhen to concentrate on innovation-related activities, such as finance and high-tech services, and for Guangzhou to focus on services that can be linked to its position as a long-term political, commercial and cultural centre in the region. However, these two cities still show a greater willingness to compete rather than cooperate with each other in enhancing their positions.

For most second- and third-tier cities in the region, the more viable choice is service sector-supported rather than service sector-led development. This means focusing on those business services that can support (or promote) their current industrial foundations. It will include, above all, 'regular business services' (type A) that respond to the common demand from the city's local economic activities, especially the demand from local manufacturing firms. Most of these services will fulfil a principally supporting function, with little export potential. However, through improving the productivity and reducing the costs of local economic sectors, they can help to increase the competitiveness of the overall economy of the city. In addition, substituting the import of these services by local service providers can also contribute to a city's employment (cf. Coffey and Polèse 1989: 23–24).

These non-core cities may also try to promote some specific type(s) of business services that can benefit from their local industrial foundations, and develop a more 'specialized business services economy' (type C). Most cities in the PRD have established a variety of industrial sectors, some of which have even formed world-class manufacturing clusters (Enright *et al.* 2005). They have the potential to take advantage of their production capability and specialist knowledge accumulated in specific industrial sectors and extend to more value-added parts of the production chain. Dongguan's recent upgrade from a manufacturing base for animation-derivative products to an emerging cluster of animation design, production and exhibition is a good example of such a development (*Chinanews* 2013). These services may only take up a niche market in the service economy, but over time they have the potential to become a new source of export. However, the production of these specialized services raises a greater challenge to the knowledge and skill base in lower-tier cities, which are even more disadvantaged (see Table 6.3) in attracting high-level service labour.

For the PRD, a refined regional 'division of labour', with higher-order business services provided mainly by two core cities, and manufacturing and more specialized service activities clustered in lower-level cities, will be a more favourable choice to improve the region's overall economic competitiveness. All cities need to reposition themselves within this new regional production network and foster more diverse comparative advantages based on their specific economic foundations.

Conclusion

This chapter has examined the process and patterns of business service development in the PRD and discussed relevant policy implications. It provides some counterweight to the currently widespread enthusiastic belief among policy makers that business services will be a more promising choice (compared to manufacturing) to achieve socioeconomic development in various kinds of cities in China. Although the analysis is centred on a specific case, the lessons learned from it hold value for other regions in China as well. Business services, especially higher-order ones, have strict requirements for the qualities of places and a very selective choice on their locations. The unique features of business services (compared with manufacturing) imply that many cities' policy interventions, which still rely heavily on their experience accumulated in the industrialization period, may have little effect while involving very high cost (Yang and Yeh 2013). This chapter argues that local policy makers should develop a better understanding of the characteristics of business service activities as well as the strengths and constraints of their individual cities, and formulate more targeted policies to promote the development of specific type(s) of business services that fit their local economic profiles.

The discussion of service sector development policies in this chapter has mainly concentrated on the strategic level. However, even if a city manages to identify which type(s) of business services economies may be suitable for its local economy, it still has to address a perhaps even tougher question: what measures should (and could) be implemented to actually foster the development of services economies? Developing a pool of highly skilled service labour is much more difficult than attracting low-wage migrant industrial workers. Generating sufficient demand to stimulate the initial creation and subsequent growth of local service firms is also incomparable to seeking external investments and markets for local manufacturing sectors. While local governments in China played a leading role in building the 'workshop of the world' in the past three decades, the options and measures left for them (especially outside core cities) in the new wave of business service sector-led development is limited. Once again, we may come back to the long-standing question: 'is it really worthwhile to expend so much effort in attempting to resist the "natural" market trends?' (Coffey and Polèse 1989: 25).

It should be emphasized that, for most cities, developing a business service sector that fits their local economies will be a long-term effort. It may take decades to restructure a city's manufacturing-based urban economy and improve its labour quality, knowledge base, institutional arrangements and social-cultural environment to a level that can meet the basic requirement of business service activities. This requires local governors to shift their focus from short-term economic growth, which was more easily realized through policy and tax incentives in the manufacturing-based development period, to more sustainable, long-term socioeconomic progress. In addition, local governors may also have to adapt to their cities' new roles in the restructured regional (and national) 'division of labour', and adopt a more cooperative rather than competitive development ideology as currently prevalent among Chinese cities. These changes probably will not be easily achieved in China's current competition-centred political-economic environment (Xu 2011). However, they will be decisive for any city or region's future development.

This chapter introduced a typology of business services economies to illustrate the diverse modes of service sector development. For a more comprehensive understanding of its policy implications, further research could look at the social and spatial consequences of various types of business services economies. This includes how different business services economies impact and restructure cities' dominant labour structure and social stratification and who are the beneficiaries of the growth of particular (high-order, specialized or offshore) service activities. A deeper understanding is needed of the social support systems and planning practices that are needed to underpin urban transitions from a manufacturing to a service sector-led economy or from one type of business services economy to another. To answer these questions, more studies (like those in this volume) drawing on detailed, city- and sector-specific information are needed.

Notes

1 The PRD is composed of nine municipalities (Guangzhou, Shenzhen, Foshan, Zhuhai, Dongguan, Huizhou, Zhongshan, Jiangmen and Zhaoqing) in China's Guangdong province. In 2012, this region accounted for about 84 per cent of GDP and 93 per cent of services production in Guangdong (GSB 2013).

2 In 2011, the PRD's services exports (US$44 billion) accounted for only less than 9 per cent of its goods exports, and only 6 per cent of its services exports involved relatively higher-order business services (GYP 2012).

3 Unlike in the classification in Table 6.1, outsource/offshore services are also perceived as 'high value-added', 'high-tech' and 'high-growth' by the local policy makers in the PRD (DCGP 2013).

Acknowledgements

I would like to thank the three editors of this book (particularly Dr Bart Lambregts) for their constructive comments and suggestions at various stages of the manuscript. Of course, any errors or omissions remain my sole responsibility.

References

ADB (Asian Development Bank), 2012. *Asian Development Outlook 2012 Update: Services and Asia's Future Growth*. Mandaluyong City, Philippines: Asian Development Bank.

AWDC (Antwerp World Diamond Council), 2013. *The Global Diamond Report 2013: Journey Through the Value Chain*. Antwerp: Antwerp World Diamond Council.

Bassens, D., Derudder, B. and Witlox, F., 2010. Searching for the Mecca of finance: Islamic financial services and the world city network. *Area*, 42 (1), 35–46.

Bennett, R.J., Bratton, W.A. and Robson, P.J.A., 2000. Business advice: The influence of distance. *Regional Studies*, 34 (9), 813–828.

Chinanews, 2013. Dongguan dongman chanye: congzhi daoliang de huali zhuanshen [Dongguan animation industry: from quantity to quality]. www.dongman.gov.cn/xinwen/pinglun/201310/t20131011_774864.htm. Accessed 9 January 2015 (in Chinese).

Coffey, W.J., 2000. The geographies of producer services. *Urban Geography*, 21 (2), 170–183.

Coffey, W.J. and Polèse, M., 1989. Producer services and regional development: A policy-oriented perspective. *Papers of the Regional Science Association*, 67, 13–27.

Cumbers, A., 2000. Globalization, local economic development and the branch plant region: The case of the Aberdeen oil complex. *Regional Studies*, 34 (4), 371–382.

Daniels P.W., 1985. *Service Industries: A Geographical Appraisal*. London: Methuen.

Daniels P.W., 2013. The transition to producer services in China: Opportunities and obstacles. *In*: A.G. Yeh and F.F. Yang, (eds). *Producer Services in China: Economic and Urban Development*. London and New York: Routledge, 29–51.

Daniels, P.W. and Moulaert, F., (eds). 1991. *The Changing Geography of Advanced Producer Services*. London and New York: Belhaven Press.

DCGP (Department of Commerce of Guangdong Province), 2013. *The Development Plan for Guangdong Service Outsourcing Industries*. www.gddoftec.gov.cn/dept_detail.asp?deptid=1042&channalid=1642&contentid=17095. Accessed 9 January 2015 (inChinese).

Dossani, R. and Kenney, M., 2007. The next wave of globalization: Relocating service provision to India. *World Development*, 35 (5), 772–791.

Economic Daily, 2011. Jiakuai fazhan sanchan fuwuye, cujin chanye jiegou youhua shengji [Accelerating the development of the tertiary service sector to promote the optimization and upgrading of economic structure]. www.zgcqjjw.com/Html/?723.html. Accessed 9 January 2015 (in Chinese).

Economist, The, 2012. Manufacturing: the end of cheap China. www.economist.com/node/21549956. Accessed 9 January 2015.

Enright, M., Scott, E.E. and Chang, K.M., 2005. *Regional Powerhouse: The Greater Pearl River Delta and the Rise of China*. Singapore: John Wiley & Sons.

Fortune China, 2013. *Top 500 Companies in China 2013*. www.fortunechina.com/fortune500/c/2013-07/16/2013C500.htm. Accessed 9 January 2015 (in Chinese).

Ghani, E. and Kharas, H., 2010. The service revolution in South Asia: An overview. *In*: E. Ghani (ed.). *The Service Revolution in South Asia*. New York: Oxford University Press, 1–32.

GSB (Guangdong Statistical Bureau), 1999. *Guangdong Wushi Nian* [Fifty Years of Guangdong]. Beijing: China Statistics Press (in Chinese).

GSB, 2001, *Guangdong Statistical Yearbook*. Beijing: China Statistics Press (in Chinese).

GSB, 2012. *Guangdong Statistical Yearbook*. Beijing: China Statistics Press (in Chinese).

GSB, 2013. *Guangdong Statistical Yearbook*. Beijing: China Statistics Press (in Chinese).

GSB and OPCGP (Office for the Population Census of Guangdong Province), 2012. *Tabulation on the 2010 Population Census of Guangdong Province*. Beijing: China Statistical Press.

GYP (Guangdong Yearbook Press), 2012. *Guangdong Yearbook*. Guangzhou: Guangdong Yearbook Press (in Chinese).

HKCSD (Hong Kong Census and Statistics Department), 2011. *Hong Kong AnnualDigest of Statistics*. www.statistics.gov.hk/pub/B10100032011AN11B0100.pdf. Accessed 9 January 2015.

Illeris, S., 1994. Proximity between service producers and service users. *Tijdschrift voor Economische en Sociale Geografie*, 85, 294–302.

Li, J.F., Gu, N.H. and Chen, J.X., 2008. 30 years' development of the tertiary sector in China. *In*: D.T. Zhou, (ed.). *China: 30 Years of Reform and Opening-Up (1978–2008)*. Beijing: Social Sciences Academic Press, 452–489 (in Chinese).

Lin, G.C.S., 2005. Service industries and transformation of city-regions in globalizing China: new testing ground for theoretical reconstruction. *In*: P.W. Daniels, K.C. Ho and T.A. Hutton, (eds). *Service Industries and Asia-Pacific Cities: New Development Trajectories*. London and New York: Routledge, 283–300.

Lu, H., 2008. Dali fazhan shengchanxing fuwuye, cujin woguo chanye jiegou youhua shengji [Promoting the optimization and upgrading of China's industrial structure through developing producer services]. *Forward Position in Economics*, 2, 68–73 (in Chinese).

Metters, R. and Vargas, V., 2000. A typology of de-coupling strategies in mixed services. *Journal of Operations Management*, 18 (6), 663–682.

NBS (National Bureau of Statistics), 2011. *China Statistical Yearbook*. Beijing: China Statistics Press.

Sassen, S., 2001. *The Global City: New York, London, Tokyo*. Princeton: Princeton University Press.

Shen, K., 2011. Xiandai fuwuye: jingji zhuanxing de biyou zhilu [Modern services: the necessary road to economic transition]. *China Urban Economy*, 11, 86–87 (in Chinese).

Sit, V.F.S. and Yang, C., 1997. Foreign-investment-induced exo-urbanisation in the Pearl River Delta, China. *Urban Studies*, 34, 647–677.

Taylor, P.J., Derudder, B., Faulconbridge, J., Hoyler, M. and Ni, P., 2014. Advanced producer service firms as strategic networks, global cities as strategic places. *Economic Geography*, 90 (3), 267–291.

Tholons, 2014. *Top 100 Outsourcing Destinations: Regional Review*. www.tholons.com/TholonsTop100/pdf/Tholons_Top_100_2014_Rankings_&_Report_Overview.pdf. Accessed 9 January 2015.

Wood, P., 2009. Knowledge intensive business services. *In*: R. Kitchin and N. Thrift, (eds). *International Encyclopedia of Human Geography*. Oxford: Elsevier, 37–44.

Xu, C.G., 2011. The fundamental institutions of China's reforms and development. *Journal of Economic Literature*, 49 (4), 1076–1151.

Yang, F.F. and Yeh, A.G., 2013. Spatial development of producer services in the Chinese urban system. *Environment and Planning A*, 45 (1), 159–179.

Yeh, A.G.O., 2005. Producer services and industrial linkages in the Hong Kong-Pearl River Delta Region. *In*: P.W. Daniels, K.C. Ho and T.A. Hutton, (eds). *Service Industries and Asia-Pacific Cities*. London and New York: Routledge, 150–173.

Yeh, A.G.O. and Yang, F.F., 2013. Producer services and China's economic and urban development: Introduction and overview. *In*: A.G.O. Yeh and F.F. Yang, (eds)., *Producer Services in China: Economic and Urban Development*. London and New York: Routledge, 3–27.

Zhang, X. and Kloosterman, R.C., forthcoming. Connecting the 'workshop of the world': intra- and extra-service networks of the Pearl River Delta city-region. *Regional Studies*, DOI: 10.1080/00343404.2014.962492.

7 Hong Kong as an offshore trading hub

Thomas J. Sigler and Simon XB. Zhao

Introduction

Cities play an important role in the world economy, mediating flows of capital and information within complex global production networks (GPNs). The increasing importance of advanced business services (ABS) in orchestrating these flows has cast so-called Global Cities into the limelight, focusing attention on the local practices and processes that facilitate international economies. 'Offshore' services constitute a growing component of the service economy, and although the offshoring of particular business processes is regarded as significant (Gereffi 2006), only recently has substantial scholarly attention focused on the offshoring of services and the territorial implications thereof (Beerepoot and Hendriks 2013, Haberly and Wójcik 2015). This is attributable to the fact that the offshoring of services has lagged behind manufacturing, and that it is less conspicuous and not as well understood, as the range and complexity of services is virtually infinite. Moreover, much of this activity is deliberately obfuscated and secretive, as regulatory and/or tax compliance is often why services are offshored in the first place.

Within Asia, Hong Kong has become a recognised Global City through its service agglomeration, much of which involves offshore service activities. As a special administrative region (SAR) of China, Hong Kong features a *laissez-faire* market orientation with historical roots as a colonial *entrepôt*, and plays an important role in the global economy as an intermediary connecting Mainland China to the world at large. Since the handover of Hong Kong and the adjacent New Territories by the United Kingdom in 1997, this role has expanded and Hong Kong has become a prominent Global City (Chiu and Lui 2009) and a global financial centre (Lai 2012) with a range of complementary services.

Although trade has always been a core function of the Hong Kong economy, the meteoric rise of China as the 'world's workshop' beginning in 1979 has led to enhanced business opportunities for both local and multinational corporations in Hong Kong with linkages to the Mainland. Since the handover, Hong Kong has transitioned from a regional services hub to a global one, with growth driven by several key industries, among them tourism, transportation, ABS and a handful of trade-based services including transhipment, re-exportation and 'offshore trade'.

This chapter provides an analytical overview of Hong Kong's role in offshore trading – the practice of purchasing, or arranging the purchase of, goods that never physically enter or leave the territory. This shift from physical intermediation to transactional intermediation carries weighty implications for Hong Kong's territorial development as offshore trading is considerably less land and labour intensive than previous regimes of entrepôt trade.

The rise of offshore trade as a complement to Hong Kong's other trade-based industries is an indication of the dynamic nature of its economy and is seen as a harbinger of a movement away from trade in goods toward an almost exclusively services-oriented economy. The chapter concludes with a discussion of the local implications of the rise in offshore trading in Hong Kong in the context of a globalised shift toward offshoring more broadly.

Hong Kong in context

Hong Kong is a territory of 1,104 km^2 that lies at the mouth of the Pearl River along the South China Sea. Having grown from a relatively small British outpost into a cosmopolitan metropolis in less than a century, Hong Kong's 7.2 million inhabitants enjoy one of the highest standards of living in the region with a gross domestic product (GDP) per capita (at purchasing power parity) of nearly US$51,000 (CIA 2014). Along with Macau, Hong Kong is one of two SARs of the People's Republic of China (PRC) under the 'one country, two systems' framework that allows it to function as a capitalist exclave that is fundamentally decoupled from the Mainland. Although greater integration has been gradually implemented through a series of Closer Economic Partnership Agreements (CEPAs), Hong Kong's government operates autonomously from the PRC in most respects, and is a nominally democratic territory (Zhao *et al.* 2012).

Given its colonial history and particularistic juridical status, Hong Kong has a well-established entrepôt economy, dating to well before its emergence as a Global City. Although the British operated in Hong Kong alongside several other treaty ports, power coalesced in Hong Kong in the late nineteenth century as a Chinese capitalist class developed (Chiu and Lui 2009). It first served as a trans shipment port for migrants from its Chinese hinterland, and later as an intermediary for the brokerage of goods entering and leaving China (Chiu and Lui 2009). It was during this period that a suite of 'local' British institutions such as Swire and Jardine took root, which would over time grow into large multinational conglomerates specialising in Sino-Anglo trade (Jones and Khanna 2006). As the global economy shifted and China became increasingly introverted in the wake of World War II, Hong Kong replaced Shanghai as the region's main financial centre, giving rise to scores of 'native' banks that had strong regional ties to disparate areas of the Mainland. As beneficiaries of Hong Kong's involvement in both UK sterling and US dollar trading, these banks held a strong position in supporting various types of intermediary trade, enjoying relatively high returns due to the lack of exchange controls that many overseas banks faced (Schenk 2002). From the 1970s onward, Hong Kong shifted increasingly toward financial intermediation. Monetary stability and innovations within the financial industry attracted scores of large multinational banks, which gradually replaced smaller 'native' banks through mergers (Jao 1980, Schenk 2002, Chiu and Lui 2009: 62–63). This development into a regional financial centre laid the foundation for Hong Kong to emerge as a global financial centre decades later.

To diversify against an overreliance on financial and trade-related services, however, Hong Kong's industrialisation was also promoted to complement its intermediary role. Enabled by policies supporting economic openness, Hong Kong's industrial transformation took root in the 1950s, and by the 1970s it had become a world-leading producer, gradually transitioning from textiles to electronics and other high-value goods. At the time, Hong Kong's free-market orientation contrasted with the Mainland's policies prioritising endogenous industrial development over export-oriented growth. Szczepanek (1986 [1958]) argues that despite the apparent similarities, Hong Kong emerged ahead of Taiwan, Macau and Singapore early on largely because of its well-suited deep-water port, market-oriented regulatory environment, and a steady flow of migrants and capital from the neighbouring province of Guangdong. Furthermore, the territory's colonial systems (e.g. British law, English language) made it a logical choice for Western firms looking to outsource production to cheaper labour markets (Au *et al.* 2000: 30).

However, triggered by China's decision to open its market to external trade, 1980 marks the year that Hong Kong's economy began to shift back toward a trade and services orientation. For the first time since the Chinese Revolution in 1949, the PRC government sought to pursue a semi-mercantilist model based on export-oriented industrialisation, as Japan and other 'Asian Tigers' had done just years prior. In China, manufacturing industries were developed, first in China's five initial special economic zones (SEZs), and later throughout eastern China (Cartier 2001). The implication of this was that over the course of the decades to follow, much Hong Kong-based industry moved across the border to neighbouring Guangdong province. This led to a fundamental restructuring of Hong Kong's economy and labour force, as manufacturing fell from its mid-1970s peak of over 40 per cent of total employment to less than 20 per cent by 1991 and 3 per cent in 2012 (Hsieh and Woo 2005, Census and Statistics Department 2014).

Although many predicted the demise of Hong Kong preceding the British withdrawal and the concurrent exodus of local manufacturers leading up to the mid-1990s, Hong Kong has emerged as a significant global centre of trade-related services (Tao and Wong 2002) and ABS, particularly finance (Chu 2008). As Table 7.1 details, Hong Kong's intermediary role has persisted over time, but has changed forms considerably.

Given that manufacturing was at the forefront of Hong Kong's economy through the mid-twentieth century, the resurgence of its entrepôt role was fundamentally predicated upon the opening up and consequent transformation of southern China into an industrial Goliath. In fact, much of the void that was left by the outflux of manufacturing was filled by the opportunities created by entrepôt trade rooted in re-exportation and transhipment of Mainland goods. Between 1980 and 2013, the number of manufacturing firms contracted from

Table 7.1 Hong Kong's key economic roles over time

	Key activities	*Territorial status*	*Time period*
Entrepôt trade, mark I	East–West mercantile trade; regional trans-shipping	British colony	1840s–1940s
Export-oriented industrialisation	Manufacturing for export; regional financial centre	British colony	1940s–1970s
Entrepôt trade, mark II	Re-exportation; hubbing; transhipping; trade intermediation	British colony (to 1997); Special Administrative Region (from 1997)	1980–present
Development of higher-order services	Financial services; offshore trading; re-exportation	Special Administrative Region; Global City	1997–present

45,025 to 11,586, while the number of firms engaged in ABS increased six-fold to 66,767, and in wholesaling and trade nearly trebled to 180,905 (Census and Statistics Department 2014). As production moved to southern China beginning in the 1980s, Hong Kong developed several niche roles mediating between the Mainland and global economies, enhanced by the fact that deregulation by the PRC government created (somewhat counterintuitively) additional demand for intermediation (Sung 1991: 123).

Hong Kong's emergence as a trade intermediary vis-à-vis its role in offshore trade, transhipments, and re-exports (discussed below) is well supported by information-based views on intermediation (Feenstra and Hanson 2004). Though most academic work in this domain has focused on financial intermediation, information-based perspectives on intermediaries find that their advantage lies in the diffusion of risk and the reduction of transaction costs tied to market monitoring activities (Diamond 1984). As Rauch and Casella (2003) contend, trade breaks down where factor endowment ratios are far apart. In other words, Hong Kong's intermediary role helps bridge the informational and systemic discrepancies between China and the world at large – an advantage that has been accentuated by enhanced demand since the 1980s.

Hong Kong's re-exportation economy

Since the PRC's great economic awakening, one of Hong Kong's core intermediary functions has been re-exportation – a process in which firms import goods from China and distribute them onward to a final destination, or vice-versa.[1] Hong Kong's re-exportation industry represents HK$3.3 trillion (around US$425 billion) in economic activity per annum. Re-exportation and related activities comprise a significant proportion of the Hong Kong economy. With an average (mean) of six employees per firm, the sector is comprised primarily of small- and medium-scale firms that form the core of Hong Kong's global supply chain hub.

Hong Kong's intermediary firms play an important role in distribution networks as re-exporters, performing a variety of functions for both the buyer and seller including quality sorting, and 'matchmaking' – essentially finding producers able to fill orders to distributors' specifications. As Feenstra and Hanson (2004) note, Hong Kong's 'middlemen' have an informational advantage that benefits them in conducting business between China and distant markets, and Rauch and Trindade have shown that ethnic Chinese business and social networks have a considerable quantitative impact on international trade by helping to match buyers and sellers (2002: 116), with Hong Kong merchants' connections in greater China as exemplary of this. This informational advantage comprises multiple dimensions, including well-developed international connections in banking and trade; social linkages to the global Chinese diaspora; knowledge of both local and global customs; freedom of information (which is limited in Mainland China); as well as a 'head start' in certain industries – particularly textiles and electronics – all of which allow Hong Kong's re-exporters to understand the inner workings of globalised supply chains.

Much of Hong Kong's re-export activity falls under the category of 'outward processing', whereby raw materials are acquired on the world market and sent onward to China for further value-adding (Feenstra and Hanson 2004). However, though Hong Kong's intermediaries play an important role in re-exportation for the purposes of facilitating trade, the avoidance of tariffs and quotas[2] through transfer pricing – the sale of goods between two closely related parties – is also significant. Even though Hong Kong has increased its scrutiny of related-party transactions in recent years, the legislation remains poorly defined (Pahlman and Webb 2012), and as Feenstra and Hanson contend, 'there is some evidence that Hong Kong traders shift income from high-tax destination markets to Hong Kong through transfer pricing, as re-export markups are higher where corporate income tax rates in destination markets are higher' (2004: 33).

The growth of Hong Kong's re-export trade since the 1980s has created economies of agglomeration centred on trade-related services (Sung 2005: 2), which are strongly supported by the Hong Kong government under a developmentalist framework. It houses one of the world's largest trade-related services clusters, and has developed advanced infrastructures to host its intermediary activities. Hong Kong International Airport currently ranks first in cargo throughput (Airports Council International 2014), and the Port of Hong Kong was the world's busiest container port until 2004 and remains the world's second busiest transhipment port after Singapore. These support Hong Kong's role as a transhipment hub, in which goods are aggregated from smaller ports to comprise larger shipments to be deployed along major global cargo routes.

As a component of Hong Kong's economy, however, re-exportation is declining in relative importance. As Figure 7.1 demonstrates, offshore trading has surpassed re-exportation in economic impact, and is now more significant as a percentage of overall trade with the Mainland (Sung 2005).

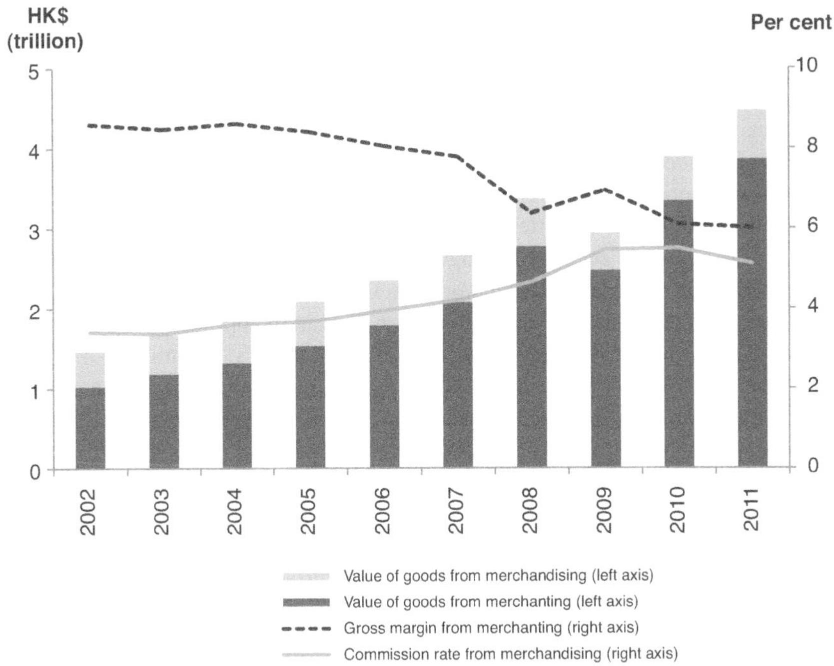

Figure 7.1 Offshore trade in Hong Kong by type, 2002–2011

Source: Census and Statistics Department (2012).

Offshore trading

Offshoring is an umbrella term that applies to many business processes in a variety of industries. Fundamentally, offshoring involves the movement of particular business functions from one jurisdiction to another in order to reap the benefits of favourable regulatory, labour or tax conditions. China's emergence as a pre-eminent industrial economy has been predicated on the offshoring of manufacturing, just as the emergence of India as one of the world's ICT leaders is a result of the offshoring of technology services (cf. Kleibert and Krishnan in this volume). Analogous to the offshoring of manufacturing and services, offshore trade involves the brokering of goods in a third-party jurisdiction – in this case Hong Kong – without them ever physically entering the territory.

Offshore trading comprises two related processes: merchanting and merchandising. Merchanting involves the purchase and sale of goods by Hong Kong-based establishments that take ownership of the goods involved. This often involves the direct sale of goods by subcontracted entities in Mainland China. Merchandising is the practice of arranging the purchase and sale of goods outside Hong Kong based on the buyer's specifications. This can involve a range of services, including sourcing, procurement, shipment and contracting, but in contrast to merchanting, establishments engaged in merchandising never take ownership of the goods involved (Leung *et al.* 2008, Census and Statistics Department 2013). While merchanting activities consist primarily of small and medium-sized firms trading products to and from China, merchandising more often involves trade in bulk goods with fixed prices (e.g. commodities) for which quality sorting and related services are less of a concern. Although this also involves trade with China, it is more likely to involve state-owned entities, with Hong Kong acting as an 'escrow' site. Both are able to leverage access to Hong Kong's capital, using letters of credit from their customers in order to obtain commercial finance (HKTDC 2012).

The rise of offshore trading in Hong Kong began in approximately 1991 (Sung 2005: 13) and has grown steadily to HK$4.5 trillion (US$580 billion) as of 2011 (Census and Statistics Department 2013). Unlike re-exportation, which primarily involves consumer goods such as electronics (54 per cent) and textiles (8 per cent), a substantial proportion of offshore trade is in fuels (40 per cent), indicative of rising energy demand in Mainland China. Thus, while re-exportation relies heavily on small firms trading in consumer goods, offshore trade is comprised of larger firms trading with Mainland state-owned corporations. These companies use Hong Kong as an offshore hub for obtaining commodities such as fuels and ores and agricultural products, which are more easily tradable from a distance, as prices are determined more by global supply and demand than local market conditions and preferences. The most common destinations of offshore traded goods in Hong Kong are Mainland China (39 per cent) and the United States (17 per cent), followed by Singapore (7 per cent), Japan (6 per cent) and the United Kingdom (4 per cent) (Census and Statistics Department 2012).[3]

Although both merchanting and merchandising are increasing in volume in Hong Kong, merchanting is a more common practice, representing more than 86 per cent of offshore trade (Figure 7.2).

As Figure 7.2 shows, profit margins (enumerated as gross margin and commission rate for merchanting and merchandising respectively) are converging, although merchanting remains slightly more lucrative. This may be explained by the fact that Hong Kong firms are more involved in the merchanting process than in merchandising, and thus better able to add value through the services they provide.

Hong Kong's increasing reliance on offshore trading represents three complementary processes at work. First, as Hong Kong's human population has grown and business activity has expanded, the territory has become physically saturated, and new development – particularly of expansive infrastructures – is both costly and logistically difficult. Wages are considerably higher in the territory than elsewhere in the region, and space is limited. Hong Kong International Airport (Chek Lap Kok), for example, was the most expensive ever built upon completion in 1998, as nearly 10 km^2 of adjacent seabed had to be reclaimed for its construction. Furthermore, at the core of the exodus of manufacturing in the 1980s and 1990s were not only rising wages, but a lack of scalability, which the vast hinterland of Mainland China ultimately provided. In such a space-constrained environment, heavy

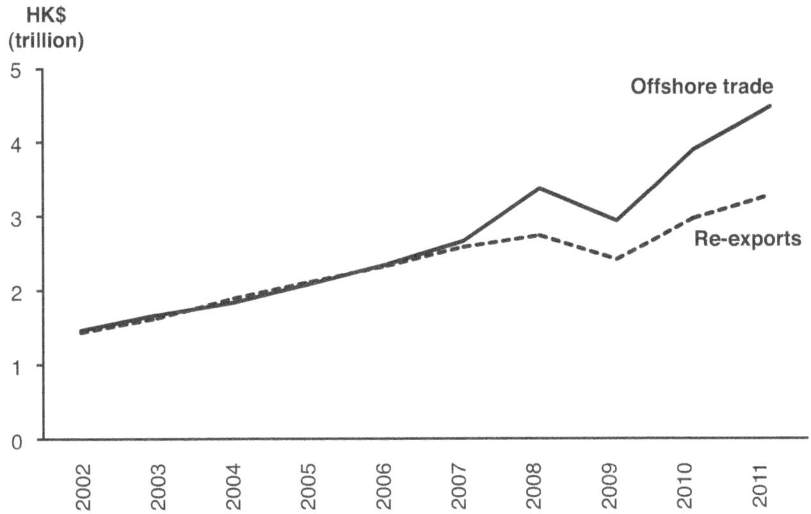

Figure 7.2 Total value of offshore trade and re-export in Hong Kong, 2002–2011
Source: Census and Statistics Department (2012).

industry – such as the port facilities associated with entrepôt trade – does not hold a particularly bright future. As Sung (2005) argues, it is likely that low value-adding sectors, particularly the vestiges of Hong Kong's manufacturing economy and re-exportation centred on the city's hub functions, will ultimately be completely 'shorn', and replaced by more capital- and knowledge-intensive, rather than labour- or space-intensive, industries.

Second, the development of China's spatial economy has obviated the need for many goods to pass through Hong Kong (Enright and Mak 2005). Increasing sophistication of production processes, improved port infrastructures and ever-greater integration with export markets have meant that Chinese producers are better equipped to ship their products directly to consumer nations, and that Chinese consumers can import directly from the global marketplace. Five of the world's top ten container ports are now located in Mainland China, including first-ranked Shanghai and Shenzhen – just a few kilometres north of Hong Kong (Journal of Commerce 2012).

Although this would seem to reduce Hong Kong's place along the value chain, it has in fact increased demand for the transactional services the territory provides. Chinese producers often require the services of an intermediary in Hong Kong, given the informational advantages they have acquired over time. As information-based views on intermediation posit, it is often less costly and/or risky for the merchanting service to coordinate with multiple suppliers and ensure legal and regulatory compliance than for importers to do themselves (Leung *et al.* 2008: 119). Furthermore, as re-exportation through Hong Kong becomes less important,

Hong Kong's intermediaries seek new opportunities mediating trade outside of the territory. As Leung *et al.* (2008: 121) note:

> while the Mainland may have developed the requisite port facilities and the necessary logistics expertise to handle direct shipments, there still exist important gaps in the supply chain that Hong Kong service providers can fill – such as finding overseas buyers and meeting their quality standards, as well as sourcing raw materials and parts and co-ordinating work with other suppliers

Third, due to a burgeoning middle class and an expanding consumer market more generally, China has become one of the world's most significant importers, both of finished goods as well as raw materials and semi-finished goods. China is now the world's third largest importer, increasing annual import volume from a mere US$20 billion in 1980 (National Bureau of Statistics 2012) to more than US$1.6 trillion in 2012 (CIA 2014). This creates further intermediary opportunities for Hong Kong-based firms, as the same informational advantage that allows Chinese exporters to find and negotiate outside market opportunities facilitates the inverse as well. China represents the largest source of export earnings for Hong Kong firms and creates significant potential as the Mainland market matures.

The implications of service export development in Hong Kong

Hong Kong has gone from being a net service importer to a considerable service exporter in a short period of time. In 1998, just after the handover, Hong Kong imported more than HK$120 trillion in services, composed primarily of manufacturing services. Though Hong Kong currently imports HK$594 trillion in services, it exports more than HK$764 trillion in services with transport, travel and financial services accounting for the bulk of activity (Census and Statistics Department 2014). Offshore trading is a component of Hong Kong's trade in services that is unaccounted for by these categories, as merchants derive profits and commission from the mediation of goods that never enter the territory.

The rise of offshore trading as a component of a larger trade-based economy in Hong Kong is explained several factors relating to its advantageous position in global networks: the diffusion of transactional risk, preferential access to market information, as well as economies of scale and agglomeration (Townsend 1978, Sung 1991: 28–33). As Jessop and Sum (2000) suggest, the territory's transition from manufacturing to services in the 1980s and 1990s was driven by a combination of state-led entrepreneurial 'glurbanisation' in southern China and firm-led 'glocalisation' within Hong Kong – both of which were externally focused and leveraged pre-existing cultural and economic linkages. Furthermore, the expansion of offshore trade is driven by the fact that China's expansion as both a large export and import market creates enhanced demand for a centralised source of information and access to capital. Hong Kong provides both, as its traders have a long history of China-related intermediation, and its emergence as a global financial centre

Table 7.2 Composite employment estimates by industry, 2001–2012

Industry	*2001*		*2012*		*Absolute change*	*Proportional change*
			Number	*Proportion*	*Number*	*Proportion*
Trading and sales (Import/export, wholesale and retail trades)	**835 900**	**25.7 %**	**899 200**	**24.6 %**	**7.6 %**	**–1.1 %**
Import and export trade	*505 000*	*15.5 %*	*517 600*	*14.2 %*	*2.5 %*	*–1.4 %*
Wholesale	*70 300*	*2.2 %*	*64 000*	*1.8 %*	*–9.0 %*	*–0.4 %*
Retail trade	*260 600*	*8.0 %*	*317 600*	*8.7 %*	*21.9 %*	*0.7 %*
Public administration, and social and personal services	**738 200**	**22.7 %**	**936 900**	**25.6 %**	**26.9 %**	**2.9 %**
Advanced business services	**523 900**	**16.1 %**	**710 300**	**19.4 %**	**35.6 %**	**3.3 %**
Financing and insurance	*178 100*	*5.5 %*	*228 800*	*6.3 %*	*28.5 %*	*0.8 %*
Real estate	*92 700*	*2.8 %*	*126 700*	*3.5 %*	*36.7 %*	*0.6 %*
Professional and business services	*253 000*	*7.8 %*	*354 700*	*9.7 %*	*40.2 %*	*1.9 %*
Logistics (transport and related services)	**304 400**	**9.4 %**	**317 600**	**8.7 %**	**4.3 %**	**–0.7 %**
Construction	**289 400**	**8.9 %**	**291 300**	**8.0 %**	**0.7 %**	**–0.9 %**
Accommodation and food services	**250 100**	**7.7 %**	**268 500**	**7.3 %**	**7.4 %**	**–0.3 %**
Manufacturing	**193 400**	**5.9 %**	**111 500**	**3.0 %**	**–42.3 %**	**–2.9 %**
Information and communications	**94 300**	**2.9 %**	**101 800**	**2.8 %**	**8.0 %**	**–0.1 %**
Utilities	**16 500**	**0.5 %**	**14 600**	**0.4 %**	**–11.5 %**	**–0.1 %**
Others [(1)]	**9 600**	**0.3 %**	**5 300**	**0.1 %**	**–44.8 %**	**–0.1 %**
Total employment	**3 255 600**	**100 %**	**3 657 100**	**100 %**	12.30 %	

Source: Composite employment estimates by Census and Statistics Department (2012)

Note: (1)Including the industries of agriculture, forestry and fishing; and mining and quarrying.

ensures that Chinese firms can access global capital markets and vice-versa. The Hong Kong stock exchange is the world's sixth-largest by market capitalisation and it is common for Chinese companies to list shares simultaneously on Mainland exchanges (either Shenzhen or Shanghai) and in Hong Kong, known locally as 'H-shares' (Callen *et al.* 2009). Both transactional and financial intermediation help anoint the Mainland's industrial economy, and Hong Kong further acts as a sink for offshored capital.

On a local scale, the transition from industrial colony to Global City focusing on service exports has carried significant implications for Hong Kong's residents. Manufacturing jobs have nearly disappeared from Hong Kong (see Table 7.2), and the economy has become ever-more bifurcated between high-wage jobs in ABS and the rest of the economy (Chiu and Lui 2009).

Between 2001 and 2012, the key sources of labour market growth were ABS (+35.6 per cent), public, social and personal services (+26.9 per cent), and although trading and sales increased in absolute importance (+7.6 per cent), their relative importance actually declined as wholesale trade employment contracted. Within these sectors, professional and business services were Hong Kong's highest-growth subsector, representing the expansion of offshore trading activities.

The transition toward a services orientation has implications for Hong Kong's working class, as offshore trade contributes even less to the employment than re-exports, and its expansion thus furthers a polarising effect on labour in Hong Kong (He 2007: 5), supporting Sassen's (1991) theory that Global Cities are sites of inequality. It also carries gendered implications, with thousands of service works from the Philippines and other neighbouring countries forming a shadow service economy catering to the local élite (Chiu and Lui 2004). As such, Hong Kong is an offshore destination not only for capital, but for labour originating from elsewhere in the region.

Although income inequality has risen across the majority of industrial sectors (Lui 2013), a greater worry for Hong Kong residents is the increasing cost of housing, which has become the least affordable in the world (Einhorn 2014). Tens of thousands of Hong Kongers live in so-called 'cage' homes, generating significant concern about living conditions amid some of the highest human densities in the world. Hong Kong's torrid real estate market is a direct result of the territory's position as an offshore site, and acts a repository for the fortunes of Mainland industrialists.

On a global scale, however, Hong Kong's large-scale transition toward a services-oriented exclave runs parallel to the fundamental reordering of the global economy that offshore economies suggest more broadly. Hong Kong's increasingly corporeal position as a Global City and international offshore financial centre is easily identified through its residential and commercial spaces catering to China's élite. As Urry (2013: 232) suggests, contemporary Hong Kong:

> seems to function as an offshore territory for China similar to how it functioned for Britain before ownership was transferred to China in 1997. Chinese elites thus require their own offshore centre, governed at a distance

and deploying a hybrid British and Chinese façade to conceal the scale of the tax avoidance/evasion passing through.

Capital and information – the two critical components of Hong Kong's contemporary economy – pass across space with greater ease than goods and people, and are what give the territory a competitive advantage over Shanghai, Shenzhen, Guangzhou and Beijing in trade-related and financial intermediation. The clinical separation of Hong Kong's political and economic regimes under the 'one country, two systems' framework enables locally based firms to leverage preferential access to both, filling an important lacuna in China's economic development. Hong Kong's role thus parallels that of Singapore, Dubai and other offshore capitalist exclaves more broadly (Sigler 2013), insofar as the activities that are carried out within the territory complement fundamental business activities that firms find to be cumbersome, difficult, expensive or outright impossible on the Mainland.

Conclusion

The offshore world is increasingly fundamental to the global economy. The continued presence of numerous offshore jurisdictions proves this to be true, combined with the fact that the volumes of capital that they mediate are ever-increasing. As we have discussed above, offshore trade in Hong Kong has very clearly defined spatial dimensions and indicates a movement even further toward an almost entirely services-based economy (Wong 2002: 9). In contrast to other observations of offshoring in the region (Beerepoot and Hendriks 2013), however, the case of Hong Kong symbolises the concentration of business activities at the upper echelons of the value chain, with knowledge and information as key resources, as opposed to cheap labour.

Hong Kong is both physically and metaphysically an offshore centre for China. This role involves multiple industries, and increasingly those that are capital and information intensive rather than labour or land intensive, representing a shift from physical intermediation to transactional intermediation. Hong Kong's economy is led by several large-scale conglomerates that are able to mediate between East and West with relative ease, leveraging access to capital, information and economies of scale (Chiu and Lui 2009: 118–120). This parallels the rise of Japan's *keiretsu*, which seized the intermediary opportunities created by linguistic and cultural barriers, long-standing geographic isolation and distance from foreign markets and capital faced by many would-be exporters in the mid-twentieth century (Yamamura 1976). Just as Japan ultimately became a leading industrial economy on account of international integration by its industrial conglomerates, Hong Kong's intermediaries are paving the pathway for the unification of the Chinese economy with the global marketplace.

Hong Kong's position as an intermediary is to be interpreted with caution, however, as its continued profitability is neither fixed nor a guaranteed boon for the local population. Just as manufacturing activities migrated to Mainland China in the 1980s, it is entirely possible that offshore trading activities will no longer need to be 'offshore' in the future. Given that a substantial proportion of offshore trading activity occurs around bulk commodities, this trade may increasingly be 'onshored', as tax, legal and regulatory frameworks are harmonised between key trading partners. Furthermore, much of Hong Kong's emergence as *the* offshore intermediary for a globalising China was due to serendipity and path dependence, as long-established social and economic linkages enabled it to flourish in a post-colonial context. Since the 1980s, the Chinese diaspora has spread ever-farther afield (Ma and Cartier 2003) and Shanghai, Beijing, Taipei and Singapore have all become significant Global Cities (GaWC 2014) in the Sinosphere. Furthermore, given an increasingly reliance on knowledge and information intensive industries, it is inauspicious that Hong Kong's public expenditure on education is a mere 3.5 per cent per annum – well below the average of 6.3 per cent among the countries of the Organization for Economic Co-operation and Development (OECD 2014, World Bank 2014).

Ultimately, it is not so much that 'traditional industry' has disappeared from Hong Kong as the fact that the line between manufacturing and services has increasingly blurred, as trade-related services are still a fundamental part of the production process (Tao and Wong 2002). The recent emergence of service exports as Hong Kong's main economic driver, with offshore trading as a fundamental element, demonstrates that intermediary services serve important purposes within GPNs. With greater economic integration through CEPA, service exports to the Mainland are likely to continue growing, thus maintaining Hong Kong's niche role as an intermediary service provider (Ramón-Berjano *et al.* 2011). In addition to this growth, Hong Kong remains a global supply chain hub housing many small and medium firms engaged in physical trading.

Complex global networks require increasingly specialised services to facilitate production, exchange and even consumption (e.g. marketing), and Hong Kong has emerged not only as China's primary intermediary but as one of the world's greatest offshore 'middlemen'. This has underpinned its ascent as a Global City, with the strong presence of ABS serving to support regional firms, leading to dynamic spatial outcomes over time.

However, as the 2014 'Occupy Central' demonstrations highlight, the nature of a dual system from which the populous feels estranged is tenuous, and the expansion of offshoring threatens to further destabilise the existing socioeconomic order, affecting local job markets, real estate prices and ultimately quality of life. The case of Hong Kong thus serves as an illustrative case concerning both the advantages and the perils of an increasing reliance on offshore services, and while the economic benefits are relatively clear, the social implications may not crystallise until more about service offshoring is understood. As such, studying offshore economies and the physical spaces that mediate transnational flows is increasingly important, and future research should seek to better understand the territorial implications of offshoring from geographic, legal and social perspectives.

Notes

1 It is worth noting that while Hong Kong's re-export role initially mediated the flow of goods from China, data from 2012 indicate that the mainland is actually a net receiver of re-exported goods (Census and Statistics Department 2013).

2 In 2005, there was a sudden resurgence of textiles 'Made in Hong Kong'. This was not the result of a sudden awakening by the local textile industry, but rather by a surge in 'outward processing arrangements' (OPAs) with plants in China to export Chinese textiles so as to circumvent restrictive quotas (The Straits Times 2005) that were vestiges of multi-fibre arrangements (MFAs), which until 2005 imposed limits on textile and garment exports from developing countries. Though this proved ephemeral, such tactics are often used and underlie re-exportation in some cases.

3 Statistics for offshore trade by category and country refer to merchanting. Data for merchandising are unavailable as goods are never taken possession of by Hong Kong companies.

References

Airports Council International, 2014. *ACI World Traffic Statistics*. www.aci-na.org/content/aci-world-traffic-statistics [accessed 17 February 2014].

Au, K., Peng, M.W. and Wang, D., 2000. Interlocking directorates, firm strategies, and performance in Hong Kong: Towards a research agenda. *Asia Pacific Journal of Management*, 17(1), 29–47.

Beerepoot, N. and Hendriks, M., 2013. Employability of offshore service sector workers in the Philippines: opportunities for upward labour mobility or dead-end jobs? *Work, Employment & Society*, 27(5), 823–841.

Callen, J.L., Lai, K. and Wei, S.X., 2009. *Understanding the Variation of Foreign Share Price Discounts: A study of dual-listed Chinese firms*. www-wiwi.uni-muenster.de/me/downloads/Veroeffentlichungen/Paper-Callen-Helsinki-neu2.pdf [accessed 20 February 2014].

Cartier, C., 2001. *Globalizing South China*. Oxford: Blackwell.

Census and Statistics Department, 2012. *Tables E055-E059*. Hong Kong Government. www.censtatd.gov.hk/hkstat/sub/sp454.jsp [accessed 7 February 2014].

Census and Statistics Department, 2013. *Offshore Trade in Goods*. Hong Kong Government. www.censtatd.gov.hk/hkstat/sub/so454.jsp [accessed 11 February 2014].

Census and Statistics Department, 2014. *Hong Kong Monthly Digest of Statistics*, February 2014. www.statistics.gov.hk/pub/B10100022014MM02B0100.pdf [accessed 26 February 2014].

Chiu, S.W. and Lui, T.L., 2009. *Hong Kong: Becoming a Chinese global city*. Abingdon UK: Routledge.

Chiu, S.W. and Lui, T.L., 2004. Testing the global city-social polarisation thesis: Hong Kong since the 1990s. *Urban Studies*, 41(10), 1863–1888.

Chu, Y.W., 2008. Deconstructing the global city: unravelling the linkages that underlie Hong Kong's world city status. *Urban Studies*, 45(8), 1625–1646.

CIA (Central Intelligence Agency), 2014. *CIA World Factbook*. Available from: www.cia.gov [accessed 17 February 2014].

Diamond, D.W., 1984. Financial intermediation and delegated monitoring. *The Review of Economic Studies*, 51(3), 393–414.

Einhorn, B., 2014. The world's freest economy is also its least-affordable housing market. *Bloomberg Businessweek*. www.businessweek.com/articles/2014-01-21/the-worlds-freest-economy-is-also-the-least-affordable-housing-market [accessed 21 January 2014].

Enright, M.J. and Mak, V., 2005. Hong Kong's trading industry: challenges from mainland China. *In:* A.F. Farhoomand, (ed.). *Small business management and entrepreneurship in Hong Kong: A casebook*. Hong Kong: Hong Kong University Press.

Feenstra, R.C. and Hanson, G.H., 2004. Intermediaries in entrepôt trade: Hong Kong re-exports of Chinese goods. *Journal of Economics & Management Strategy*, 13(1), 3–35.

GaWC (Globalization and World Cities Research Network), 2014. *The World According to GaWC 2012*. www.lboro.com/gawc/world2012.html [accessed 27 May 2014].

Gereffi, G., 2006. *The New Offshoring of Jobs and Global Development*. Geneva: International Institute for Labour Studies.

Haberly, D.and Wójcik, D., 2015. Tax havens and the production of offshore FDI: an empirical analysis. *Journal of Economic Geography*, 15(1), 75–101.

He, X., 2007. *An Evaluation of the Intermediation role of Hong Kong in Chinese Foreign Trade*. Working Paper No. 15/2007. Hong Kong: Hong Kong Institute for Monetary Research.

HKTDC (Hong Kong Trade Development Council), 2012. *Import and Export Trade Industry in Hong Kong*. http://hong-kong-economy-research.hktdc.com/business-news/article/Hong-Kong-Industry-Profiles/Import-and-Export-Trade-Industry-in-Hong-Kong/hkip/en/1/1X000000/1X006NJK.htm [accessed 21 May 2014].

Hsieh, C.T. and Woo, K.T., 2005. The impact of outsourcing to China on Hong Kong's labor market. *The American Economic Review*, 95(5), 1673–1687.

Jao, Y.C., 1980. Hong Kong as a regional financial centre: evolution and prospects. *In*: C.K. Leung, J.W. Cushman and G. Wang, (eds). *Hong Kong: Dilemmas of growth*. Canberra: The Australian National University.

Jessop, B. and Sum, N.L., 2000. An entrepreneurial city in action: Hong Kong's emerging strategies in and for (inter) urban competition, *Urban Studies*, 37(12), 2287–2313.

Jones, G. and Khanna, T., 2006. Bringing history (back) into international business. *Journal of International Business Studies*, 37(4), 453–468.

Journal of Commerce, 2012. *The JOC Top 50 World Container Ports, 20–27 August*. www.joc.com/sites/default/files/u48783/pdf/Top50-container-2012.pdf [accessed 18 February 2014].

Lai, K., 2012. Differentiated markets: Shanghai, Beijing and Hong Kong in China's financial centre network. *Urban Studies*, 49(6), 1275–1296.

Leung, F., Chow, K., Szeto, J. and Tam, D., 2008. Service exports: the next engine of growth for Hong Kong? *In*: H. Genberg and D. He, (eds). *Quantifying Macroeconomic Linkages between Hong Kong and Mainland China*. Hong Kong: University of Hong Kong Press.

Lui, H. K., 2013. *Widening Income Distribution in Post-handover Hong Kong*. Abingdon UK and New York: Routledge.

Ma, L.J. and Cartier, C.L. (eds). 2003. *The Chinese Diaspora: Space, place, mobility, and identity*. Lanham, MD and Oxford: Rowman and Littlefield.

National Bureau of Statistics of China, 2012. *Total Imports and Exports*. www.stats.gov.cn/english/statisticaldata/yearlydata/YB2000e/Q03E.htm [accessed 17 February 2014].

OECD (Organization for Economic Co-operation and Development), 2014. *Education at a Glance 2013 – Indicators and annexes*. www.oecd.org/edu/educationataglance2013-indicatorsandannexes.htm#ChapterB [Accessed 23 May 2014].

Pahlman, K. and Webb, K., 2012. *'Hong Kong'. A Report by KPMG*. www.kpmg.com/CN/en/IssuesAndInsights/ArticlesPublications/Publicationseries/Transfer-Pricing-Forum/Documents/TP-Forum-201203-Transfer-Pricing-HK.pdf [accessed 25 March 2013]

Ramón-Berjano, C.B., Zhao, S.X. and Ming, C.Y., 2011. Hong Kong's transformation into a service hub. *Asian Survey*, 51(4), 584–609.

Rauch, J.E. and Casella, A., 2003. Overcoming informational barriers to international resource allocation: Prices and ties. *The Economic Journal*, 113(484), 21–42.

Rauch, J.E. and Trindade, V., 2002. Ethnic Chinese networks in international trade. *Review of Economics and Statistics*, 84(1), 116–130.

Sassen, S., 1991. *The Global City: New York, London, Tokyo*. Princeton, NJ: Princeton University Press.

Schenk, C.R., 2002. Banks and the emergence of Hong Kong as an international financial center. *Journal of International Financial Markets, Institutions and Money*, 12(4), 321–340.

Sigler, T.J., 2013. Relational cities: Doha, Panama City, and Dubai as 21st century entrepôts. *Urban Geography*, 34(5), 612–633.

The Straits Times, 2005. Textile wars spark revival for 'Made in HK', *The Straights Times*, 3 October, p. 17.

Sung, Y.W., 1991. *The China-Hong Kong Connection: The key to China's open door policy*. Cambridge UK, New York, and Oakleigh Australia: Cambridge University Press.

Sung, Y.W., 2005. The evolving role of Hong Kong as China's middleman. *International Conference of the Asia-Pacific Economic Association*. Tokyo, Japan.

Szczepanik, E.F., 1986 [1958]. *The Economic Growth of Hong Kong*. Westport, CT: Greenwood Press.

Tao, Z. and Wong, Y.R., 2002. Hong Kong: from an industrialised city to a centre of manufacturing-related services. *Urban Studies*, 39(12), 2345–2358.

Townsend, R.M., 1978. Intermediation with costly bilateral exchange. *Review of Economic Studies* 45(3), 417–425.

Urry, J., 2013. The super-rich and offshore worlds. *In* T. Birtchnell and J. Caletrío, (eds). *Elite Mobilities*. Abingdon UK and New York: Routledge.

Wong, R.Y.C., 2002. The role of Hong Kong in China's economic development. *Working Paper Series*, 2002–26. Kitakyushu: The International Centre for the Study of East Asian Development.

World Bank, 2014. *Public Spending on education, total (% of GDP)*. http://data.worldbank.org/indicator/SE.XPD.TOTL.GD.ZS/countries [Accessed 23 May 2014].

Yamamura, K., 1976. General trading companies in Japan: their origins and growth. *In* H. Patrick, (ed.). *Japanese Industrialization and Its Social Consequences*. Berkeley: University of California Press.

Zhao, S.X., Chan, Y. and Ramón-Berjano, C.B., 2012. Industrial structural changes in Hong Kong, China under one country, two systems framework. *Chinese Geographical Science I*, 22(3), 302–318.

8 Where footloose jobs and mobile people meet

The peculiar case of the Japanese call centre industry in Bangkok

Bart Lambregts

Introduction

It is becoming increasingly clear in the main how services offshoring transforms the global geography of services production. Most visibly, the trend spurs the growth of new 'offshore' services production centres in places – found across the world but in South and Southeast Asia in particular – that offer the right mix of production factors sought by those seeking to relocate their business processes offshore. Cities such as Bangalore, Mumbai, Manila, Delhi and Chennai have come to be recognized as major recipients of offshored business processes in the services domain and enjoy considerable employment, spending and associated gains in effect (see Beerepoot and Vogelzang, Kleibert, Krishnan, Kunmar and Marasigan in this volume). Less clearly visible, but very real nonetheless, are the job losses suffered in the places from where the business processes are offshored (e.g. Blinder 2009, Breznitz and Zysman 2013, Rubalcaba 2007). It mostly concerns places in high-wage countries, but since geographically disaggregated records of job losses caused by services offshoring are not systematically kept, it is much harder to construct a shortlist of major 'losers' than it is to shortlist the major 'winners'.

Underexposed as well, are the offshoring practices taking place in the shadow of mainstream developments. Much popular and scholarly attention naturally focuses on what is happening in those places emerging as the most profound beneficiaries of the services offshoring trend (see e.g. Dossani and Kenney 2009, Eltschinger 2007, Kleibert 2015). It is not a coincidence that most of these places are located in countries where English is widely spoken. This for instance holds for all but one of Tholons top ten so-called 'established' outsourcing destinations (Tholons 2014), suggesting – rightfully so – that a majority of services offshoring takes place in the English-speaking world. It is only logical, however, that there is a world to discover beyond this particular language domain as well. The same competitive pressures that prompt American, British and Australian firms to engage in services outsourcing and offshoring are also felt by firms operating elsewhere in the world. However, an important difference for such firms is that unless they hail from former colonial powers such as Spain, Portugal or France that managed to 'leave behind' their language after decolonization, their opportunities to offshore any business process requiring the original language to be mastered, are much more limited. In other words, firms from countries that do not enjoy the advantage of there being overseas low-wage destinations where the same language is spoken face a much more challenging services offshoring environment.

A relevant question is how firms from such economies cope with the challenge of not having access to same-language, low-wage 'backyards' for easy offshoring. Can the challenge be overcome and if so in what way(s)? To look beyond the spotlights and to engage with such questions contributes to the development of a more comprehensive understanding of how services offshoring unfolds and may draw attention to the existence of alternative modes of services offshoring and particular niches. Insights so generated, moreover, may help firms and local economies that so far have remained at the periphery of the services offshoring wave but wish to partake, to generate ideas about how to possibly do so.

This chapter aims to expose at least some of what has remained underexposed about services offshoring so far. It examines the service offshoring practices of Japanese firms in Bangkok, with a focus on contact services. Bangkok is currently reputedly the most important offshore destination for Japanese contact services. The city that otherwise has remained relatively untouched by the services offshoring wave (ranked rather modestly at place 85 in Tholons top 100 in 2014), has over the past decade become the seat of a small but flourishing collection of Japanese language contact centres. Here, some 500 mostly young Japanese work to service the Japanese home market while being paid local, 'Thai' wages. This chapter takes a closer look at this unconventional example of services offshoring. It explores the strategies and motives of the Japanese contact centre firms involved, looks into the motives of the Japanese workers filling the cubicles, and reflects upon its possible wider implications.

The chapter proceeds as follows. The next section describes the early experiences of Japanese firms in outsourcing and offshoring contact services. It helps to explain the more recent move to Bangkok made by some of the firms, which is detailed in the section thereafter with attention for motives, strategies and experiences. The chapter then looks into the motives and strategies of the employees manning the work station. The concluding section reflects upon the implications of the practice revealed.

Contact services offshoring by Japanese firms: early experiences

Over the past decades, Japanese manufacturing firms have enthusiastically embraced outsourcing and offshoring as ways to improve business performance. In search of cheaper inputs, market access and (human) resources no longer available at home, Japanese manufacturers of all trades have spun dense production networks across East and Southeast Asia and beyond (see also Iguchi in this volume). In notable contrast, services offshoring by Japanese firms has lagged behind, both compared to manufacturing as well as compared to services offshoring by North American and European firms (Ito *et al.* 2007, Todi 2013, Tomiura *et al.* 2013). This is not to say that Japanese firms do not outsource and/or offshore services activities at all. The world's third economy (IMF 2014) boosts a sizable service sector the members of which are as keen as their peers elsewhere to reduce operational costs, increase productivity, concentrate on core business processes and improve competitiveness. In fact, Japan is considered to be the largest market for services outsourcing and offshoring in the Asia Pacific region with the potential revenues in the contact centre outsourcing sector alone amounting to several billions US dollars per year (William *et al.* 2006).

Initially, Japanese firms tried to reduce the operational costs involved in the production of back-office and customer services by relocating these activities from expensive first-tier cities such as Tokyo and Osaka to cheaper locations elsewhere in Japan (William *et al.* 2006). While this helped to achieve some level of cost reduction, it did not offer an escape from national regulations putting strict limits on the flexible use of labour. Especially services outsourcing firms felt adversely affected, since these laws prevented them from being able to quickly adjust the amount of labour hired to the ever-fluctuating amount of work in hand. When, in addition, labour shortages became more pressing (Zhang and Kawabata 2013), the logical next step for these firms was then to look for greener pastures overseas. These were initially found in China, and within China notably in Dalian. Here, several decades of Japanese rule in the first half of the twentieth century and the subsequent survival of comprehensive Japanese language education (with Japanese being taught from elementary school until university level) had created one of the very few sizable overseas concentrations of non-Japanese Japanese-speaking people. Towards the end of the 1990s, Dalian's local political leaders and entrepreneurs were quick to recognize the opportunities created by Japanese firms' emerging desire to bring the production of IT-enabled services offshore. In a successful process of 'strategic coupling' (MacKinnon 2012, see also Kleibert in this volume) they fine-tuned local assets to the needs of the emergent (Japanese) offshore services scene and as such prompted the rise of Dalian and its wider region as one of East Asia's foremost offshore service production centres (Freeman 2005, Kobayashi 2014, Zhang and Kawabata 2013) and the 'back-office of Japan' (Metters and Verma 2008).

Dalian soon became the base for a variety of firms producing services for the Japanese market. These included subsidiaries and shared service centres of Japanese corporations (captive offshoring), Japanese services outsourcing firms, Chinese services outsourcing firms and Western services outsourcing firms, with many of them primarily targeting the Japanese market (Zhang and Kawabata 2013). In the first stages, activities offshored to Dalian included both voice-based and non-voice services, with a focus on IT-intensive services (e.g. data processing and software engineering). While the language and IT skills mastered by the local labour force sufficed for the various non-voice activities, it soon appeared that they fell short for the voice-based services. The level of Japanese spoken by local workers was in fact satisfactory, but many lacked a deep enough understanding of the Japanese etiquette governing economic and customer transactions. Mastering intonation and different levels of politeness, being able to sense customer's emotions, knowing exactly when and how deeply to apologize: they are all essential to maintaining good customer relations in Japan. When it appeared that this lack of 'cultural proximity' (Metters and Verma 2008) adversely affected customer satisfaction, interest among Japanese firms to move voice-based services offshore started to wane (William *et al.* 2006).

Onshore in Japan, however, high operational costs (even in second-tier cities) and rigid labour legislation – in spite of gradual changes in the direction of flexibilization (Keizer 2010) – continued to weigh down on the services outsourcing sector. With Japanese firms gradually becoming more comfortable with outsourcing customer care and contact centre processes, the market for such services admittedly grew, but so did the number of market players. By 2005 several dozens of services outsourcing firms competed for a share in the domestic, Japanese language contact services outsourcing market (William *et al.* 2006). Stiff competition kept margins low and encouraged outsourcing firms to continue looking for cost-reducing strategies, with the option to go offshore never completely disappearing from the table.

Most players involved by then had developed the insight that successful offshore delivery of customer care and other contact services (e.g. telemarketing) to the domestic market would require either extensive training of non-Japanese staff (to teach them the language and familiarize them with Japanese transactional etiquette) or the overseas employment of 'real' Japanese. Neither of the two was ideal: the former would involve substantial and time-consuming investments and the latter was constrained by the lack of large Japanese population concentrations in low-cost environments overseas.

The move to Bangkok

One of the largest overseas concentrations of Japanese nationals is found in Bangkok. According to the Ministry of Foreign Affairs of Japan (MOFA) only Los Angeles, New York and Shanghai host larger Japanese populations (Newsclip.be 2009). The number of Japanese residing in Bangkok is not exactly known. MOFA (2014) puts the number of Japanese nationals residing in all of Thailand at about 56,000 (for 2012), but according to the 2010 Thai Population and Housing Census, Bangkok alone is home to 63,000 Japanese (National Statistical Office of Thailand no date). However, irrespective of the exact number, Bangkok's Japanese community is likely to be the largest by far in a low-cost business environment (Shanghai is more expensive). The presence of so many Japanese in Bangkok is first and foremost the product of Thailand's popularity since the 1970s, and accelerating in the decades following, as a production site for Japanese manufacturers. Bangkok and its neighbouring provinces are home to hundreds of Japanese manufacturing firms, notably in the automobile and electronic appliances industries, and over time these have attracted a wide spectre of Japanese-run supporting services. These include among others services in the field of logistics, engineering, finance, recruitment and other business services. It reportedly has made the Japanese chamber of commerce in Thailand (over 1,500 corporate members in 2014) one of Japan's biggest chambers of commerce abroad (see www.jcc.or.th/) and also spurred the growth of rich ecology of services supporting expatriate life (e.g. Japanese restaurants, shops, entertainment venues, Japanese language education facilities).

The first Japanese services outsourcing firms to tap into Bangkok's Japanese labour potential started to arrive about a decade ago. One of the country's largest services outsourcing firms, Transcosmos Inc., arrived in 2004. By successfully negotiating with the Thai authorities an exemption from the law prescribing that a firm in Thailand shall employ at least four full-time Thai employees for every non-Thai employee, it paved the way for others to follow. Masterpiece Group, another large player, opened its doors in 2007, and by then was the fifth Japanese operator to deliver Japanese language contact services from Bangkok. According to the founder and managing director of a recruitment agency providing services to the sector, Bangkok is currently home to about ten Japanese call centres, including smaller outsourcing firms such as BPO Bangkok, BBS Thailand, Intec Systems Bangkok and Delivery Thai, and a small number of captive centres operated notably by Japanese insurance companies. Together they operate anything between 400 and 1,000 seats, with numbers fluctuating according to the development of demand (Interview MD recruitment agency 8 February 2012).

During interviews, the managing directors (MDs) of two of the largest Japanese services outsourcing firms in Bangkok confirmed that their company's move to Bangkok had been mainly cost driven. Lower office rents, the opportunity to pay lower wages and Thailand's more permissive labour legislation (as compared to Japan's) in combination enable the firms to save 40 to 50 per cent on operation costs (Interview MD recruitment agency 8 February 2012). Risk management was mentioned as an additional reason to establish overseas operations. Should for instance an earthquake stall operations in Japan, then offices overseas would be able to mitigate the consequences (Interview MD Japanese services outsourcing firm 31 May 2012). The two firms had previously tried delivering contact services from various places in China (Dalian, Chengdu, Beijing), but while the firms were happy to continue their non-voice operations there, voice-based services had mostly been retracted due to quality concerns. Both MDs appeared convinced that voice-based services targeted at the Japanese market can only be satisfactorily produced by Japanese themselves.

None of the MDs interviewed was aware of there being any other offshore location in the region, if not the world, from where voice-based services are delivered to the Japanese home market at any significant scale. In their view and experience, Bangkok basically has it all: competitively priced but yet representative office space, good enough ICT infrastructure, a wide variety of (Japanese) supporting services to choose from (e.g. Japanese recruitment agencies), modern-day urban comfort at affordable costs (making it easier for people to accept low wages), longstanding and warm bilateral relations between the two nations (making it easier to negotiate special deals), flexible labour legislation, a substantial Japanese community to recruit employees from and, finally, an image and reputation that appeals to many (young) Japanese at home. The last of these is of particular importance since, in spite of its respectable size, the local Japanese community does not represent a large enough labour pool to satisfy the recruitment needs of the various contact services centres. To fill all the seats it is necessary to recruit people in Japan as well, with some of the interviewees asserting that actually most of the seats are filled with people freshly recruited from Japan (Interview MD Japanese services outsourcing firm 26 June 2012, Interview MD recruitment agency 8 February 2012). While the interviewees could easily think of other places in the region offering a low-cost environment, a firm-friendly labour regime, adequate infrastructure and acceptable supporting services, they all agreed that none of these could compete with Bangkok for the city's appeal to Japan's younger generations and thus for ease of recruitment and thus for the firms' ability to keep wages relatively low (i.e. adjusted to local price levels).

The relations between the Japanese contact services centres and their Bangkok/Thai environment are thin. The contact centres are basically Japanese owned and managed operations, employing Japanese labour (with the help of Japanese recruitment services), servicing the Japanese domestic contact services market. Compared to countries such as Malaysia, India and the Philippines, Thailand's efforts to promote the development of an offshore services industry are limited at best. The Japanese firms moving into Bangkok received little support other than the admittedly crucial exemption from the 'you shall hire four Thai for every single foreigner' rule. A trickle of information exchange is said to take place between some of the Japanese and some Thai services outsourcing firms (Interview MD Japanese services outsourcing firm 31 May 2012, Interview MD Thai services outsourcing firm 21 June 2012), and of course certain auxiliary services (such as IT maintenance and housekeeping) are bought from Thai suppliers. At least one company was pondering the idea of engaging with Thai educational institutes to explore if Thai students can be taught Japanese language and conversation skills at a level answering to the firms' specific needs (Interview MD Japanese services outsourcing firm 26 June 2012). If this were to work out, in due time it could reduce the firms' dependency on Japanese workers and their possibly changing preferences.

Mobile labour

The employees of Japanese call centres in Bangkok are typically employed on one- or two-year contracts and earn wages in the range of US$900–1,300 per month (Interview MD recruitment agency 8 February 2012). That is less than half of what a similar job would pay in Japan (*New York Times* 2010) and a salary that puts one at the lower end of 'middle income' in Bangkok. Who are those 400 to 1,000 Japanese operating the telephones and managing the email accounts? And what motivates them to trade life in Japan for what would seem a much more uncertain and less well-paid existence in Bangkok?

As noted, most of the people concerned are reportedly freshly recruited from various parts of Japan and thus relative newcomers to Bangkok. The firms seek to employ people with high-school education at least and a service-oriented attitude. The younger of age and women are preferred, but the more mature are not excluded and in practice many cubicles are eventually occupied by men (Interview MD recruitment agency 8 February 2012, Interview former MD Japanese services outsourcing firm 26 May 2012).

The call centres in Bangkok naturally attract Japanese who are interested in living and working abroad and in Thailand in particular. According to the recruitment MD, pull factors seem to be more important than push factors, with an important pull factor being the promise of finding a more relaxed living and working environment in Thailand. In his view, two groups of candidates can be distinguished. First there are those with ambitions to start a career in Thailand. They see the call centre job as a way to get a foot on the ground in the country (the job comes with a non-immigrant visa, a work permit and enough money to survive), to acquire knowledge about job opportunities and hiring practices in the local labour market, and to build up credentials. The last of these is not so much to do with possible skills gained in the contact centres but much more with demonstrating that one has 'managed' the transition from living and possibly working in Japan to living and working in Thailand. Many Japanese firms beyond the contact services sector are reluctant to hire Japanese newcomers to Thailand, especially if the job carries managerial responsibilities. Such firms want to be as sure as possible that the person they hire is capable of managing the transition and to a reasonable degree is 'streetwise' in Bangkok and its environs. Someone who has worked in Bangkok for a year or two, even if only in a call centre, has proven that he or she is up to the challenge and not likely to quit because of transition issues (Interview MD recruitment agency 8 February 2012).

Next to those using call centre work in Bangkok as a stepping stone to a more serious career in Thailand, there are others who are primarily interested in living an uncomplicated life in Bangkok. For them the job is just the job, and the job is fine as long as it provides enough income to live in reasonable comfort and as long as it does not become too demanding or starts to affect life after office hours as well (Interview MD recruitment agency 8 February 2012). This category resembles the Japanese 'lifestyle migrants' previously identified by Sato (2001) and Ono (2005, 2009) among others. According to these authors, a combination of bleak labour market prospects at home, stress-producing social and corporate conventions, and growing wanderlust among young Japanese in particular, have since the 1990s fuelled the growth of a class of young people who are very keen to move abroad – not primarily to pursue a career but rather to seek pleasure and improve their quality of life. To quantify their numbers is a challenge, but based on yearly outmigration numbers and the fact that the share taken by traditional expatriate packages is decreasing (*New York Times* 2010) there may be thousands, perhaps tens of thousands leaving the country with these intentions each year and perhaps more willing to do so. The bleak labour market factor is of interest in particular, as it connects to certain issues discussed above. The services outsourcing firms referred to the admittedly relaxing but in their view still stringent limits applying to the use of non-regular, flexible labour as one of the reasons to move activities offshore. On the other side of the spectre, however, the reality faced by young Japanese entering the labour market is a completely different one. The drive towards labour flexibilization hardly affects the virtually untouchable older generations still hired on lifetime employment conditions. As a result, it is the newcomers to the labour market that bear the brunt. Whereas in better days lifetime employment with the first company joined was a near certainty for most college and university graduates, these days competition is fierce and temporary contracts more often than not the only prize to win (Bloomberg 2010). It means that for many young Japanese, access to job security is probably as limited at home as it is abroad, which obviously makes it easier for other considerations such as the pursuit of a more laid-back lifestyle to gain the upper hand and become decisive in migration decisions.

According to Ono (2005, 2009), Thailand appeals particularly strong to these people because of its (imagined) laid-back atmosphere, the relatively cheap cost of living and its exotic appeal. Many of those having made the move became first acquainted with the country through holiday travels or visiting previously migrated friends. Obviously, the presence of such a large Japanese community in Bangkok boasting all possible services a newcomer might need makes it relatively easy to arrive there (cf. Saunders 2010).

Concluding remarks

Early 2011 the telecom provider Orange decided to outsource and relocate 40 call centre jobs from Darlington (county Durham) in the UK to an IBM-managed facility in Manila, Philippines. It reportedly made the affected staff the following offer: their job could remain theirs if they would agree to relocate with it – not as pampered expatriate employees but hired on local terms, entitled to a monthly salary of about US$300 and an allowance covering for the cost of laundry and rice. Outrage best describes the response, prompting Orange to quickly issue apologies and a denial (*Independent* 2011). One might wonder if the response possibly would have been less unforgiving if the offer had been to move with the job to Thailand, which also in the UK enjoys quite a solid reputation as a pleasant place to spend at least some period of time.

This chapter has shown that for the Japanese, the concept of moving both work and people to a lower-cost but yet agreeable overseas location like Bangkok seems to work well. It answers to firms' desire to produce tradable services at lower costs while keeping the quality of the services delivered at the highest possible level. Simultaneously it offers workers who wish to broaden their geographic horizon – be that because of pull or push factors or a combination of both – to capitalize upon their (unique) language skills and cultural baggage, either as a way to finance a temporary stay abroad or as a first step towards a more serious career away from home.

The benefits of the model for the receiving economy at first glance look rather limited. The small but apparently thriving Japanese call centre industry in Bangkok hitherto has operated largely in almost splendid isolation from the Thai economy that surrounds it. In that sense the model has much in common with that of the traditional export processing zone, with the notable difference that the latter at least offers direct (albeit often poorly defined) employment opportunities for the local labour force. The benefits for the Thai economy so far have remained largely limited to the spending effects of the employees, and to the rents, service fees and taxes paid by the firms. Yet, the industry is still young and there seems to be potential for additional, more important spillover effects to develop. The very recent two-pronged expansion of the activities of Transcosmos in Bangkok offers a glimpse of what may be possible. First, the opening in March 2015 of a 200-seat Thai-language contact centre providing services for the Thai domestic market may well impact the Thai contact services outsourcing sector, which so far has remained a comparatively modest affair. Much will depend on the extent to which the new centre, which enjoys access to Transcosmos' 45 years of global experience in delivering outsourced services, manages to set a new standard in the Thai services outsourcing world. If it does, it will likely force Thai players to raise their game and as such trigger change in the sector at large. Second, Transcosmos' late 2014 decision to make Bangkok the seat of its headquarter office for the Association of Southeast Asian Nations (ASEAN) region represents a significant move up the value chain. It means that in addition to straightforward services production, accumulation of regional command and control functions will take place. These functions will require higher-level human resource inputs and locate decision-making powers in Bangkok. While it remains to be seen to what extent non-Japanese will have access to these managerial jobs, the prestige thus generated for the city is a nice bonus.

Finally, the same factors inciting young Japanese to venture abroad for work may gain relevance for European and American youngsters as well. The global financial crisis and its aftermath have pushed unemployment and notably youth unemployment in the US and many European countries to very high levels. Currently, more than five years after the height of the crisis, job growth in many countries is picking up only slowly, with much of that growth in short-term and insecure (or 'flexible') work. Meanwhile, speculation, notably in Europe, about the continent entering a 'Japanese scenario' entailing a prolonged period of subdued economic growth is rife and some countries have already gone as far as to advise their younger citizens to not wait for the good old times to return but instead to seek employment abroad (*Financial Times* 2012). If this is to become a real trend, offshoring contact services 'Japanese style' may become a viable model for more countries with a language 'handicap'. In Thailand, the first genuine – i.e. not a so-called 'boiler room' – multi-language contact centre employing European nationals to service the German, Italian, Spanish and French domestics markets has already opened its doors. Time will tell if it remains an isolated case or the trailblazer for a new industry. Beyond dispute, however, is that the traditional core–periphery distribution of economic opportunity and work is gradually changing, with the landscape assuming increasingly polycentric features (Scott 2012). Developing countries that are perceived to offer a good-enough quality of life and that are both willing to and capable of sustainably embedding new modes of work into their economies will be well positioned to reap the benefits of this change.

References

Blinder, A.S., 2009. How Many U.S. Jobs Might Be Offshorable? *World Economics*, 10 (2), 41–78.

Bloomberg, 2010. Japan 'Ice Age' Returns as Student Joblessness Soars to Record. 12 March. www.bloomberg.com/apps/news?pid=newsarchive&sid=aSj9Cvt0AZHg

Breznitz, D. and Zysman, J., 2013. *The Third Globalization. Can Wealthy Countries Stay Rich in the Twenty-First Century?* Oxford and New York: Oxford University Press.

Dossani, R. and Kenney, M., 2009. Service Provision for the Global Economy: The Evolving India Story. *Review of Policy Research*, 26 (1–2), 77–104.

Eltschinger, C., 2007. *Source Code China: The New Global Hub of IT Information Technology Outsourcing*. Hoboken, NJ: Wiley.

Financial Times, 2012. Spanish Youth Urged to Seek Work Abroad. 2 May. www.ft.com/intl/cms/s/0/f2018cf0-9467-11e1-8e90-00144feab49a.html?siteedition=uk

Freeman, Thomas L., 2005. *The World Is Flat: A brief history of the twenty-first century.* New York: Picador.

IMF (International Monetary Fund), 2014. *World Economic Outlook: Legacies, Clouds, Uncertainties*. Washington, DC (October): IMF.

IMO (International Organization for Migration), 2013. *World Migration Report 2013 – Migrant Well-being and Development*. Geneva: IOM.

Independent, 2011. Orange Denies Manila Move. 19 April. www.independent.co.uk/news/uk/home-news/orange-denies-manila-move-2269632.html

Ito, B., Tomiura, E. and Wakasugi, R., 2007. *Dissecting Offshore Outsourcing and R&D: A Survey of Japanese Manufacturing Firms*. RIETI Discussion Paper 07-E-060. www.rieti.go.jp/jp/publications/dp/07e060.pdf.

Keizer, Arjan B., 2010. *Changes in Japanese Employment Practices: Beyond the Japanese model*. London and New York: Routledge.

Kleibert, J.M., 2015. Expanding Global Production Networks: The emergence, evolution and the developmental impact of the offshore service sector in the Philippines. Amsterdam: Dissertation Universiteit van Amsterdam.

Kobayashi, M., 2014. Industrial Cluster Formation and Development: Software Development Outsourcing Industry in Dalian. *Annals of Business Administrative Science*, 13, 183–197.

MacKinnon, D., 2012. Beyond Strategic Coupling: Reassessing the firm-region nexus in global production networks. *Journal of Economic Geography*, 12 (1), 227–245.

Metters, R. and Verma, R., 2008. The History of Offshoring Knowledge Services. *Journal of Operations Management*, 26, 141–147.

MOFA (Ministry of Foreign Affairs), 2014. Japan-Thailand Relations (Basic Data). www.mofa.go.jp/region/asia-paci/thailand/data.html

National Statistical Office of Thailand, no date. 2010 Population and Housing Census. http://web.nso.go.th/en/census/poph/cen_poph_10.htm.

Newsclip.be, 2009. シンガポール・マレーシアの在留邦人急減　外務省調査 [Singapore and Malaysia show sharp decrease in number of Japanese residents according to a Ministry of Foreign Affairs investigation]. 7 September. www.newsclip.be/article/2009/09/07/9596.html.

New York Times, 2010. Many in Japan Are Outsourcing Themselves. July 21. www.nytimes.com/2010/07/22/business/global/22outsource.html?pagewanted=all&_r=0.

Ono, Mayumi, 2005. *Young Japanese Settlers in Thailand: The pursuit of comfort and alternative lifestyle.* Working Paper 4, The Institute of Contemporary Japanese Studies, Waseda University.

Ono, Mayumi, 2009. Japanese Lifestyle Migration/Tourism in Southeast Asia. *Japanese Review of Cultural Anthropology*, 10, 43–52.

Rubalcaba, L., 2007. *The New Service Economy: Challenges and Policy Implications for Europe*. Cheltenham: Edward Elgar.

Sato, Machika, 2001. *Farewell to Nippon: Japanese Lifestyle Migrants in Australia*. Melbourne: Trans Pacific Press.

Saunders, D., 2010. *Arrival City: How the Largest Migration in History Is Reshaping Our World*. London: Heinemann.

Scott, A.J., (2012) *A World in Emergence, Cities and Regions in the 21st Century*. Cheltenham (UK)/Northampton (MA/USA): Edward Elgar.

Tholons, 2014. *2014 Tholons Top 100 Outsourcing Destinations: Regional Overview*. www.tholons.com/TholonsTop100/pdf/Tholons_Top_100_2014_Rankings_and_Report_Overview.pdf

Todi, Y., 2013. Offshoring by Japanese Small and Medium Enterprises. *In*: A. Bardhan, D.M. Jaffee and C.A. Kroll, (eds). *The Oxford Handbook of Offshoring and Global Employment*. Oxford University Press, 252–275.

Tomiura, E., Ito, B. and Wakasugi, R., 2013. Offshoring and Japanese Firms. *In*: A. Bardhan, D.M. Jaffee and C.A. Kroll, (eds). *The Oxford Handbook of Offshoring and Global Employment*. Oxford University Press, 229–251.

William, A. Shukla, S. and Nizam, M., 2006. *Asia Pacific Market Insights: The Rising Sun: Understanding Japan, the Largest Contact Center Outsourcing Market in the Asia Pacific Region*. Frost & Sullivan Market Insight. www.frost.com/sublib/display-market-insight.do?id=85891967.

Zhang, Yan and Kawabata, Nozomu, 2013. *The Formation of the Software and Information Services Industry in Dalian, China*. Discussion Paper No.2. Center for Data Science and Service Research, Tohoku University. www.econ.tohoku.ac.jp/econ/datascience/DDSR-DP/no2.pdf

Part III

Labour and industrial organization in the latest wave of globalization

Challenges, opportunities and transformations

9 Exclusion in Asia's evolving global production and service outsourcing

Rene E. Ofreneo

Introduction

There are two significant global developments in the world today – the slow-moving economic recovery of Europe and North America, and the continuing surge of Asia's share in the global economy. These twin developments have given rise to the question that is increasingly posed by international development agencies – *is the twenty-first century Asia's century?* The Asian Development Bank (ADB) unequivocally has declared that it is, asserting the following:

> Asia is in the middle of a historic transformation. If it continues to follow its recent trajectory, by 2050 its per capita income could rise sixfold in purchasing power parity terms to reach Europe's levels today. It would make some 3 billion additional Asians affluent by current standards. By nearly doubling its share of global gross domestic product (GDP) to 52 percent by 2050, Asia would regain the dominant economic position it held some 300 years ago, before the industrial revolution.
>
> (ADB 2011: 3)

Per the ADB treatise, Asia is now regarded to be the world's growth engine, since the economies of North America and Europe are declining in relative terms. This shift in the global economic power equation is accentuated by the rise of China as the world's biggest economy, and the weak recovery of Europe from the global financial and economic crisis.

However, it is difficult to find any trade union or civil society organization in the Asia-Pacific that is exultant over the ADB proclamation or is ecstatic over the prognosis that the twenty-first century is Asia's century. To them, the more important concern is addressing the endemic poverty and inequality that have remained widespread across the Asian continent despite or because of the processes of economic globalization. There are huge social and economic deficits and imbalances virtually everywhere – at the national, regional and global levels (see World Bank 2012, Dreze and Sen 2013).

This chapter uses the metaphors 'Factory Asia' and 'Service Asia' to provide a critical analysis of Asia's integration in globalized systems of production in industrial goods and offshore services and examines how both have led to increasing differentiation within labour markets. The chapter particularly focuses on trade union critiques that these developments have eroded labour rights and weakened the labour movement. The chapter analyses the struggle of trade unions against rising precarity or casualization of work. The chapter concludes that fostering inclusive and sustainable growth in Asia requires a major rethinking of Asia's integration in global production networks.

The chapter draws heavily from the materials published by the International Trade Union Council (ITUC), Asia-Pacific Regional Organization of Union Network International (UNI-Apro) and the Asia Monitor Resource Center (AMRC), a labour resource centre based in Hong Kong. References to union perspectives in this chapter are derived from these sources and longstanding interactions and discussions with their representatives.

Asia's integration in global value chains: a brief historical overview

Under globalization goods and services can be traded globally much easier (see Baldwin 2013, Pratap 2014). For trade unions in developing Asia, the internationalization of production was seen as part of a 'new international division of labour' or NIDL. The German researchers Frobel *et al.* (1980) wrote that the decline of employment in the garments, textile and leather industries of Europe in the 1970s was due to the migration of labour intensive factories to the developing world where labour cost were lower. This migration was accompanied by the increased specialization of the developed world in more skills-, technology- and capital-intensive industries. The NIDL gave rise to the development of labour-intensive, low-technology, industries such as garments, toys, electronics assembly that were located in export-processing zones (EPZs) where unions were strictly regulated or even forbidden. The MNCs were the main drivers of this NIDL, either as investors in developing countries or as contractors-partners of manufacturers based in the latter, in the relocation of labour intensive industries from the developed world and in the final marketing and distribution of products processed in the developing world.

Baldwin (2013) and Kimura (2013) argue that global production networks (GPNs) have developed in a geographical or regional way because MNCs organize global production based on locational advantages such as presence of market, transport, power and 'agglomeration' or concentration of small producers linked to major producers. For example, Thailand emerged as a hub for car production given the formation of a community of inter-linked car-parts makers. In short, labour cost is a major but not the only determinant of an MNC's decision to invest or outsource production in certain countries. This has given rise to Japan's (and South Korea's and Taiwan's) 'Factory Asia', made up of firms producing auto and electronics parts and components in different countries of East and Southeast Asia based on their specialization and strategic advantage (see Edgington and Hayter 2013, Felker 2003).

At any rate, Asia – under the industrial dynamics fuelled by MNCs' decisions to invest or contract out manufacturing – has become the world's workshop, producing varied industrial goods for the global market. But given the dynamics of capitalist development, some destination countries for global industrial outsourcing have themselves developed the capacity to participate in the industrial relocation business such as what is happening today in the case of China, which is similar to what happened to the Asian newly industrialized countries (NICs) after these countries had achieved a high level of industrial sophistication.

The tradability revolution and the rise of 'Service Asia'

Services were once thought to be non-tradable for they are usually bought and sold *in situ* (see Kloosterman, Beerepoot and Lambregts in this volume). Thus, when the General Agreement on Services (GATS) was included among the trade agreements to be enforced by the World Trade Organization (WTO) beginning 1995, there were lots of debates and criticisms. The trade unions and civil society organizations (Ng and Ofreneo 2000) claim that GATS is an instrument for the global 'commodification' of services and paves the way for MNCs to dominate the service sector of developing countries. This is so because the primary mode of service trading recognized by GATS is the recognition of the right of foreign service providers such as banks and insurance companies to set up shop (Mode 3) in the economy of a participating WTO member state.

As a result the global trade in services has grown rapidly in the last two decades. In 2013, Pascal Lamy, the WTO's director general, proudly proclaimed that half of global trade is now in trade in services or what the WTO calls as a general 'trade in tasks'. The shift towards services is amply documented by UNCTAD in its 2004 *World Investment Report.* The report validates the earlier observation by trade unions that the main drivers of the international trade in services are indeed the MNCs themselves. However, the most dramatic development in the global trade in services is the phenomenal rise of outsourcing and offshoring of service activities that used to be done in the home countries of MNCs (see UNCTAD 2004, World Bank 2007). Due to advances in ICT and telecommunications such as the development of cyber-speed internet communications and voice-over internet protocols or VOIP, American and European multinationals requiring back-office support such as customer services, billing and purchasing, financial reconciliations, airline ticketing and reservations, editing and publishing and so on have discovered that it is much cheaper to outsource or 'offshore' these activities to business process outsourcing (BPO) facilities located in India, Philippines, Malaysia and other low-cost sites of the world (see also Kleibert in this volume).

The services being outsourced and delivered online have become increasingly diverse and sophisticated. *Plunkett's Outsourcing & Offshoring Industry Almanac 2011* reported the increased outsourcing of more knowledge-based activities requiring judgement and analysis such as research and development (R&D), legal research, patent research, architecture, design, engineering, website development, market research, tax preparations and so on. These activities are collectively placed under the category 'knowledge process outsourcing' (KPO). UNCTAD (2004) describes the rise of ICT-enabled offshoring, marketing and delivery of 'corporate service functions' such as those undertaken by the ITES-BPO firms in developing countries as the 'tradability revolution'. ICT advances have solved the problem of information storage through digitization as well as the problem of transporting and exchanging data needed by the offshoring/outsourcing companies. The pioneers in the ITES-BPO outsourcing are the MNCs such as General Electric and the big companies listed in Fortune 500. However, smaller firms have now joined the business of service offshoring (see Beerepoot and Lambregts 2015), which has truly gone global. The offshoring business has also spawned the rise of multinational contract service providers such as Convergys, ICT Group, Sitel and Sykes. Like MNCs setting up production facilities in different countries, these MNC contract service providers also set up ICT facilities in as many countries as needed to serve clients in different time zones.

In Asia, the favourite offshoring destinations are India and the Philippines because of the availability of a huge pool of English-speaking and ICT-literate workers (see Krishnan, Kleibert, Raquiza in this volume). India has focused on higher value-adding ICT services such as customized IT programming and problem-solving research consulting. The Philippines has become the world's leading site for online customer or call centre business operations, although there is a rising trend in the non-voice BPO services. However, the global ITES-BPO industry is also rapidly spreading in other Asian countries, including the non-English speaking countries such as China.

Characteristics of an evolving labour market in the ITES-BPO sector

The processes of economic globalization during the last three decades have led to radical changes in the economy of many Asian countries. Most have become outward looking and active participants in the global production networks of MNCs as well as in the global trading of services. The globalization processes are also changing the skylines of many Asian cities, from the smoke-filled factory cities producing varied products for the global market (for examples, Guangdong in China, Phnom Penh in Cambodia, Medan in Indonesia and Dhaka in Bangladesh) to the 'offshore service cities' of Bangalore-Chennai-Hyderabad of India and Cebu-Quezon City of the Philippines, which are wired to North America, Europe and Australia.

The problem is that despite current economic growth and the projection that Asia will be the world's growth engine, unemployment rates remain high in Asia and not all who have jobs enjoy stable income and decent work standards. The Asia-Pacific Organisation of the International Trade Union Confederation (ITUC-AP 2007: 1), in its 2007 Founding Conference, lamented that:

> Globalisation has failed to deliver the promised decent living standards and has not benefited working people as a whole in the Asian and Pacific region. Economic injustice arising from globalization is distinctly visible in the region. The gap between the haves and have-nots is ever widening. The race to the

bottom still continues. Economic and social deficits in globalization often lead to deficit in democracy and further tension and hostilities as we see in many parts of the region.

In short, many workers in Asia have not benefited from globalization and its growth upsides in the region. Asian workers who produce parts of the twenty-first century technology gadgets such as the iPhone, iPad, computers and their operating chips will in most cases never be able to own any of them. They are excluded from the consumer market for these products by their low wages and benefits.

Who are the excluded?

The workers who are excluded from current economic growth in Asia can be clustered under two major categories. First, the *vulnerables*. As defined by the ILO *Employment Indicators* (ILO 2009), 'vulnerable employment' is the total of 'own-account' or self-employed workers who operate farms or micro family businesses/activities in the informal economy, and the 'contributing family members' (counted in some countries as 'unpaid family workers') who cannot find better quality jobs outside home or family. The total of the two is considered by the ILO as the size of the informal economy. In 2010, the share of the vulnerables in the total employment is 50 per cent for East Asia and 78 per cent for South Asia, with Southeast Asia registering 62 per cent (see Table 9.1). This illustrates that global integration is unable to create (decent) jobs for all as Factory Asia does not hire everybody.

The Asia Monitor Resource Center (AMRC) devoted the 2008 issue of the *Asian Labour Law Review* (see Lee *et al.* 2008) to the situation of informal sector workers in the different Asian countries. The conclusion that emerged from the publication is that informality is part of the coping mechanism of workers who cannot get jobs, good or bad, in the narrow formal sector of developing Asia. In short, informal work, generally unprotected or not covered by the formal labour law system, is rooted in the joblessness or near joblessness in many Asian countries that forces many workers to accept substandard employment.

Deeper global integration does not automatically lead to inclusive and sustainable job creation. The UNDP Human Development Report for Asia-Pacific (2006) emphasized that growth has been jobless for some Asian countries, as reflected in East Asia's job record: 337 million jobs created in the 1980s and only 176 million

Table 9.1 Vulnerable employment in Asia, 2010

	Vulnerable employment (total in millions)	*Vulnerable employment as a percentage*
East Asia	407.4	49.6
Southeast Asia and the Pacific	181.4	62.3
South Asia	480.5	78.4

Source: ILO (2012).

jobs in the 1990s. The ILO report for Asia-Pacific in 2011 also highlights the remarkable divergence between high gross domestic product growth and low employment growth (see Table 9.2) illustrating that recent economic growth comes without new jobs. China has the highest GDP growth and yet it also has the lowest employment growth, with the exception of slumping Japan.

The second major group or category of excluded workers are the *precarious paid workers* who are hired in the formal or organized sector of the economy (see Standing 2010). They are excluded in the sense that their job tenures are generally precarious and they get only a pittance for the work or service that they render. Arne Kalleberg and Kevin Hewison (2013: 271) define 'precarious work' as work characterized by 'uncertainty, instability, and insecurity of work in which employees bear the risks of work (as opposed to businesses or the government) and receive limited social benefits and statutory entitlements'. They argue that precarious work, which is a reality in the large informal economy, is widespread in the formal sector with the globalization of production. Simply put, 'precarity' means the 'informalization' or 'casualization' of work in the formal sector through short-term or flexible hiring arrangements and limited compensation or benefits to the workers.

The growing informalization of work in Asia is what Pratap (2014) documented in his book *Emerging Trends in Factory Asia*, a comprehensive summation of various studies of the AMRC on the labour situation in GPNs of MNCs such as Samsung and Toyota and in globalized industries such as garments and electronics. He writes that GPNs generally 'lock in' workers in low-wage and insecure jobs. This is because the MNCs' primary motivation for the relocation of labour-intensive industries and processes is to take advantage of lower-cost labour in labour-surplus economies. With the ability of modern corporations to atomize production into simpler tasks and distribute production tasks in a fragmented

Table 9.2 Average annual growth in GDP and employment, selected Asian-Pacific countries, 2001–2008 (per cent)

Country	*GDP growth*	*Employment growth*
China	10.5	0.9
India	7.0	2.4
Indonesia	5.4	1.7
Japan	1.4	-0.1
Korea, Republic of	4.4	1.4
Malaysia	5.7	1.8
Mongolia	8.2	3.2
Pakistan	5.3	3.7
Philippines	5.3	2.8
Sri Lanka	6.0	1.7
Thailand	5.2	1.7
Viet Nam	7.6	2.0

Source: ILO (2011).

manner, such as what is happening in GPNs, work can be done by workers with low levels of skills and education. With widespread poverty and with families unable to support children to finish college education, factories have no problem recruiting workers for such jobs. In China, the recruits, composed mainly by rural migrants who are escaping poverty and limited job opportunities in the countryside, end up as poorly paid factory casuals or construction workers in the cities.

The Asia-Pacific Organization (AP) of the International Trade Union Council (ITUC), formerly known as the International Confederation of Free Trade Unions (ICFTU), reaffirms the above AMRC findings. The ICFTU/ITUC has been denouncing in varied conferences and meetings the informalization phenomenon and its deleterious impact on unionism and labour protection. The ITUC-AP, together with the global union federations (GUFs), has reported that all its affiliates in the Asia-Pacific are affected by the increasing informalization of work almost everywhere. As far back as 1996, at its regional conference in the Philippines, the ICFTU-AP expressed anger at this process, which it dubbed 'de-formalization' of the labour market. It (ICFTU-AP 1996: 9) explained the de-formalization process as follows:

> Employers are increasingly resorting to contracting out work to workers who work on contract basis with the employer or with contractors engaged by the employers to do the work concerned. In other cases certain work is farmed out to workers who then either work at the employers' premises or at some other locations such as their homes. These workers are the most exploited and employers shirk off their legal obligations and responsibilities as employers once they resort to such work arrangements.
>
> Apart from the above, part-time work, flexi-work and temporary work are also on the increase. The advance of technology is also increasing the number of teleworkers who usually work at home most of the time. These workers are also usually not provided with the legal protection due to workers such as social security including occupational health and safety protection, as well as basic workers' rights of representation through unions.

In 2007, or 11 years later, the ITUC-AP, which replaced the ICFTU-AP, bewailed the fact that this de-formalization process had become widespread. The ITUC-AP declared that the 'globalization of capital has led to increased flexibility in the labour market converting 'formal employment' into 'informal employment' or 'atypical work' (ITUC-AP 2007). The ITUC-AP (2007: 4) described atypical work as 'characterized by its contingency, transitoriness, different working conditions compared to regular workers in the same job, and precariousness of employment such as part-time job, dispatched workers, temporary or contractual workers, and workers in special employment arrangements under subcontracts or commission'. The ITUC-AP document noted that all these phenomena in the formal labour market were increasing sharply.

Are ITES-BPO service workers exempt from precarity?

A key issue is whether IT/ICT workers working in the emerging ITES-BPO sector are exempt from processes of the informalization of work. They are paid much higher than the ordinary workers in factories or in service industries such as retailing and are regarded to form a new middle class as argued by various authors in this edited volume (see Krishnan; Hatekar and More; Beerepoot and Vogelzang in this volume).

A first critical remark is that despite rapid employment growth, the ITES-BPO workforce in Asia still constitutes only a minority of the overall workforce. For example, India's ITES-BPO workforce is estimated to be 4 million (Central Statistics Office 2010) and as such only a fraction of India's labour force of over 400 million people. In the Philippines, the BPO workforce is now estimated to have reached 1 million, 17 years after the first call centre was established in 1997. In contrast, the total Philippine workforce is about 41 million. In both cases the employment is largely based in the main cities of both countries, which could lead to an increasing urban–rural divergence of economic development as investment is heavily concentrated in already more-developed regions of the country (see also Kleibert 2015).

As to the quality of jobs, some differentiation ought to be made. IT programmers who have regular tenures are most well off among the ITES-BPO workers but they are only a small number compared to the number of BPO workers, who are hired on a project-to-project basis depending on the business contracts bagged by the Indian, Philippine and other Asian service-providing vendors. For example, customer service provided by a vendor for a client such as General Electric may be good only for one year which makes it very rare that BPO firms offer workers regular employment contracts.

There are also studies on how the stressful working conditions in the BPO sector, especially in the call centres, have contributed to the huge number of drop-outs despite the higher compensation BPO workers are getting compared to minimum wage earners (see Taylor and Bain 2005, Thite and Russel 2010, Marasigan in this volume). The stressful working conditions are well-known – work done mainly at nighttime or flexibly based on the 24/7 schedule of services provided by the vendors, dedicated nature of work (meaning workers cannot just leave their respective cubicles), intensive camera monitoring of the workers, periodic review of workers' performance online, limited breaks, limited time to answer or service a client (for example, maximum four minutes per client), abusive clients, very cold temperature inside the workplace and very hot outside the buildings, and so on and so forth (see, for example Fabros 2009, Cruz and Valisno 2014).

Deepening inequality amid rapid growth

Rapid growth without creating jobs for large parts of the labour force can deepen inequality (see Krishna and Nederveen Pieterse 2008, Standing 2010, Dreze and Sen 2013). Rapid growth without any social and labour rules or regulations can also deepen inequality, a reality taking place across the region even before the term 'globalization' became part of the economic vocabulary in the 1990s. Due to historical, economic, political and even geographic reasons, there was already a great deal of unevenness in the overall development of Asia and the Pacific in the decades before.

Deepening of inequality can generate mass resentment and can destabilize societies. This is why the ADB has been raising alarm bells on the serious social and economic implications of the scissor movement of growth and inequality. The ADB also chose the theme 'Confronting Rising Inequality in Asia' for its 2012 *Asian Development Outlook* publication. The ADB mentioned that the percentage of the population living at US$1.25 a day was reduced by more than a half between 1990 and 2010. Then it raised the red flag: the 'performance in growth and poverty reduction has, however, been accompanied by rising inequality within many countries' (ADB 2012: 38). Specifically, it found out that 11 out of 28 Asian countries with comparable data experienced a deepening in inequality, as measured by the standard Gini coefficient. Table 9.3 shows that the 11 countries with rising inequality belong to the three subregions of East Asia, Southeast Asia and South Asia. Moreover, the giant globalizers, China and India, have both registered rapid growth and deeper inequality. China is aptly described by Hansjörg Herr (2011: 16) as a country transformed from one 'with a relatively equal income distribution to a country with a very unequal one', with China's Gini coefficient of 30.0 in the mid-1980s swinging upward to 41.5 by 2007. This leads to the observation that an increasing differentiation is emerging between people with access to the new economic opportunities and those who are confronted with various forms of exclusion.

The ILO (2011) also noted that the Asian region, apart from having the largest concentration of the world's working poor, is also vulnerable to global shocks. For example, 87 million of the region's workforce was estimated by the ILO to be out of work in 2007, before the onset of the global financial crisis. In 2010, the number of the unemployed had risen to 92 million. Rising inequality can be seen in the consumption or expenditure patterns among income classes, particularly between the top 20 per cent and the bottom 20 per cent. A World Bank East Asia report (2011) noted that in the Philippines the top 20 per cent outspends the bottom 20 per cent by about nine times, in Cambodia by about eight times and in Thailand by seven times.

Declining wage income share

A significant contribution of the ILO to the inequality discourse is its analysis of declining share of wages in GDP or in the national income. The ILO (2011: 49) writes that 'Wage growth is lagging behind labour productivity growth, and the share of wages in national GDP is declining throughout the region'. The decline is most dramatic in China, with the All-China Federation of Trade Unions (ACFTU) officially estimating the decline of the wage income share vis-à-vis the GDP to be 20 per cent since the liberalization of the economy, as cited by the same ILO report (2011: 49). To a certain extent, such disproportionate sharing of income has

Table 9.3 Trends in inequality: Gini coefficients in select Asian countries, 1990s and 2000s (per cent)

	1990s	*2000s*
East Asia		
China	32.4	43.4
South Korea	24.5	28.9
Mongolia	33.2	36.5
Taiwan	31.2	34.2
South Asia		
Bangladesh	27.6	32.1
India	32.5	37.0
Nepal	35.2	32.8
Pakistan	33.2	30.0
Sri Lanka	32.5	40.3
Southeast Asia		
Cambodia	38.3	37.9
Indonesia	29.2	38.9
Lao PDR	30.4	36.7
Malaysia	47.7	46.2
Philippines	43.8	43.0
Thailand	45.3	40.0
Viet Nam	35.7	35.6

Source: ADB (2012).

contributed to the increase in the number of labour disputes in China. Labour disputes rose from 100,000 in 1998 to 250,000 in 2004, and then more than doubled to 690,000 in 2008 (ILO 2011: 50). The response of the Chinese government to the labour unrest and other grassroots-based protest actions, mainly at the community and town/city level, is a pledge to build a more 'harmonious society' with social protection for all.

The skewed distribution of jobs and incomes is most vividly reflected in the production and marketing of goods done by Factory Asia. While Asia is a beneficiary in terms of jobs, its share of wages is woefully low. This is best illustrated by the case of the famous iPod, which is designed and marketed by the Americans and assembled by Taiwanese-owned factories in China (see Table 9.4). Sold in 2006 at the American market at $299, the iPod gave American companies $163, $132 to parts suppliers from other Asian countries, and only $4 to Chinese workers doing assembly. However, the positive side for China: about 30 per cent of the iPod jobs are created within China.

The 2012 ADB report *Confronting Rising Inequality in Asia* affirms the general observation that wage share in Asia is declining vis-à-vis capital share (65–67). Thus, according to the ADB, wage growth is also lagging behind labour productivity growth. Per ADB estimates, all the Asian economies saw a decline in wage share from the mid-1990s to the mid-2000s. For the research arm of the ILO, the International Institute for Labour Studies (IILS 2011), the decline of wage share in Asia for the same period was about 20 per cent.

Trade union perspectives on the race to the bottom

The World Bank, in its *Renaissance* paper on Asia (Gill and Kharas 2007: 30), has a relatively simplistic explanation for the phenomenon of growing inequality in a surging Asia: 'The rise of inequality in the region can be explained in terms of the growth processes driven by economies of scale'. Thus, to the World Bank, urban–rural disparity is due to less trade opportunities in the rural areas. It also mentions that within the urban areas, the inequality is driven by the higher wage premiums given for skills and talents. As to inequality among countries, the World Bank ascribes it to the success of some countries in integrating faster in the global economy compared to the slow globalizers.

However, to the trade union movement, inequality is seen as the outcome of the narrow character of the dominant growth model being uniformly promoted by the globalizers – the neoliberal 'Washington Consensus' programme of economic deregulation, privatization, trade and investment liberalization and general opening up of the economy to speed up global integration. Such a programme tends to favour the few with a 'global reach', mainly the TNCs and some big homegrown capitalist enterprises, at the expense of the workers. The trade unions call this a 'race to the bottom'. In a forum organized by the ADB, Christopher Ng (2010, no page nos.) of UNI-Apro explained the race to the bottom and its role in the making of the global financial crisis as follows:

> The race to the bottom is instrumental in the over-production of goods and services, most of which are exported by Factory Asia and Services Asia to a handful of developed countries in the North. On the other hand, global competition is used by the exporting countries as the argument to squeeze workers' wages, benefits and basic rights such as freedom of association and collective bargaining. This naturally weakens the purchasing power of the workers of Asia and even those of the workers in the North, many of whom have lost jobs under the global production chains of footloose transnational capital.

Hence, the race to the bottom carries with it the seeds for future crises, as the race leads to global overproduction, on the one hand, and under-consumption, on the other. Under-consumption means workers of both the North and South have lost the capacity to consume and buy the products they produce because of the low wages and limited job creation by the transnational corporations (TNCs). In Asia, wages of the workers hired by the EPZ and non-EPZ firms hardly rise because of short-term flexible labour contracts and anti-union restrictions, with the process of flexibilization aided by the availability of a huge pool of unemployed and underemployed and weak labour law enforcement.

Also, the problem with Factory Asia is that it ignores the role of other sectors of society in job and wealth creation. These include the domestic industry, domestic agriculture, local artisans and producers, farmers and fisher folk and the so-called producers of 'non-tradeables' such as the self-contained indigenous peoples, who are not participating in the globalization processes. These actors in the economy are

Table 9.4 Jobs and earnings tied to iPod production in the US, China and other countries, 2006

Jobs	*Number of employees*	*Total earnings (in US$ million)*
US engineers & professionals	6,101	525.2
US non-professionals	7,789	219.2
US production	30	1.4
China engineers & professionals	555	5.6
China non-professionals	0	0
China production	11,715	18.0
Other foreign engineers & professionals	3,265	126.0*
Other foreign non-professionals	4,892	96.5
Other foreign production	7,445	72.3*

Source: Ahearn (2011).
Note: *Japan and South Korea.

marginalized under the current growth model that emphasizes, in a dogmatic manner, global trade participation and wholesale economic liberalization as the main routes to growth and development. Even domestic agriculture and food sufficiency in support of local consumption are regarded to be sacrificed in the name of global trade opening.

Conclusion: the 'rebalancing' challenge

From the foregoing outline of growth of employment through integration in globalized systems of production it is clear that growth is not inclusive. Growth is exclusionary and unequal, especially in countries that have embraced globalization in a one-sided manner by simply opening up trade and investment doors. Growth is also unsustainable when a country is dependent on fragments of production and service outsourcing processes. For example, the Philippines once had a vibrant garments industry employing around 1 million or so workers (Beerepoot and Hernandez-Agramonte 2009, Ofreneo 2009); today, it has less than 100,000 workers, after the footloose investors/contractors in the industry redirected production to lower-cost producers like those in Indochina and South Asia. Similar concerns can be raised on whether low-end activities in the ITES-BPO are also vulnerable for relocation to lower cost locations.

However, it is difficult to imagine countries opting out of the globalization processes and building up economic autarkies ala-North Korea. One lesson from the experiences of the NICs and today's China is that participation in globalization through outward-looking policy regimes does not mean abandonment of policies to help nurture a strong domestic sector, for example, the small and medium enterprises catering to the domestic market. Another lesson is that globalization does not prevent a country from pursuing a broader vision of economic development that goes beyond the narrow requirements of a narrow globalization agenda (for example, relying solely on foreign investments of MNCs) that, as highlighted in this chapter, cannot benefit everyone. Part of such a vision should be the ability of countries to upgrade its industrial and agricultural base in order to strengthen both domestic and export-led industries and create jobs in both the urban and rural areas.

References

ADB (Asian Development Bank) (2011). *Asia 2050: Realizing the Asian Century*. Mandaluyong City: ADB.

ADB (2012). *Asian Development Outlook 2012: Confronting Rising Inequality in Asia*. Mandaluyong City: ADB.

Ahearn, R. (2011). *Rising Economic Powers and the Global Economy: Trends and Issues for Congress*. Washington DC: US Congressional Research Services.

Baldwin, R. (2013). Global supply chains: why they emerged, why they matter, and where they are going. In Elms, D. and Low, P. (eds). *Global Value Chains in a Changing World*. Geneva: World Trade Organization, Fung Global Institute and Temasek Centre for Trade and Negotiations, pp. 13–59.

Beerepoot, N. and Hernandez-Agramonte, J. (2009). Post MFA-adjustment of the Philippine garments sector: women's cooperatives amidst manufacturing decline. *European Journal of Development Research* 21 (3), 362–376.

Beerepoot, N. and Lambregts, B. (2015). Competition in online job marketplaces: towards a global labour market for service outsourcing? *Global Networks* 15 (2), 236–255.

Central Statistics Office (India). (2010). *Value Addition and Employment Generation in the ICT Sector in India*. Delhi: Central Statistics Office.

Cruz, J. and Valisno, J. (2014). Travails in the call center. *BusinessWorld weekender*. Two parts: June 27–28 and July 4–5. Quezon City: BusinessWorld Publishing.

Dreze, J. and Sen, A. (2013). *An Uncertain Glory: India and its Contradictions*. Princeton, NJ: Princeton University Press.

Edgington, D. and Hayter, R. (2013). The in situ upgrading of Japanese electronics firms in Malaysian industrial clusters. *Economic Geography* 89 (3), 227–259.

Elms, D. and Low, P. (eds). (2013). *Global Value Chains in a Changing World*. Geneva: World Trade Organization, Fung Global Institute and Temasek Centre for Trade and Negotiations.

Fabros, A. (2009). Global economy of signs and selves: A view of work regimes in call centers in the Philippines. *Sociologie du travail* 51, 343–360.

Felker, G.B. (2003). Southeast Asian industrialisation and the changing global production system. *Third World Quarterly* 24 (2), 255–282.

Frobel, F., Heinrichs, J. and Kreye, O. (1980). *The New International Division of Labour: Structural unemployment in the industrial countries and industrialization in developing countries*. Cambridge: Cambridge University Press.

Gereffi, G. and Korzeniewicz, M. (eds). (1994). *Commodity Chains and Global Capitalism*. London: Praeger Publishers.

Gill, I. and Kharas, H. (2007). *An East Asian Renaissance: Ideas for Economic Growth*. Washington, DC: World Bank.

Herr, H. (2011). Perspectives on high growth and rising inequality. In H. Scherrer, (ed.), *China's Labour Question*. Munchen, Mering: Rainer Hammp Verlag, pp. 7–27.

ICFTU (International Confederation of Free Trade Unions) (2002). *A Trade Union Guide to Globalisation*. Brussels: ICFTU.

ICFTU-APRO (International Confederation of Free Trade Unions-Asia and Pacific Regional Organisation) (1996). *Building Trade Unions into the 21st Century*. Singapore: ICFTU-APRO.

IILS (International Institute for Labour Studies) (2011). *World of Work Report 2011. Making markets work for jobs*. Geneva: IILS.

ILO (International Labour Office) (2005). *Making Decent Work an Asian Goal*. Geneva: ILO.

ILO (2009). *Guide to the Millennium Development Goals: Employment Indicators*. Geneva: ILO.

ILO (2011). *Building a Sustainable Future with Decent Work in Asia and the Pacific*. Geneva: ILO.

ILO (2012). *Global Employment Trends 2012*. Geneva: ILO.

ITUC (International Trade Union Confederation-Asia Pacific) (2007). *Action Programme for United Trade Union Action in Asia and the Pacific*. Singapore: ITUC-Asia Pacific.

Kalleberg, A. and Hewison, K. (2013). Precarious work and the challenge for Asia. *American Behavioral Scientist* 57 (3), 271–288.

Kimura, F. (2013). How have production networks changed development strategies in East Asia? In: Elms, D. and Low, P. (eds). *Global Value Chains in a Changing World*. Geneva: World Trade Organization, Fung Global Institute and Temasek Centre for Trade and Negotiations, pp. 361–381.

Kleibert, J. (2015). Expanding Global Production Networks: The emergence, evolution and the developmental impact of the offshore service sector in the Philippines. PhD dissertation. Amsterdam: University of Amsterdam.

Krishna, A. and Nederveen-Pieterse, J. (2008). Hierarchical integration: The dollar economy and the rupee economy. *Development and Change* 39 (2), 219–237.

Lamy, P. (2013). Foreword. In: Elms, D. and Low, P. (eds). *Global Value Chains in a Changing World*. Geneva: World Trade Organization, Fung Global Institute and Temasek Centre for Trade and Negotiations.

Lee, D., Leong, A., Ofreneo, R. and Sukumaran, A. (2008). *Rights for Two-Thirds of Asia: Asian Labour Law Review 2008*. Hong Kong: AMRC.

Muchhala, B. (ed.). (2007). *Ten Years After: Revisiting the Asian Financial Crisis*. Washington, DC: Woodrow Wilson Institute.

Ng, C. (2010). Post-GFC: Challenge of labour-economic policy coherence. contribution to the ILO/ADBI conference on post-crisis employment. Unpublished.

Ng, C. and Ofreneo, R. (2000). *People First in the New Economy*. Singapore: UNI Asia and the Pacific.

Ofreneo, R. (2009). Development choices for Philippine textiles and garments in the post-MFA era. *Journal of Contemporary Asia* 39 (4), 543–561.

Plunkett, J. (ed.). (2011). *Plunkett's Outsourcing & Offshoring Industry Almanac 2011*. Houston: Plunkett Research, Ltd.

Pratap, S. (2014). *Emerging Trends in Factory Asia: International Capital Mobility, Global Value Chains, and the Labour Movement*. Hong Kong: Asia Monitor Resource Centre.

South Centre (2013). *Global Value Chains (GVCs) from a Development Perspective*. Geneva: South Centre.

Standing, G. (2010). *The Precariat: The New Dangerous Class*. London: Bloomsbury Academic.

Taylor, P. and Bain, P. (2005). 'India calling to the far away towns': the call centre labour process and globalization. *Work, Employment and Society* 19 (2), 261–282.

Thite, M. and Russell, B. (2010). The next available agent: work organisation in Indian call centres. *New Technology, Work and Employment* 25 (1), 2–18.
UNCTAD (United Nations Conference on Trade and Development) (2004). *World Investment Report 2004: The Shift Towards Services*. Geneva: UNCTAD.
UNDP (United Nations Development Programme) (1999). *Human Development Report 1999*. New York: Oxford University Press.
United Nations Development Programme Regional Centre (2006). *Trade on Human Terms: Transforming Trade for Human Development in Asia and the Pacific*, Asia-Pacific Human Development Report 2006. Delhi: Macmillan India Ltd.
World Bank (2007). *Global Economic Prospects: Managing the Next Wave of Globalization*. Washington, DC: The World Bank.
World Bank (2011). *Securing the Present, Shaping the Future*, Vol. 1. Washington, DC: World Bank.
World Bank (2012). *More and Better Jobs in South Asia*. Washington, DC: World Bank.

10 How work in the BPO sector affects employability

Perceptions of ex-BPO workers in Metro Manila

Mary Leian C. Marasigan

Introduction

Global sourcing and offshoring of services is creating job opportunities for thousands of workers in developing economies (Dobbs *et al.* 2012, Dossani and Kenney 2007). In the Philippines, the pulse of this phenomenon is in the IT-enabled business process outsourcing (ITES-BPO) sector. ITES-BPO jobs are plentiful, require a low to moderate level of skills, and provide salaries that are much higher compared to entry-level jobs in other sectors (Usui 2011). Since options for good jobs in the local labour market are limited, workers, many of them young, skilled and from middle-class background, flock to the ITES-BPO as soon as or even before they graduate from college. The industry's need for labour is actually such that it also opens its doors to older and long unemployed persons and other workers in circumstances that disadvantage them from accessing jobs in other sectors. However, the fact that many workers leave after several months suggests that not all is rosy in the industry. Already, a growing body of literature illuminates the realities of employment in the offshore service sector, pointing out that the challenges of the reverse hours, work monotony, and limited upward career development opportunities are important reasons for workers to exit (Taylor and Bain 1999, Thite and Russell 2010, Upadhya 2009).

A hitherto little-explored area is whether and how ITES-BPO work affects subsequent employability. Employability, in the careers and organizational management literature in recent decades, has come to be seen as key to maintaining or improving one's labour market position (Clarke 2008). While most BPO jobs are at the lower to medium segments of the value chain (Beerepoot and Hendriks 2013, Gereffi and Fernandez-Stark 2010), they need also to be seen in light of what they offer to workers in terms of new experiences not available in traditional service jobs in the labour market. BPO jobs, for instance, provide people with the opportunity to work in globally connected workplaces and engage with multicultural employers and clients, while the generally higher salaries may contribute to individual financial empowerment (Mirchandani 2004). While recognizing that BPO work presents many difficult challenges to workers that are as novel as the rewards, opportunities in BPO potentially confer labour market advantages to workers that may help enhance their employability.

This chapter aims to deepen our understanding and advancing the debate on how new IT-enabled jobs in developing countries impact on workers' career development prospects over the longer-term (see e.g. Belt and Richardson 2005, Messenger and Ghosheh 2010, Vira and James 2012). It empirically explores how work in call centres and back-office support services influences workers' subsequent employability. It does so by investigating the career trajectories of a small group of former ITES-BPO workers in Metro Manila and by examining workers' perceptions as to how work in ITES-BPO has affected their employability and their post-BPO movements in the external labour market.

Jobs in the Philippine BPO sector

The Philippines is a good example of a developing country with a thriving BPO sector providing jobs mostly to young and skilled workers but also to older and otherwise less-employable persons including returning overseas workers, the long-term unemployed, and university students. In 2014, around 1 million workers were directly employed in BPO (de Vera 2014), a number that translates to around 2.4 percent of a labour force of 41.3 million (PSA 2014). The attraction of BPO has as much to do with the lack of good jobs elsewhere in the labour market as well as with the salaries and other perks that are associated with BPO work. These jobs are seen as white-collar 'office work' in air-conditioned and modern workplaces and glamorized further by being located in big shopping malls and central business districts. The salary and incentive packages are higher compared to those in the local labour market (Amante 2010, Hechanova 2013) particularly for entry-level positions. It is also important to note that before the BPO boom, most service jobs available to young workers were low-wage, short-duration work in sales, warehouses, shopping malls (Amante 2010) and fast-food chains. In this light, the BPO industry provides a certain measure of 'upgrade' to the list of job choices in the market.

Sustainability of employment in BPO, however, is an issue. Job tenure ranges from just two months to two years (Ofreneo and Marasigan 2007) and turnover rates are anywhere from 20 per cent (Magtibay-Ramos *et al.* 2008) to 80 per cent based on anecdotal reports. The reasons for exit, from the workers' point of view, are well-known and include the nature of work, the work hours (Kuruvilla and Ranganathan 2010, Thite and Russell 2010), and the limited career development options (Bird and Ernst 2009). At the same time, BPO as a sector is also vulnerable to global business dynamics and firm-level risks, such as loss of business due to non-renewal of contract by clients or pre-termination of an existing account, which translate to threats to workers' employment security. So, while the BPO sector may be absorbing thousands of workers into its ranks and providing relatively good jobs (World Bank 2014) the rewards that workers reap, particularly financial empowerment (Mirchandani 2004), may be short-lived because sustaining employment is challenged both by the business risks and nature of work in BPO.

A broad definition of employability

Employability is all about surviving in the labour market (Thijssen *et al.* 2008) or, to be more precise, about being able to 'get a job, advance in a given job, or move to a new one if necessary' (Forrier and Sels 2003). While this sounds rather straightforward, employability is a complex concept (Clarke 2008) that defies a standard definition. One unresolved issue in the literature concerns whether employability should be defined in a narrow or a broad sense. A narrow definition focuses on individuals' qualities and attributes that employers consider as valuable traits and so emphasizes the objective employability of a person (Fugate *et al.* 2004). Over the years, however, broader definitions have been proposed. These tend to include both the labour supply and demand dimensions in an attempt to recognize the interactivity between the two and understand the implications for not only a person's objective but also his relative employability. Along this line, Hillage and Pollard (1998: 2) have defined employability as:

> the capability to move self-sufficiently within the labour market to realise potential through sustainable employment. For the individual, employability depends on the knowledge, skills and attitudes they possess, the way they use those assets and present them to employers and the context (e.g. personal circumstances and labour market environment) within which they seek work.

Building on Hillage and Pollard's definition McQuaid and Lindsay (2005) have proposed a framework of employability that aims to give contextual conditions a more balanced consideration alongside the more person-centered factors. In this framework, the components of employability are individual factors, personal circumstances, and external conditions. *Individual factors* pertain to personal attributes of workers including qualifications and educational attainment; basic, key, and high-level transferable skills; work experience; demographic factors; health and wellbeing; job-seeking skills; and adaptability and mobility. *Personal circumstances* refer to a person's social and household circumstances and responsibilities, which may facilitate or constrain one's ability to accept and perform a job or not. *External conditions* are labour demand conditions including local labour market factors, macroeconomic factors, vacancy characteristics, recruitment factors, and public support services that are employment related. This broader framework of employability is a useful analytical lens to examine the employment situation of workers in less-developed countries where external conditions such as lack of job opportunities in the labour market make it difficult for workers not only to get into entry-level jobs but also to move between different types of employment.

Forrier and Sels (2003), in addition, argue that employability should be seen as a process and assessed in light of workers' labour market position because this serves as a 'reference point' against which to compare the initial and subsequent condition of workers. This also means that because workers come from different positions they face distinctive issues and that their future labour market prospects depend on whether and how these issues are addressed. Within the field of economics, studies have suggested that a job contributes to acquisition of skills, job credentials, building informal network, and resources to aid job search (Cockx and Picchio 2012). In the field of career studies, Inkson and Arthur (2001) have suggested that having a job can also lead to a better understanding of career motivations, which may result in finding a better job match. However, depending on their labour market situation and desired job workers may have to develop different areas of their employability to successfully transition to a different type of job or sector (Cockx and Picchio 2012).

Views on employability in BPO

Several scholars have focused on the impact of BPO work on skills development and its potential implications on employability. The overriding notion is that BPO jobs and specifically, call centre jobs, do not contribute significantly to skills development because the knowledge that workers gain from the job is minimal, owing to the non-complex and routine nature of the tasks involved (Bird and Ernst 2009, Taylor and Bain 2005). There are contending views on whether the types of jobs that are being offshored to developing economies are increasingly knowledge-intensive jobs. According to some researchers, there is evidence that the situation is somewhat moving towards that direction, for instance in India (Dossani and Kenney 2007), while others suggest that the majority of jobs are still of the low-end kind (D'Cruz and Noronha 2010, Upadhya 2009). Yet other authors suggest that there is great diversity in workplace practices in the sector, particularly in call centres (Batt *et al.* 2009), suggesting that an outright dismissal of skills development in low-level jobs in BPO warrants a re-evaluation or may otherwise have to be qualified against specific cases. Two recent studies about BPO workers in India and the Philippines that indeed present more optimistic perspectives are those by Vira and James (2012) and Beerepoot and Hendriks (2013). The former found that ex-call centre agents in India are able to transfer to better-paid employment in other sectors of services similar to the verticals they serviced as call centre agents and on that basis suggest that call centre work is best seen as venue for skills acquisition. Beerepoot and Hendriks (2013) focused on call centre agents' generic skills acquisition and employability in the second-tier city of Baguio in the Philippines and found that workers perceive that their work gains them generic skills such as communication skills, interpersonal skills, business knowledge, and leadership skills. Importantly, the study argued that workers deliberately joined the sector as part of a long-term career strategy to break into the overseas labour market. The latter connects to views held by others (e.g. Bird and Ernst 2009, Ofreneo and Marasigan 2007, Pal and Buzzanell 2008) that many workers consider ITES-BPO as a convenient provider of transition employment or stop-gap jobs, implying that workers enter the sector already with a plan to transfer to a different job later on. This means that workers to begin with do not really join the sector expecting to build on factors that will help them to sustain employment.

Research methodology and respondents

The research for this chapter adopted a qualitative design using semi-structured interviews to examine the longitudinal experiences of workers who voluntary left their jobs in call centres (CC) and back-office support (BOS) in Metro Manila. Given the difficulty of locating workers who already left BPO (see also Vira and James 2012), respondents were identified through the snowball method. Between February and May 2013 and in January and February 2014, a total of 32 former ITES-BPO workers agreed to be interviewed. Each interview lasted from 45 till 90 minutes and was fully transcribed. The questions related to respondents' employment history before they joined BPO (their initial labour market position), the employability gains acquired while working in ITES-BPO, and their perceptions of how work in ITES-BPO had affected their movements on the labour market after they had left the sector. The main themes of the interview data were grouped guided by the framework of McQuaid and Lindsay (2005) described above.

The sample of 32 respondents contained 17 women and 15 men; 21 used to work in call centres and 11 in back-office support. Respondents had a mean age of 24 when they first joined the BPO sector, with the youngest joining at 18 and the oldest at 58. BPO was the first job for little over half of the respondents. In terms of educational attainment, 81 per cent had a bachelor's degree in such fields as nursing, pharmacy, engineering, IT, business, physical sciences, social sciences, mass communications, or human resources, while 19 per cent were college undergraduates. In terms of post-graduate degrees, one person was already pursuing a law degree when she entered BPO employment, while others started a Masters course during (6 per cent) or after they left BPO (12 per cent).

Labour market positions before joining and job changes after leaving the BPO

Respondents' initial labour market positions varied. Half of them had recently graduated from college without any prior work experience, while 19 per cent were still in university or otherwise pursuing higher degrees. Others, including returning overseas-based workers, had previous work experiences (25 per cent) and the rest had been out of work for at least a year (6 per cent).

In joining the BPO for the first time, 66 per cent found employment in call centres as customer service representatives (CSRs). The others started in back-office support as 'specialists' or 'analysts'. The latter entered the BPO as recent college graduates, while CSRs entered as recent graduates, students, long-term unemployed, and returning overseas workers. Just over 30 per cent of workers stayed in the BPO for less than a year, 28 per cent between one and two years, 16 per cent between one and five years, and 25 per cent were in the sector for six years or more. The majority of workers had worked for one employer (53 per cent), 25 per cent for two, and the rest for three or more.

It appeared that 69 per cent of interviewees found non-BPO employment at one time or another from the time they left BPO until the conduct of the interview. After workers left BPO, the majority (59 per cent) transitioned to new jobs in privately owned firms, government agencies, non-government organizations (NGO), or in overseas employment. Others (9 per cent) went into full-time study to finish an undergraduate degree that had been interrupted by BPO employment. Others pursued training (12 per cent). The rest became self-employed (9 per cent), retired (3 per cent), or unemployed (6 per cent). Further changes in labour market positions were noted among 28 per cent of respondents from the time they left BPO until the interview. For instance, four of those who found employment changed job(s) six months to four years after they left BPO; one managed to finish college and found related employment; three of those who pursued training found employment in the field they trained for; and one respondent who found a job post-exit had become unemployed and was still searching for a job. Table 10.1 provides a summary.

Perceived employability gains from BPO work: skills, job credentials, and access to resources

Individual factors: skills and other job credentials

There was a sense among the interviewees that their ITES-BPO jobs had brought them IT skills they would not have learned otherwise. Call centre workers said that they picked up keyboard shortcuts and techniques of using spreadsheet and office application, such as MS Work and Excel, which raised their knowledge a notch higher than 'average' users. Interviewees also believed that this learning translated to better work efficiency and effectiveness. Technical support agents learned to solve computer and internet connection problems. Younger and more 'techie' call centre workers downplayed improvements in their IT skills but long-term

Table 10.1 Workers' labour market position before, during, and after exit (n=32)

Labour market position previous to working in BPO	*BPO segment worked in*	*Employment/labour market position post-exit*
New college graduate (16)	Call centre (21)	Private sector (12)[a]
Employed in non-BPO job (6)	Back-office support (11)	Government (5)[b]
College student (5)		NGO (1)[c]
Overseas worker (2)		Overseas work (1)[d]
Long-term unemployed (2)		Study (3)
Law student (1)		Training (4)
		Self-employment (3)
		Unemployed (2)
		Retired (1)

Note: [a] regulatory affairs associate, nurse, writer, market researcher, sales and marketing officer, marketing assistant, human resource (HR) information systems officer, junior bank officer, production planner, HR specialist, sales and marketing officer, IT consultant; [b] administrative assistant, researcher, dispute adjudicator, HR specialist; [c] donor relations officer; [d] business development officer.

unemployed interviewees and older first-time BPO entrants considered these to be the highlight of their learning.

One of the main findings from the interview data was that skills, training, and other opportunities that may improve job credentials were set down according to the business line, account, or worker's position, which means that some workers had better opportunities to learn certain skills compared to others. As one interviewee reported:

> In the call centre one could learn many skills if one is assigned in quality assurance, as team leader or some other higher position. But if you're just an agent you will not learn unless your team leader teaches you. (Female, team leader, 25 February 2014)

Apart from communication skills, former call centre workers mentioned that they learned other soft skills such as customer service and multi-tasking. Others too learned related knowhow such as doing online research. One interviewee mentioned that he learned to conduct 'cold calls' and used that skill to solicit job vacancy information from companies that he hoped to work for after he left the ITES-BPO sector.

Former workers in back-office support mentioned that they learned different IT skills such as using business software such as SAP, handling databases, and processing documentation. Two workers noted that even seemingly specific work such as preparing abstracts of lease contracts helped sharpen other skills such as extracting information, noting details, and computational skills. At least one interviewee insisted that in back-office support he learned to work and supervise a team and this, in his eyes, is a skill that was highly valuable elsewhere in the labour market. In addition to skills, two interviewees were able to pursue higher studies that were partly paid for by the firm. The programme seemed intended to encourage retention, but interviewees also saw that this could be an additional credential should they leave BPO:

> As soon as I became eligible for the scholarship benefit I immediately took advantage of it and enrolled in a master's degree.
>
> (Male, former BOS, 12 January 2013)

In addition, 3 out of 11 ex-back-office support said that they became skills certified in quality management through their company-offered training in Six Sigma, a quality improvement tool (Schroeder *et al.* 2008), which is transferable and recognized across different industries.

Personal circumstances: access to resources and informal network

Work in ITES-BPO also provided interviewees with access to financial resources. Most interviewees reported that they spent (most of) their earnings on consumer goods, travel, and leisure. However, a few workers used income to finance their bachelors, higher studies, or other training. Bachelor students work in call centres to earn income to pay for tuition and allowance and they straddled between work and study during the regular semester. Immediately after they left the sector, two respondents who wanted to shift to a non-BPO job used part of their income to attend specialized training courses.

Interviewees also used income to fund the job search process, which lasted between four months to a year. Since they had income from employment a number of interviewees felt less pressured to move to the first job available. Instead they surveyed more job options before they resigned. Workers also found that the reverse work hours allowed them to go to job interviews without needing to take a leave from work:

> It also helped that we were required to be in business suit at work, so I get off my shift in the morning ready to go for a job interview.
>
> (Female, former BOS employee, 12 August 2013)

Workers also tried to find potential job referrals from informal network of colleagues. However, a few workers related that this also had a disadvantage: supervisors may discover and thwart one's attempts at leaving or, alternatively, prematurely push workers to exit. While one interviewee was able to find a new job through a co-worker, the rest found employment by accessing formal job portals and their informal network outside BPO.

Relating employability gains and (not) finding a job in the external labour market

In this section, the job search experience of the interviewees who found employment post-exit is linked with the perceived employability gains from previous ITES-BPO employment.

Individual factors versus employer expectations

Interviewees perceived that the advanced IT skills they learned in BPO contributed to finding a non-BPO job post-exit. There was a sense among interviewees that their experience, notably from back-office support, put them at par or otherwise gave them an 'IT advantage' over other jobseekers:

> I think my work in BPO1 really became my selling point to my new employer … I learned to work with different types of databases in the BPO and that is what I do now in this job.
>
> (Female, former BOS employee, 12 August 2013)

> I learned to use SAP and process documentation and apply these in my current job. We are transitioning from manual to automated system so I am helping to

> document the process. My boss said they had a hard time finding a candidate who knew how to use SAP so I guess, SAP was the most helpful skill I learned.
>
> (Female, former BOS employee, 14 March 2013)

> I told this new company that I had knowledge of SAP and other software that we used in BPO2 and that helped because they also use that software in this company.
>
> (Male, former BOS employee, 13 January 2013)

Other workers said that the soft skills they learned helped them to get hired. A nurse and former call centre agent said that her customer-service relations experience was valued positively by recruiters. The long-term unemployed who re-entered the labour force by joining a call centre mentioned that they performed better at job interviews, thanks to their call centre experience.

A common view among new college graduates was that BPO was a 'good first job' and this work experience can be an additional credential for a future job. According to a former call centre agent:

> I disliked the job, although it was also good because that job was my initiation, taught me how to go to work every day, to work with officemates, how to keep on doing a job even if you dislike talking to the customers. My long-term career plan was to finish my studies. I really considered [BPO] as a temporary thing at that time. However, that experience also helped me after like when I applied in a market research firm they also considered that at least I had some initiative to work and spend my hours productively.
>
> (Female, former call centre agent, 23 January 2013)

To be sure, the majority of respondents thought ITES-BPO could be a long-term work environment for them. For instance, new college graduates who joined some big multinational BPOs counted on an upwardly mobile career and long employment with the same firm at the beginning stage. In their eyes, multinational BPOs were prestigious 'brands' to work for and that night work was just part of the challenge. After some time, however, other concerns emerged such as security and safety during the long commutes to and from work, especially during the early hours, health effects of night work, and feelings of being socially isolated from family and friends. The extracts below show that workers quickly considered changing employment:

> A few months after we went live, people started to search for new jobs. We went to university job fairs to look for jobs though we had different ambitions – one of us wanted to be a teacher, another wanted to be a journalist … I started to ask friends if they know of any other job that I can apply for.
>
> (Female, former BOS, 14 March 2013)

> My friends back in college were in jobs related to industrial engineering, while I had an administrative job. At some point I decided that I also wanted to experience how it was to actually work in the field.
>
> (Male, former BOS, 13 January 2013).

> I thought I was running out of time not having been able to practice my nursing profession so I decided to leave.
>
> (Male, former call centre agent, 26 March 2013)

Job dissatisfaction somehow forced workers to consider other labour market options and their realization that they wanted to be in a different job helped to shape career objectives that guided subsequent job search.

Workers also perceived that BPO work is not a sufficient qualification to mitigate the demands imposed by another job. This theme came up in discussions comparing entry-level qualifications for BPO and non-BPO jobs. A consensus was that there were higher barriers to employment in white-collar occupations outside of BPO. For example, since a college degree is still an important proxy that employers use to signal productivity (McGuinness and Wooden 2009), workers who did not have a college degree were in a disadvantaged position compared those who had:

> The problem is I don't have a degree and here in the Philippines employers choose to hire those who are college graduates. As much as I would like to work in San Miguel, Smart, or Globe, I can't because these companies will not hire me.
>
> (Male, former call centre training supervisor, 16 February 2013)

At the same time, the lack of a degree could also disadvantage workers from promotion or transfer to a similar position within BPO. A former call centre team leader recalled that after a serious health problem forced him to find a day job, he realized that other centers did not want to hire him for the same position because he did not have a college degree.

Another perspective was that a job in BPO can disrupt a workers' career track. Workers can enter BPO regardless of their field of study but doing so may make it difficult for them to return. For instance, a young graduate of electrical engineering joined a back-office firm for an account dealing with finance and accounting. He was retrenched after a year due to the financial crisis in the United States, but found that his BPO experience in finance and accounting was too limited to enable him to work in that area, and at the same time he could not find employment in his original field of training. Eventually, he landed a series of short-term jobs but since he lacked a formal background in accounting and finance he was not able to find work that was sustainable over the long term:

> I immediately worked in BPO after graduation so I was not able to take the licensure exam and companies only hire licensed ECEs.
>
> (Male, former BOS employee, 26 March 2013)

Finally, the scope and similarity of previous work experiences against expectations of prospective employers brought problems for respondents. While Vira and James (2012) found that jobs in the BPO helped workers to land employment in similar verticals (industry lines), the interview data showed a more nuanced picture. For instance, several respondents in this study said that non-BPO employers preferred those who had broad knowledge and experience compared to what they have been exposed to in BPO. A respondent from an outsource HR recruitment account, for instance, had specialized tasks in BPO that did not include conducting interviews or sourcing applicants, which were typical functions in recruitment. Due to this, she got turned down by employers. Similarly, another interviewee processed purchase orders in his back-office job in procurement services but felt that it was too limited to highlight as related work experience when he applied in procurement and supply-chain management jobs outside of BPO.

Another recurrent theme in the interviews was that workers used different strategies to overcome the obstacles they faced concerning employers expectations. One common approach was to highlight other job credentials to fill in what employers and interviewees may perceive as weak areas of one's qualifications. For instance, interviewees may not have had broad experience but their advanced IT skills helped them to be considered for other positions that made use of those scarce skills. Likewise, the job applicant may not have had related work experience in the job applied for, but having a Master's degree in a related field may have helped the applicant to be selected. Two interviewees enrolled in a specialized training course that lasted six months to a year in order to update their skills and get hired in a related job:

> I needed to take training in order for companies to even consider me. Instead of related experience, I can show that I had training.
>
> (Male, former BOS employee, 15 January 2014)

They noted that there were attendant opportunity costs in pursuing training full-time instead of immediately working, but in their eyes, this improved their long-term employment prospects compared to if they only depended on their existing skills and experiences.

Personal circumstances: access to resources and informal network

Some workers used income in BPO to support further studies (Vira and James 2012). The interview results showed that students taking their bachelors also work in BPO to earn income for tuition or allowance. However, there was a sense among the relevant interviewees that balancing work and study can be a risky strategy. For instance, one interviewee completely dropped out of school, and for the rest it resulted in failing marks and prolonged years in university:

> I had difficulty balancing work and studies. I had a problem with the shift schedules because they change every so often. I cannot request my boss to give me a regular shift. Worst, on some days my shift ended at 6am and I had

> classes that start at 7am and those were labouratory classes which were more demanding.
>
> (Male, former call centre agent, 6 March 2013)

A recurrent theme that came up in discussions about workers' job search experiences is the importance of one's informal network. Those who worked in non-BPO jobs prior to joining BPO were able to tap their network of contacts from previous employment and this led to productive job finds, compared with workers whose informal network were mostly people from BPO:

> She (a client from a previous job) told me to submit a job application at the bank where she works. I was quite happy with my BPO job but I was embarrassed to turn down her suggestion. I found out that it was a really good job, so I left BPO.
>
> (Female, former BOS employee, 4 March 2013).

Interviewees who had only worked for BPO had a smaller informal network so they also used online job portals, websites, and newspapers to find job vacancies, but for them the search process was long-winded and, in the words of some, 'really difficult'.

Conclusion

This chapter aimed to contribute to our understanding of the long-term impact of BPO jobs on workers' career development, an area that is still under-researched. The study used McQuaid and Lindsay's (2005) employability framework to examine the perceptions of a small group of former ITES-BPO workers to determine their labour market destinations post-exit, the employability gains derived from BPO work, and the impacts of the latter on the former.

The study shows that ex-BPO workers move to a wide variety of labour market destinations post-exit. The majority of the workers interviewed found new employment in non-BPO sectors, similar to the findings of Vira and James (2012). In line with the findings of Beerepoot and Hendriks (2013), the majority of workers recognized that BPO work provided them with an opportunity to improve various aspects of their employability. ITES-BPO helps sufficiently skilled workers from all ages and backgrounds to gain labour market attachment. Younger workers tend to treat it as an initiation and transition job. From an employability perspective, young graduates have much to gain in terms of work experience and skills from employment in ITES-BPO, particularly if they join the right firm and account.

Employability gains appeared related to the opportunities that workers find in these jobs: BPO workers in different business lines developed different skills sets. Former call centre workers perceived that they developed communication skills in particular, while those in back-office support acquired more advanced IT skills. Likewise, depending on firms joined, a minority of the workers were able to access incentives that allowed them to pursue higher studies or otherwise earn skills certification on account of the company. However, the results also showed that young persons who work in the sector while attending university may drop out and not complete their degree. By doing so, such workers may be putting their employability at risk, given the continuing importance placed by employers in the Philippines on education as a selection criterion.

McQuaid and Lindsay (2005) suggest that the interaction of individual factors, personal circumstances, and external factors impacts on employability. The interface of these dimensions was pervasive in the job-search experiences of workers in this study. Through an examination of how employability gains facilitate or constrain the process of finding employment, this study found that BPO can confer an IT advantage to ex-back-office workers and this may result in successful movements to new jobs. At the same time, however, it was also shown that young workers found themselves constrained from being hired because the entry qualifications outside ITES-BPO are higher and employability gains from the sector only serve to supplement other existing credentials. Running through the data is a sense of awareness that BPO work cannot substitute for the more basic job qualifications imposed by employers. It explains why workers felt that they would have lower chances at another job due to lack of skills or educational qualification regardless of their BPO work experience.

This study suggests that contrary to more negative claims, BPO work, in the eyes of the workers that is, provides opportunities to build employability assets. However, whether these gains translate to improved abilities to get selected for desired jobs also depends on demand-related factors, many of which are determined by the employer. While Vira and James (2012) suggest that the sector is best seen as a skills training ground that can assist workers in getting into similar jobs in other sectors, the experiences of ex-BPO workers showed that the link between skills and employment cannot be drawn easily because other factors also complicate the process of job transition. Thus, while acknowledging that these jobs may expand workers' labour market options, it also needs to be considered that there are limitations to what BPO work can achieve for workers' employability.

In light of these findings, it would be interesting to also study the career trajectories of workers who continued to work within the BPO to find out how their career prospects compare to the prospects of those who left the sector. Likewise, it would be interesting to more systematically investigate the impact of the ITES-BPO sector on educational attainment: is the sector essentially an enabler of peoples' (further) studies or does it instead mainly encourage people to discontinue their studies?

References

Amante, M., 2010. Offshored Work in Philippine BPOs. In Messenger, J.C., Ghosheh, N., and others, (eds). *Offshoring and Working Conditions in Remote Work*. Palgrave Macmillan: New York.

Batt, R., Holman, D. and Holtgrewe, U., 2009. The Globalization of Service Work: Comparative Institutional Perspectives on Call Centers. *Industrial and Labor Relations Review* 62, 453–488.

Beerepoot, N. and Hendriks, M., 2013. Employability of Offshore Service Sector Workers in the Philippines: opportunities for upward labour mobility or dead-end jobs? *Work Employment Society* 27, 823–841.

Belt, V. and Richardson, R., 2005. Social Labour, Employability and Social Exclusion: Pre-employment training for call centre work. *Urban Studies* 42, 257–270.

Bird, M. and Ernst, C., 2009. *Offshoring and Employment in the Developing World: Business process outsourcing in the Philippines*. ILO: Geneva.

Clarke, M., 2008. Understanding and Managing Employability in Changing Career Contexts. *Journal of European Industrial Training* 32, 258–284.

Cockx, B. and Picchio, M., 2012. Are Short-lived Jobs Stepping Stones to Long-Lasting Jobs?*. *Oxford Bulletin of Economics and Statistics* 74, 646–675.

D'Cruz, P. and Noronha, E., 2010. Employee Dilemmas in the India ITES-BPO Sector. In: Messenger, J.C. and Ghosheh, N., (eds). 2010. *Offshoring and Working Conditions in Remote Work*. Palgrave Macmillan: Basingstoke.

de Vera, Ben, 2014. Employment in BPO sector hits 1-M mark. *Inquirer.net*. http://business.inquirer.net/177150/employment-in-bpo-sector-hits-1-m-mark [Accessed 5 November 2014].

Dobbs, R., Madgavkar, A., Barton, D., Labaye, E., Manyika, J., Roxburgh, C., Lund, S. and Madhav, S., 2012. *The World at Work: Jobs, pay, and skills for 3.5 billion people*. McKinsey Global Institute.

Dossani, R. and Kenney, M., 2007. The Next Wave of Globalization: Relocating service provision to India. *World Development* 35, 772–791.

Forrier, A. and Sels, L., 2003. The Concept of Employability: A complex mosaic. *International Journal of Human Resources Development and Management* 3, 102–124.

Fugate, M., Kinicki, A.J. and Ashforth, B.E., 2004. Employability: A psycho-social construct, its dimensions, and applications. *Journal of Vocational Behavior* 65, 14–38.

Gereffi, G. and Fernandez-Stark, K., 2010. *The Offshore Services Value Chain*. Working Paper 5262. The World Bank: Washington, DC.

Hechanova, M.R.M., 2013. The Call Center as a Revolving Door: A Philippine perspective. *Personnel Review* 42, 349–365.

Hillage, J. and Pollard, E., 1998. *Employability: Developing A Framework for Policy Analysis*. Research Brief No. 85. http://webarchive.nationalarchives.gov.uk/20130401151715/www.education.gov.uk/publications/eOrderingDownload/RB85.pdf [Accessed 28 May 2014].

Inkson, K. and Arthur, M.B., 2001. How to be a Successful Career Capitalist. *Organizational Dynamics* 30, 48–61.

Kuruvilla, S. and Ranganathan, A., 2010. Globalisation and Outsourcing: Confronting new human resource challenges in India's business process outsourcing industry. *Industrial Relations Journal* 41, 136–153.

Magtibay-Ramos, N., Estrada, G. and Felipe, J., 2008. An Input–Output Analysis of the Philippine BPO Industry. *Asian-Pacific Economic Literature* 22, 41–56.

McGuinness, S. and Wooden, M., 2009. Overskilling, Job Insecurity, and Career Mobility. *Industrial Relations: A Journal of Economy and Society* 48, 265–286.

McQuaid, L. and Lindsay, C., 2005. The Concept of Employability. *Urban Studies* 42, 197–219.

Messenger, J.C. and Ghosheh, N., others, 2010. *Offshoring and Working Conditions in Remote Work*. Palgrave Macmillan: New York.

Mirchandani, K., 2004. Practices of Global Capital: Gaps, cracks and ironies in transnational call centres in India. *Global Networks* 4, 355–373.

Ofreneo, R.E., Ng, C. and Marasigan-Pasumbal, L., 2007. Voice for the Voice Workers: Addressing the IR Concerns in the Call Center/BPO Industry of Asia. *Indian Journal of Industrial Relations* 42, 534–557.

Pal, M. and Buzzanell, P., 2008. The Indian Call Center Experience: A case study in changing discourses of identity, identification, and career in a global context. *Journal of Business Communication* 45, 31–60.

PSA, 2014. *Highlights of October 2014 Labour Force Survey (No. Vol. 18, No. 32)*, Labstat Updates. www.bles.dole.gov.ph/PUBLICATIONS/LABSTATpercent20UPDATES/vol18_32.pdf. [Accessed 17 December 2014].

Ramesh, B.P., 2004. 'Cyber Coolies' in BPO: Insecurities and vulnerabilities of non-standard work. *Economic and Political Weekly* 39, 492–497.

Schroeder, R.G., Linderman, K., Liedtke, C. and Choo, A.S., 2008. Six Sigma: Definition and underlying theory. *Journal of Operations Management, Special Issue: Research in Supply Chain Quality* 26, 536.

Taylor, P. and Bain, P., 1999. 'An Assembly Line in the Head': Work and employee relations in the call centre. *Industrial Relations Journal,* 30, 101–117.

Taylor, P. and Bain, P., 2005. 'India calling to the far away towns: The call centre labour process and globalization. *Work Employment Society* 19, 261–282.

Thijssen, J.G.L., Heijden, B.I.J.M.V. der, Rocco, and T.S., 2008. Toward the Employability – Link Model: Current employment transition to future employment perspectives. *Human Resource Development Review* 7, 165–183.

Thite, M. and Russell, B., 2010. The Next Available Agent: Work organization in Indian call centres. *New Technology, Work and Employment* 25, 2–18.

Upadhya, C., 2009. Controlling Offshore Knowledge Workers: Power and agency in India's software outsourcing industry. *New Technology, Work and Employment* 24, 2–18.

Usui, N., 2011. *Transforming the Philippine Economy: 'Walking on Two Legs'*. Asian Development Bank. http://adbdev.org/sites/default/files/publications/28754/file/economics-wp252.pdf. [Accessed 3 October 2014].

Vira, B. and James, A., 2012. Building Cross-Sector Careers in India's New Service Economy? Tracking former call centre agents in the national capital region. *Development and Change* 43, 449–479.

World Bank, 2014. *Philippine Economic Update: Pursuing Inclusive Growth through Sustainable Reconstruction and Job Creation*. World Bank: Washington DC.

11 Corporatisation and standardisation of the security services industry catering to ITES-BPO firms in Mumbai

Randhir Kumar

Introduction

The expanding body of literature on global value chains (GVCs) and global production networks (GPNs) has produced rich insights into the networked structure of production across national boundaries (see Coe *et al.* 2004, Gereffi *et al.* 2005, Henderson *et al.* 2002). The key strength of the GPN framework is its capacity to reveal the spatial configurations, governance structures and regional value capturing practices of cross-border firms. Several studies have analysed how 'lead firms' engage in and foster capacity building and industrial upgrading processes and how local (clusters of) firms are affected (Ernst and Kim 2002, Giuliani *et al.* 2005). These studies, when combined, provide a comprehensive account of GPN governance, embeddedness, upgrading and regional value capture. Notwithstanding these achievements, it has been emphasised that additional research is required to understand the wider societal impacts of GPN operations in a particular local or regional setting (Coe and Hess 2013, Kelly 2013). Most studies analysing the regional outcomes predominantly trace the direct input–output linkages of lead firms, which has raised concerns on how GPN as an analytical framework could tackle place-based changes that are indirectly linked with global production of goods and services (Kelly 2013).

According to Kelly (2013), important local changes are often experienced at some degree of separation from the GPNs themselves. In close relation, Coe and Hess (2013) emphasise that for a more comprehensive understanding of regional outcomes it is essential to look beyond the key production structures and incorporate other place-based changes in the analysis as well. One such additional dimension is the circuit of capital generated through the 'back-end' processes of GPNs. These include the business and employment opportunities created in utility services, such as security, housekeeping and cab services. It is frequently assumed that these opportunities are simply absorbed by the local market, i.e. captured by local utility service providers. Questions as to if and how local utility service markets are affected when GPNs 'touch down' in a local economy are not often raised or researched. Yet, it is probable that such markets are affected, especially in places that experience rapid and intense insertion in GPNs, such as Mumbai. The arrival of substantial numbers of international 'lead firms' in a local economy is likely to generate utility services demand that is new not only in quantitative but also in qualitative terms. International client firms are likely to demand more sophisticated services and adhere to the 'global' utility services standards maintained in the production networks they are part of. Moreover, the arrival of international lead firms may also attract global utility service providers to the local economy. Global utility services firms, such as CBRE, G4S, ISS and TOPSGRUP, have emerged in recent decades to provide seamless and universal standard utility services to global clients in particular. Upon arrival they have the capacity to seriously shake-up and increase competition in local utility service markets. Insertion of a local economy in GPNs, in sum, is likely to trigger changes in both the local practice of utility service delivery (e.g. more sophisticated demand leading to upgrading of service products and processes) and in the staffing of the playing field (e.g. inviting new players to the game). While this creates opportunities for local businesses and the local labour force, it could also lead to local businesses getting crowded out by global firms.

This chapter examines how the arrival and subsequent boom in Mumbai of the ITES-BPO industry has transformed the local security services industry. It is interesting to concentrate on the security service industry for two reasons. First, security is an important aspect for ITES-BPO firms. The activities that are offshored often involve privacy-sensitive information (e.g. payroll data, medical files, credit card details etc.) that companies do not like to see compromised. Most, if not all, ITES-BPO firms dealing with sensitive data apply strict and extensive security standards and procedures to ensure that no physical or virtual security breaches occur at their premises (Oshri *et al.* 2011). Kleibert (2014: 15) observes that many international ITES-BPO firms (in Mumbai) are like heavily guarded fortresses and secretive about their business details. Such an approach towards information and physical security stimulates demand for security services that match the expected benchmark of ITES-BPO firms. Second, the international ITES-BPO firms have triggered a transformation in security services, where local security enterprises have gradually been adopting features of big corporate businesses. Large multinational corporations currently dominate the segment of providing security solutions for ITES-BPO firms. The main question stated above is explored by identifying: a) the requirements firms must meet to become the preferred security service provider for an international ITES-BPO service firm; and b) the perceptions of local security service providers as to their opportunities to serve international client firms, specifically in the context of the emerging global standards in security services.

The chapter is structured as follows. The section below summarises the theory used for this study. What follows is a description of the fieldwork site and the methodology used for collecting the empirical data. Next, the critical factors and prerequisites for having access to international firm's service contracts are identified, followed by a discussion on emerging global standards and the position of local vendors in the overall private security industry of Mumbai. The concluding section comments on the emerging transformation in the private security service industry in Mumbai and identifies new avenues for research.

Corporatisation of the security sector and emergence of global standards in service delivery

With more industries and sectors taking the shape of GPNs, the incentives for lower-order, client-following service providers to corporatise and go global become stronger. There have been changes in the world economic scenario for international business as the firm-specific assets are becoming mobile across national boundaries (Dunning 2009). With the expansion of global capital, the private security corporations (PSCs) too have become transnational and expanded their outreach, especially in fast-growing markets of developing countries (Abrahamsen and Williams 2009). There are some basic differences in the motives for internationalisation between ITES-BPO and security firms. While the locational decision of ITES-BPO firms is influenced by a combination of resource-seeking, market-seeking, efficiency-seeking and strategic asset-seeking motives (see Dunning 2009), security service multinational enterprises (MNEs), such as Group4Securicor (G4S), largely expanded across the world through client-following motives and seeking new markets. For example, the impetus for international security agencies such as Securitas to enter the Indian market was propelled by their multinational clients who expanded in India (Talwar 2014).

Traditionally, transnationalisation was the exclusive domain of manufacturing and technology-related service activities. In the past two decades, low-end utility services, such as private security and housekeeping, have taken a similar trajectory and expanded their service delivery across borders. In the early 1990s, the utility service sector in the United Kingdom (UK) became dominated by a few corporate firms, who later evolved into large, transnational corporations. Three corporate firms held 60 per cent market share in the security segment, while only five firms accounted for a third of the cleaning services contracts in the UK (Castree *et al.* 2003). At present, the world's largest private security corporation, G4S operates in more than 120 countries and employs around 620,000 people. It features in the FTSE 100 index and reported a total turnover of £7.4 billion in 2013 (G4S 2013). The global private contract security services market had total revenue of US$188.9 billion in 2012 and according to estimates by Freedonia (2013) it will be a US$244 billion industry by 2016. The World Trade Organization has enabled the international expansion of G4S and similar firms through the General Agreement on Trade in Services (GATS), which allowed for greater international competition in security service delivery (Abrahamsen and Williams 2008). In India, the liberalisation is said to have changed the face of private security from a traditionally unorganised workforce to well-managed manpower. In order to attract foreign players, prior to 2005, the Government of India had allowed 100 per cent foreign direct investment in the private security sector.

Compliance with global standards is now a *sine qua non* for entry into globalised production networks (Nadvi 2008). In businesses having a global outreach, adopting certain standard processes and protocols are beneficial in two ways. First it provides a common language for the participants in global supply chains and introduces an 'external point of reference' for intermediate goods and service providers (Hawkins *et al.* 1995). As the service or product quality can vary from provider to provider, having 'global standards' facilitates the transnational firms in maintaining the expected quality across locations (Kleindl 2006). With the emergence of global firms in security services, such as G4S and Securitas, security services and products are increasingly being standardised at the global level. These firms, who distinguish themselves with recognisable logos and uniforms, have introduced their own process and quality standards, which has been referred as 'McDonaldisation' of security services (van Steden and de Waard 2013). The second benefit of adopting global standards is in securing business opportunities. Meeting international product, process and labour standards has become essential for becoming a supplier for lead firms and integration in GPNs (Nadvi *et al.* 2011, Nadvi and Waltring 2004, Ponte and Gibbon 2005). Specifically in the case of developing countries, the lead firm's supplier selection policy and delivery parameters are increasingly dependent on the ability to match the expected product or service quality and labour standards (Hawkins *et al.* 1995).

To monitor highly dispersed suppliers, lead firms have put in place various auditory and certification measures (Nadvi *et al.* 2004, Tewari and Pillai 2005). While first party (auditory) certification relies solely on self-monitoring, second party certification shifts monitoring to trade bodies or users of products and services. In case of third party certification, the monitoring is transferred to neutral and independent auditors (Hawkins *et al.* 1995). There is a range of actors engaged in defining and certifying operational standards, including private business associations, chambers of commerce, civil society, trade unions and consumer groups (Nadvi and Waltring, 2004). Among them, an important organisation in devising standards is the ISO (International Organisation for Standardisation), which includes national standards organisations from 138 countries (Nadvi and Waltring 2004). In order to boost business opportunities and positive image creation, many low-end service providers apply for the independent certifications such as ISO (Brody 2006).

Although there are merits of having global standards, the idea has also met criticism. The key issue involves the 'initiators' of standards and its implications on the participation of local firms. It has been observed that while developing countries' enterprises are expected to comply with global standards, they have little say in devising them (Dicken 2010, Nadvi and Waltring 2004, Schmitz 2004). Global standards have been criticised for often being explicitly or implicitly devised along Northern priorities, which fail to incorporate Southern stakeholders views (Blowfield and Dolan 2008, Tallontire 2007). Another concern is related to the unintended consequences of erecting market access barriers for local players who lack the capacity to comply with global standards (Neilson and Pritchard 2010). The codes of conduct have implications for who can comply successfully with global standards. Large corporate firms are generally well equipped to meet the standards, while it constrains the participation of small independent entities based in developing countries as they are not always capable of upgrading.

Methodology

This research is based on semi-structured interviews conducted during the period November 2012 to July 2013. A total of 42 semi-structured interviews were conducted with 23 representatives of international ITES-BPO firms and independent security consultants, and 19 representatives from various types of security service providers. Through this selection it was possible to get both the client perspective and the service providers' viewpoint. The international ITES-BPO service firms with an office in Mumbai were identified from NASSCOM's database. The security officers and security consultants of ITES-BPO firms were interviewed to understand the process of selecting vendors (i.e. the security service providers). Further questions focused on quality requirements, benchmarking, auditing and maintenance of service standards.

For vendors serving ITES-BPO firms, questions focused on the method of approaching the clients and negotiation processes to obtain service contracts. Details on expected service standards, compliance, competition and level of professionalism in delivering the solutions were also discussed. For the vendors who did not serve the ITES-BPO firms, questions concentrated on the entry barriers experienced and on the perceived business opportunities. Interviews took between 20 to 60 minutes and were mostly recorded and transcribed. In some cases, where recording was not permitted, notes were taken and written out on the same day.

Overview of Mumbai's private security industry

With flexible global sourcing and production structures, the risks of operating in unfamiliar environments have increased, which demands integrated security solutions ranging from intelligence, risk analysis, security system design, manned guarding, electronic and information security and emergency response services (Abrahamsen and Williams 2009). For their security needs, international ITES-BPO firms in Mumbai typically have one regional security head along with a couple of security officers directly on their payroll. Their ground-level security personnel are sourced through third party vendors such as G4S or Securitas. The alternate model is that even the security head and the subordinate officers are on the payroll of a facilities management agency (e.g. CB Richard Ellis Group) and security vendors provide the lower-ranked personnel.

Before the 1990s, the security service industry in India was highly fragmented. A plethora of low-quality, poorly managed private security enterprises dominated the field. Before economic liberalisation of India in 1991, the private security service domain was shielded from international competition and the sector did not witness a marked improvement in quality or service standards. Respondents emphasised that the concepts of electronic and information security were largely unknown and the typical image of a private security guard was that of an unskilled, poorly educated, rural migrant guarding a premise. With the liberalisation in 1991, the entry of both international ITES-BPO service firms and private security corporations (PSCs) was enabled. This had substantial impact on the growth trajectory of the Indian security service industry. The economic developments in sectors such as infrastructure and retail, together with robust growth in financial services, IT parks, industrial complexes contributed to rising demand for higher-quality security services. International PSCs entered the Indian market and simultaneously a few big Indian security firms also emerged. These big firms, by lobbying hard, managed to get the Private Security Agencies Regulation Act (PSARA Act) adopted in 2005 and so curbed the mushrooming of new substandard security firms. In 2013, the Indian private security service industry was estimated to be worth about $6.15 billion (FICCI-EY 2013).

Three segments of vendors/service providers engaged in delivering security services can be identified in Mumbai. Most prominent are the corporate firms of both foreign and Indian origin. These firms have operations in Mumbai as a part of their pan-Indian or global operations. Due to their widespread business activities, the number of employees and the revenue generation is substantial (see Table 11.1). The second segment comprises the state government run security firm called Maharashtra State Guard Board (MSGB). The outreach of MSGB is limited to Mumbai and some other districts of Maharashtra and it primarily serves the security needs of government offices. MSGB acts both as a regulatory authority and as a security service provider for the city of Mumbai. According to MSGB Act of 1981, it is mandatory for both the private security vendors and their clients to seek an exemption from MSGB. This means that when client firms want to hire security services from private security providers, they must seek permission from MSGB and pay a levy. The corporate security firms and MSGB have a relatively long history of operation and their details on yearly turnover, number of branches and employee strength have been compiled in Table 11.1. The third segment of the security service industry constitutes the numerous small agencies with only local operations. They mostly cater to low-end clients such as residential complexes, small offices, warehouses, budget hotels etc.

Security demands of ITES-BPO firms and access to business opportunities

Various respondents highlighted that for a vendor to become the preferred security service provider for an international ITES-BPO firm, four prerequisites must be met. First is the ability to deliver security services across India and/or across the world. Second is the capacity to maintain pre-specified service standards. Third is the ability to comply with local labour standards. Fourth is being able to act as a one-stop solution for multiple support service needs. These four factors have initiated a series of transformations in the security service industry of Mumbai (and India in general), as presently these criteria have become an operational benchmark for being considered a professional player in the security service industry. These factors also have strong implications for the type of vendors who could enter into a business agreement with ITES-BPO firms.

The first service criterion for serving ITES-BPO firms is to have pan-Indian or global operations. Client firms have standardised their security parameters across all their international or pan-Indian offices, and therefore it is typical for ITES-BPO firms to have a single global (or pan-Indian) partner for catering to the security needs at multiple locations. Business deals with multi-office ITES-BPO firms are usually negotiated centrally and later executed in specific regions. With

Table 11.1 Corporate players in the Mumbai private (contractual) security sector

Name of security service provider	*Headquarters*	*No. of employees*	*Turnover yearly (US$)*	*Year of est. and no. of branches in India*	*Certifications*
G4S	Crawley (UK)	657,000 (global), 160,000 (India)	11.07 billion (2012)	1989 200	ISO 9000: 2001, QMS (BSI)
TOPSGRUP	London (UK)	100,000 (global)	50.98 million (2011)	1990 70 branches	ISO 9001: 2008
NISA	Mumbai (India)	45,000 (India)	41.70 million (2012)	1973 45 branches	ISO 9001: 2008
SIS	Mumbai (India)	60,000 (India)	108.69 million (2012)	1973 75 branches	ISO 9001: 2000, BS 7499, BS 7858
BIS	Mumbai (India)	50,000 (India)	53.37 million (2012)	1976 53 branches	ISO 9001–2008
MSGB	Mumbai (India)	70,000 (Mumbai and Thane)	73.29 million (2012)	1981 5 branches (only Mumbai)	State government undertaking
ISS-SDB	Singapore	530,000 (Global), 26,000 (India)	14.74 billion, (2012)	1901 72 branches	ISO 9001: 2000

Source: Company websites.

their financial ability and locational outreach, corporate security service providers secure most ITES-BPO firms' contracts. In addition to international PSCs, Indian players too have been focusing on expansion and improving their outreach by covering an increasing number of cities. This is a marked shift in the Indian security service industry, as prior to the 1990s, security firms were mostly localised and city specific. Dealing with a single partner reduces administrative hassle and provides an opportunity for longer-term strategic collaboration. As the security officer of an international investment banking firm put it:

> Go to our Bangkok office or New Delhi office and you won't find much difference. You will get the same security checks and protocols in all our locations. We have standardized the whole system and therefore prefer to have a single global partner who is aware of our needs. We are global players and

of course would prefer someone of our stature (here G4S) to serve as security vendor.

(Security head of a foreign investment bank in Mumbai, interview 18 March 2013)

The corporate vendors are also required to have the capacity to scale up or scale down the operations. In cases where the client firms decide to have a new office space, or close down operations from a location, the vendors are expected to flexibly cater to the changing requirements. The vendors are also required to supply additional guards for occasional events and summits. At times, the client firms have a policy of sourcing global services from a particular vendor and even if other competent players are locally available at cheaper rates, the contracts will still be awarded to the pre-specified vendor.

The second service criterion concerns the quality of service delivery. Once selected for the task, the vendor is informed by the security officer of an ITES-BPO firm about the services standard he is expected to deliver. For instance, the security officer prepares a detailed quality requirement (QR) of security guards' physical attributes and educational qualifications to be provided by the vendors. This requires PSCs to improve their recruitment strategy and workforce management practices, which were previously a lesser priority. Good-quality service and security personnel are costly and ITES-BPO firms are willing to pay above market rates to obtain the desired quality of service and personnel. Table 11.2 provides an outline of the charges of guards hired from different types of security service providers in Mumbai. Hiring a guard from MSGB is cheaper but ITES-BPO firms tend to avoid the MSGB due to its cumbersome and bureaucratic mode of operation. They prefer to seek exemption and pay a levy for getting permission to hire, in their opinion, more qualified guards from corporate vendors.

Corporate vendor firms assure a high quality of service delivery by securing relevant international process certifications from agencies such as the ISO and BSI (British Standards Institution). Before the arrival of international client firms, the

Table 11.2 Rates charged and wages paid by different types of security vendors

Type of service provider and their client base	*Guard rates charged to clients per month (in US$)*	*Guards' wages per month in US$)*
Corporate firms serving offshore firms/MNEs	486.34 (approx.)	194.54–243.17
MSGB* having government offices as clients	291.81	162.11
Local firms having residential complexities as clients	113.48–129.69	81.06–97.27

Source: MSGB website and field data.

Note: *While the charges of corporate and local firms are negotiable, the MSGB has fixed charges and a pay scale for their security guards.

local PSCs usually did not invest much in branding and getting recognition/certifications from independent authorities. At present almost all Indian corporate security firms have obtained the necessary certification as part of positive self-projection or a promotional strategy. There are several other standard certifications that are directly relevant for security services. A detailed listing of the process certifications of different types of vendors in Mumbai has been compiled in Table 11.3.

Having certifications for various delivery parameters imbibes a sense of confidence among clients about the reliability of service provision. The quality of service delivery is further maintained by regular internal and external (third party) audits. The audit reports play a role in subsequent renewal of service contracts of the prevailing service provider.

The third criterion for selecting a service provider involves their ability to adhere to labour standards. The Indian security service industry is known for its poor implementation of labour standards. Most notable, the unorganised PSCs catering to small clients (e.g. residential complexes) indulge in workforce exploitation practices (Boga 2012). Some Indian corporate PSCs have transformed themselves by paying more attention to compliance with labour standards. This shift is motivated by the auditory requirements and ethical guidelines of the international client firms, which require vendors to assure that they do not violate local labour

Table 11.3 Global process standards of offshore security service firms

Compliances and their nature (mandatory/voluntary but beneficial)	*Corporate vendors*	*MSGB*	*Local vendors*
ISO 9001:2008 QMS certified by the BSI (voluntary but beneficial)	Yes	No	No
Social welfare benefits (mandatory)	Yes	Yes	Yes (to a limited extent)
Single point of contact (mandatory)	Yes	No	No
Capacity to pass internal and external (third party) audits (mandatory)	Yes	Yes	No
Use of modern technology (walkie-talkie, scanner, CCTV, computers, alarms)	Yes	Yes (to a limited extent)	No
Training (high quality)	Yes	No	No
IFPO for key managers and security officers	Yes	No	No
RoHS (Restriction of use of hazardous substances) compliant security hardware products	Yes	No	No
International standards in electronic and fire security systems, such as UL (Underwriters Laboratories), CE (Conformité Européene), VdS (Verband der Sachversicherer) etc.	Yes	No	No

Source: Company websites and field data.

laws. This is of vital importance for reputation-conscious international client firms, who as principle employers do not wish to get into legal issues caused by erroneous behaviour by their local service providers. Indian labour law deems the principal employer responsible when the vendor fails to timely deposit the Provident Fund and Employee State Insurance Corporation contributions of contractual security guards. Therefore, other than undertaking due diligence to supervise deposition of mandatory benefits, the ITES-BPO firms usually choose service providers who have a good reputation of complying with labour standards.

The fourth parameter for selecting vendors is the ability to provide a variety of support services such as housekeeping and building/facilities management services. A vendor that can provide multiple services is usually preferred over those who could only provide security services. The trend of diversifying into allied activities is becoming common among corporate players who are trying to transform from mere 'security service providers' to providers of a 'one-stop solution' for all low-end utility service needs. For instance, G4S not only provides security solutions, but has also ventured into activities such as provision of housekeeping, building management and cab drivers, directly or through sister companies. Similarly, Indian corporate firms, such as SIS, have also diversified their service portfolio for additional value capture from their existing client base. The branch head of a prominent Indian corporate security service provider noted:

> We consider housekeeping and building management as an allied service, so other than security, our marketing person also offers housekeeping and other building management services to client. Since we provide a single contact point for coordinating with the client firms, it is hassle free administration for them.
>
> (Branch head of an Indian corporate security service provider, interview 12 February 2013)

Perceptions of local firms of global standards and certifications

With the emergence of global standards another issue is how local service providers perceive the opportunities to serve international client firms. Local firms in most cases lack the ability to upgrade and deliver the required service quality. The small local service providers are also constrained in securing the necessary certifications from the various certifying agencies mentioned in Table 11.3, often also because of financial reasons. The special emphasis placed by ITES-BPO firms on following global standards in security service delivery has raised the entry barriers for local players and further curtailed their chances to compete.

Small local firms also lack the necessary funds and expertise to provide the required level of workforce training or invest in professional management. From the interviews with managers and owners of local security service providers, it became clear that they do not see the ITES-BPO firms as potential clients. Their business model is focused on serving the lower-profit, cost-conscious market segments such as residential complexes, warehouses, small hotels, and local offices. As emphasised by a manager of a small local vendor:

> We don't reach to the customer base of large MNCs. We simply can't compete with big players who are brand names and are strategically placed in the industry. We don't have capacity to fulfil their [MNC] requirements and have to be content with small assignments, involving limited number of people and a thin profit margin.
>
> (Manager of a local security vendor, interview 4 February 2013)

When the ITES-BPO firm's security heads were asked about hiring local security providers, the responses were unanimously negative. This was because decision-making is not always done at the regional office in Mumbai and choosing a local player would require some serious reasoning. The bias towards corporate firms was articulated by the security officer of a foreign ITES-BPO firm:

> What is the value add provided by the local vendor, which our global vendor can't provide? Ok, the local vendor can be cheaper but that is not the only criteria for choosing our service providers. We don't run behind petty gains. It's not only that we hire a branded player on basis of their name and fame but they also work hard to maintain the quality of service delivery through regular supervision and feedback.
>
> (Security officer of a US-based bank in Mumbai, interview 27 September 2012)

It is common for lead firms in GPNs to exercise various forms of power over the other chain actors and make decisions about which other actors (contractors, suppliers etc.) will access the chain and under what conditions (Bair 2008, Humphrey and Schmitz 2002). The decision-making powers are often located at a distance, meaning that the decision-makers have limited knowledge of or interest in local providers, which put the latter in a disadvantageous position. The inability of local firms to access this market has strengthened the 'corporatisation' of security services catering to the international ITES-BPO firms. This selective access to the indirect business opportunities of ITES-BPO firms has further widened the gap between corporate and small (local) vendors. Unlike manufacturing GPNs, there is neither 'crowding in' (i.e. growth of new domestic security service providers catering to ITES-BPO firms) nor 'crowding out' (exit) of local small firms (see Moran 1998, Shepherd and Stone 2013). Instead, in the case of Mumbai, ITES-BPO firms have amplified the divide between the corporate and local players engaged in the security service industry.

Conclusion

The arrival of international ITES-BPO firms to Mumbai has brought about several transformations in the city's security services industry. With the international ITES-

BPO firms came international security providers who have stimulated upgrading of the managerial and operational structure for quality service delivery and improved compliance with labour standards. The upcoming trend among the service providers is to showcase a process-driven approach through securing various certifications from private accreditation agencies. Another key change in the industry is that the corporate players are diversifying into related segments (e.g. housekeeping and building management services), thus promoting themselves as a 'one-stop solution' for all support service needs. Corporate security firms invest in reputation (brand) building and networking, which helps them to secure profitable contracts of ITES-BPO firms. The corporatisation of the security sector has led indigenous Indian corporate security firms to expand their international presence. For instance, SIS security, in an attempt to go global, has acquired Chubb security of Australia. Likewise, TOPSGRUP is trying to improve its international presence by opening new offices abroad and shifting the firm's headquarter from India to UK.

This chapter has highlighted the competitive advantages of corporate vendors that enable them to secure service contracts of international ITES-BPO firms. While the organised corporate PSCs have successfully upgraded to cater to international clients' demands, the local, small and unorganised players are still far behind. Small local players cannot meet the service standards set by independent certifying agencies. Small local players are also unable to invest in upgrading and securing the necessary certifications or the desired quality of workforce and managerial staff. The entry of corporate vendors (both national and global) and the stringent service criteria of ITES-BPO firms make it difficult for small local security agencies to compete. Even if there are competent local vendors present, still the corporate firms will bag the contracts due to higher level of trust placed on them. It is evident that only handful of global and Indian (corporate) players are discretely benefitting from the business opportunities generated through the 'back-end' processes of service GPNs. The local implication of international ITES-BPO firms is that they have amplified the segmentation between big corporate and small local security service providers. Further research should focus on how the operations of ITES-BPO firms have affected other segments of support service providers (viz. facilities management and cab services). It might also explore how the job terms and benefits of support service workers (security guards, cleaners and cab drivers) are influenced by the labour policies of the international ITES-BPO firms.

References

Abrahamsen, R. and Williams, M.C. (2008). Public/Private, Global/Local: The Changing Contours of Africa's Security Governance. *Review of African Political Economy*, *35*(118), 539–553. doi:10.1080/03056240802569219

Abrahamsen, R. and Williams, M.C. (2009). Security Beyond the State: Global Security Assemblages in International Politics. *International Political Sociology*, *3*(1), 1–17. doi:10.1111/j.1749-5687.2008.00060.x

Bair, J. (2008). Analysing Global Economic Organization: Embedded Networks and Global Chains Compared. *Economy and Society*, *37*(3), 339–364. doi:10.1080/030851408 02172664

Blowfield, M.E. and Dolan, C.S. (2008). Stewards of Virtue? The Ethical Dilemma of CSR in African Agriculture. *Development and Change*, *39*(1), 1–23. doi:10.1111/j.1467-7660.2008.00465.x
Boga, D. (2012). Mumbai security men working in worst of conditions. *Daily News Analysis*, 23 July Mumbai. www.dnaindia.com/mumbai/report-mumbai-security-men-working-in-worst-of-conditions-1718479
Brody, A. (2006). The Cleaners You Aren't Meant to See: Order, Hygiene and Everyday Politics in a Bangkok Shopping Mall. *Antipode*, *38*(3), 534–556.
Castree, N., Coe, N., Ward, K. and Samers, M. (2003). *Spaces of Work: Global Capitalism and Geographies of Labour*. London: SAGE.
Coe, N.M. and Hess, M. (2013). Global Production Networks, Labour and Development. *Geoforum*, *44*, 4–9. doi:10.1016/j.geoforum.2012.08.003
Coe, N.M., Hess, M., Yeung, H.W., Dicken, P. and Henderson, J. (2004). 'Globalizing' Regional Development: A Global Production Networks Perspective. *Transactions of the Institute of British Geographers*, *29*(4), 468–484.
Dicken, P. (2010). *Global Shift: Mapping the Changing Contours of the World Economy*. London: SAGE.
Dunning, J.H. (2009). Location and the Multinational Enterprise: A Neglected Factor? *Journal of International Business Studies*, *40*(1), 5–19. doi:10.1057/jibs.2008.74
Ernst, D. and Kim, L. (2002). Global Production Networks, Knowledge Diffusion, and Local Capability Formation. *Research Policy*, *31*(8–9), 1417–1429. doi:10.1016/S0048-7333(02)00072-0
FICCI-EY (2013). *Private Security Services Industry: Securing Future Growth*. New Delhi: FICCI-EY. http://ficci.com/publication-page.asp?spid=20329
Freedonia (2013). *World Security Services to 2016*. www.freedoniagroup.com/World-Security-Services.html
G4S (2013). *Annual Report and Accounts 2013*. West Sussex: G4S. www.g4s.com/~/media/3A387C7DC35049C6950D738F6AEBDB88.ashx
Gereffi, G., Humphrey, J. and Sturgeon, T. (2005). The Governance of Global Value Chains. *Review of International Political Economy*, *12*(1), 78–104. doi:10.1080/096922905 00049805
Giuliani, E., Pietrobelli, C. and Rabellotti, R. (2005). Upgrading in Global Value Chains: Lessons from Latin American Clusters. *World Development*, *33*(4), 549–573. doi:10.1016/j.worlddev.2005.01.002
Hawkins, R., Mansell, R., Skea, J., Mansell, R. and Skea, J. (1995). *Standards, Innovation and Competitiveness: The Politics and Economics of Standards in Natural and Technical Environments*. Cheltenham: Edward Elgar.
Henderson, J., Dicken, P., Hess, M., Coe, N. and Yeung, H. W.-C. (2002). Global Production Networks and the Analysis of Economic Development. *Review of International Political Economy*, *9*(3), 436–464. doi:10.1080/09692290210150842
Humphrey, J. and Schmitz, H. (2002). How Does Insertion in Global Value Chains Affect Upgrading in Industrial Clusters? *Regional Studies*, *36*(9), 1017–1027.
Kelly, P.F. (2013). Production Networks, Place and Development: Thinking through Global Production Networks in Cavite, Philippines. *Geoforum*, *44*, 82–92. doi:10.1016/j.geoforum.2011.10.003
Kleibert, J.M. (2014). *Islands of Globalisation: Changing Spatial Divisions of Labour and Enclavisation*. Amsterdam: UVA. Retrieved from http://urbanstudies.uva.nl/working-papers/working-papers/working-papers/content/folder/working-paper-series-no.07.html

Kleindl, B. (2006). *International Marketing* (1st edn). Mason, OH: Thomson Spouth-Western

Moran, T.H. (1998). *Foreign Direct Investment and Development: The New Policy Agenda for Developing Countries and Economies in Transition*. Washington DC: Peterson Institute for International Economics.

Nadvi, K. (2008). Global Standards, Global Governance and the Organization of Global Value Chains. *Journal of Economic Geography*, *8*(3), 323–343. doi:10.1093/jeg/lbn003

Nadvi, K., Lund-Thomsen, P., Xue, H. and Khara, N. (2011). Playing Against China: Global Value Chains and Labour Standards in the International Sports Goods Industry. *Global Networks*, *11*(3), 334–354. doi:10.1111/j.1471-0374.2011.00329.x

Nadvi, K., Thoburn, J., Thang, B.T., Ha, N.T.T., Hoa, N.T. and Le, D.H. (2004). Challenges to Vietnamese Firms in the World Garment and Textile Value Chain, and the Implications for Alleviating Poverty. *Journal of the Asia Pacific Economy*, *9*(2), 249–267. doi:10.1080/1354786042000207362

Nadvi, K. and Waltring, F. (2004). Making Sense of Global Standards. In H. Schmitz (ed.), *Local Enterprises in the Global Economy: Issues of Governance and Upgrading*. Cheltenham: Edward Elgar.

Neilson, J. and Pritchard, B. (2010). Fairness and Ethicality in their Place: The regional dynamics of fair trade and ethical sourcing agendas in the plantation districts of South India. *Environment and Planning A*, *42*(8), 1833–1851.

Oshri, I., Kotlarsky, J. and Willcocks, L.P. (2011). *The Handbook of Global Outsourcing and Offshoring*. New York: Palgrave Macmillan.

Ponte, S. and Gibbon, P. (2005). Quality Standards, Conventions and the Governance of Global Value Chains. *Economy and Society*, *34*(1), 1–31. doi:10.1080/0308514042000329315

Schmitz, H. (2004). Globalised Localities: Introduction. In H. Schmitz (ed.), *Local Enterprises In The Global Economy*. Cheltenham: Edward Elgar Publishing.

Shepherd, B. and Stone, S.F. (2013). *Global Production Networks and Employment: A Developing Country Perspective*. OECD Trade Policy Papers, No. 154. OECD Publishing. http://dx.doi.org/10.1787/5k46j0rjq9s8-en

Tallontire, A. (2007). CSR and Regulation: Towards a framework for understanding private standards initiatives in the agri-food chain. *Third World Quarterly*, *28*(4), 775–791. doi:10.1080/01436590701336648

Talwar, B. (2014). Private security management firms mushroom in Gurgaon. *The Economic Times*, 9 January. http://articles.economictimes.indiatimes.com/2014-01-09/news/46030224_1_security-solution-private-security-security-service

Tewari, M. and Pillai, P. (2005). Global Standards and the Dynamics of Environmental Compliance in India's Leather Industry. *Oxford Development Studies*, *33*(2), 245–267. doi:10.1080/13600810500137947

Van Steden, R. and de Waard, J. (2013). 'Acting like chameleons': On the McDonaldization of Private Security. *Security Journal*, *26*(3), 294–309. doi:10.1057/sj.2013.18

Part IV

Offshore services and the making of a new middle class

12 The rise of India's new middle class and the role of offshoring of services

Neeraj Hatekar and Kishore More

Introduction

In recent years, the middle class has been a focus of much critical commentary across the world. Countries such as India, Brazil, China and South Africa have seen an unprecedented rise in the number of people who have risen out of poverty in recent years. This is a significant development in as much as it represents a large number of people who are no longer poor, or at least less vulnerable to economic shocks. The increasing size of the new middle class has led researchers and policy makers to ask questions about the role of these classes in promoting democracy, strengthening institutions and encouraging inclusiveness. The politics of the new middle class has also been extensively commented upon. In Tunisia, Egypt, Turkey, Brazil and India, recent protests have been led not by the poor, but by the middle class, by people with higher than average incomes (Fukuyama 2012). The business world too, has been excited about the rise of a 'global middle class' for a little over a decade now. A Goldman Sachs report indicated that spending by the world's middle three quintiles will rise from the current 31 per cent to around 50 per cent of the world's income by 2050 (Wilson and Dragusanu, 2008). Among commentators of the new middle class in India, it is common to connect the rise of the new middle class with the onset of the process of economic reforms in 1991 (Fernandes 2006). After the economic reforms, the Indian economy opened out substantially, increasingly trading with the rest of the world. Exports of services, in particular offshoring services, have been an important component of India's economic policy post-liberalization.

Offshoring of services could, in principle, contribute to an expansion of the middle class in developing countries. The key idea is that offshoring creates significant livelihood opportunities, both direct as well as indirect, which in turn allow the poor to climb out of poverty and join the middle classes. Employment in the offshoring sector has been expanding. Table 12.1 indicates the volume of employment generated by offshoring services.

In 2014, the sector is expected to provide direct employment to 3.1 million people, and added to this, an estimated 10 million people are employed in an indirect fashion (NASSCOM 2014). This means that for every one job directly generated, the sector generates 3.2 indirect livelihood opportunities.

Given the sizeable employment effects generated by the offshore service sector, its role in giving rise to a new middle class has been a matter of considerable

Table 12.1 Professionals employed in the Indian ITES-BPO sector

	2006	*2007*	*2008*	*2009*	*2010F**
IT services and software exports	513,000	690,000	877,000	958,000	993,000
BPO exports	415,000	553,000	635,000	738,000	768,000
Domestic market	365,000	378,000	450,000	500,000	525,000
Total	1,293,000	1,621,000	1,962,000	2,196,000	2,286,000

Source: NASSCOM (2010).
Note: F* = Forecast.

interest. A strand of this literature focuses on the cultural transformation that new workers in the sector have to undergo in order to become a 'global service worker'. In the process, the literature argues, the worker undergoes a significant transformation in cultural outlook and consumption patterns, thereby producing and reproducing the 'new middle class' (Sandhu 2008). For India, NASSCOM estimates that 58 per cent of the workforce in the offshore sector comes from second- and third-tier cities in India. Infosys, one of the largest recruiters in the sector, in 2010 claimed that 40 per cent of their new recruits came from rural backgrounds, with a majority of them having one or more parents having dropped out of education before finishing high school (Rastogi and Pradhan 2011).

The significance of the offshore service industry as a provider of opportunities notwithstanding, how important is its role in creating a new middle class in India? This is the principle question that this chapter deals with. In addition, there are a host of sub-questions that we look at. Do people automatically become 'middle class' when provided with well-paying jobs, irrespective of the social strata from which they originate? Which forms of social, cultural and economic capital (such as education, credentials, skills) determine the chances of becoming part of the new middle class? More importantly, who are the new middle class? Fernandes (2006) identifies this group as structurally consisting mainly of English-speaking urban white-collar segments of the middle class who are benefiting from new employment opportunities. But as Fernandes herself is quick to clarify, the heart of the construction of this social group rests on the implicit assumption that other social groups including an upwardly mobile working class can join this segment by adopting specific cultural markers like the purchase of particular commodities and brands that signify upward mobility. However, is a rise in income inevitably linked to the acquisition of the social and cultural trappings that are associated with the middle class? What are the potentialities within various social groups that are upwardly mobile to become new middle class in this sense? Do all such groups always end up becoming middle class or is there some contingency involved? Do all upwardly mobile social groups necessarily deploy the kind of economic and cultural capital on their way up or is the adaption of such markers conditional on certain kinds of in-group dynamics? These are important questions. In particular, we are interested in knowing how empirically valid is Fernandes's characterization of the new middle class as those consisting primarily English-speaking urban white-collared segments? Or are the groups forming the new middle class different from these?

How does one test empirically this type of questions? Typically, the data available in the Indian context are a single cross-section of observations rather than a panel. In any case, 'upwardly mobile' is an elusive concept when it comes to concrete situations. The same social group, or even the household, might face several vicissitudes in a cyclical fashion over time. Its economic fortunes might wax and wane, being temporarily upward or downwardly mobile, making identification in a single cross-section quite difficult. It might be better, when we only have a single cross-section of observations, to restrict ourselves to those who are way above the poverty line, in the sense of being 'comfortably non-poor' – those who have not yet made that transition to using the cultural, social and economic markers of the existing middle class. So the important question, from an empirical testing point of view is regarding the potential among those groups who are not poor, or are well above poverty line, in becoming new middle class. What are the constraints and potentialities for these groups to deploy the various types of social, cultural and economic capital, and consume the kind of commodities and services that would mark them as new middle class? In the context of urban India, who are these groups? The chapter first examines this question in an all India context, for rural as well as urban India, using National Sample Survey data on Consumption Expenditure for 2004–2005 and 2011–2012. The chapter then looks at a detailed case study of primary data on unorganized sector households in Mumbai (Bombay) collected in 2011.

How many are the new middle class?

All observers agree that there has been a substantial expansion of the middle class in India in recent times. An influential definition of the middle class in terms of per day per capita expenditure has been proposed by Bannerjee and Duflo (2007). Drawing upon a survey of 13 developing countries, Bannerjee and Duflo define the lower middle class as those who have a per capita daily consumption expenditure between US$2 and $4 in 1993 purchasing power parity (PPP) prices.

According to the Bannerjee-Duflo scheme, various classes are defined as follows (all measurements are in 1993 PPP prices):

- Lower class: Daily per capita consumption expenditure less than $2
- Middle class: Daily per capita consumption expenditure between $2 and $10
- Lower middle class: Daily per capita consumption expenditure between $2 and $4
- Upper middle class: Daily per capita consumption expenditure between $6 and $10
- Upper class: Daily per capita consumption expenditure above $10

At an all India level, we have figures for consumption expenditure categories based on the data provided by the qinquennial rounds on consumption expenditure conducted by the National Sample Survey Organisation (NSSO). In this chapter, we use the data provided by the NSSO 55th Round for the year 1999–2000, 61st round for the year 2004–2005 and the 68th round for the year 2011–2012. Using the PPP exchange rate data for 1993, the above figures were converted from US dollars to Indian rupees (Rs). We then used the GDP deflator to calculate the corresponding figures for the years 1999–2000, 2004–2005 and 2011–2012. The final figures in Rs, corresponding to the relevant cut-offs for the various rounds are thus:

- 2011–2012 prices (NSSO 68th round)
  - \$2=Rs39.46
  - \$4= Rs78.92
  - \$6= Rs118.38
  - \$10= Rs197.30
- 2004–2005 prices (NSSO 61st round):
  - \$2= Rs24.68
  - \$4= Rs49.36
  - \$6= Rs74.04
  - \$10= Rs123.40
- 1999–2000 prices (NSSO 55th round):
  - \$2= Rs20.34
  - \$4= Rs40.68
  - \$6= Rs61.02
  - \$10= Rs101.70

Using these figures, we can examine the changes in the size of the middle class over the corresponding years (Table 12.2).

These figures reveal some striking facts. Most importantly, middle class expansion did not automatically happen with India's economic liberalization. India began its economic reforms process in 1991. But between 1999–2000 and 2004–2005, we do not see a substantial expansion of the middle class. In fact, the relative size of the middle class underwent a marginal decline in this period at an all India level from 28.95 per cent of the population to 27.9 per cent of the population. There was actually a relative increase in the size of the lower classes. There was a

Table 12.2 Class composition of Indian population 1999–2000 (per cent)

Class	*All India*	*Rural*	*Urban*
Lower	70.68	79.63	44.03
Middle	28.95	20.29	54.70
Lower middle	23.61	18.28	39.46
Upper middle	1.46	0.41	4.61
Upper	0.38	0.08	1.27

Source: NSSO: 55th Round.

Table 12.3 Class composition of Indian population 2004–2005 (per cent)

Class	*All India*	*Rural*	*Urban*
Lower	71.38	81.39	41.84
Middle	27.93	18.39	56.09
Lower middle	21.83	16.15	38.59
Upper middle	1.93	0.54	6.00
Upper	0.69	0.22	2.07

Source: NSSO: 61st Round.

Table 12.4 Class composition of Indian population 2011–2012 (per cent)

Class	*All India*	*Rural*	*Urban*
Lower	47.82	58.16	21.99
Middle	50.27	41.44	72.35
Lower middle	37.13	34.85	42.83
Upper middle	4.12	1.54	10.58
Upper	1.90	0.40	5.66

Source: NSSO: 68th Round.

marginal expansion in the relative size of the urban middle class, but a more than offsetting decline in the size of the rural middle class. However, there was an increase in the size of the upper middle class, at an all India level, as well as at the rural and the urban areas.

By contrast, the period between 2004–2005 and 2011–2012 seems to have witnessed a dramatic swelling of the middle class across all categories. At an all India level, the size of the middle class increased from just about 28 per cent to a little over 50 per cent! By any standards, this is a huge increase in the size of the middle class over a span of just about seven years. In absolute terms, the size of the middle class increased from 304.16 million to 604.29 million, an almost doubling of the middle class. However, during 1999–2005, the size of the middle class increased from 289.7 million to 304.16 million, or a mere 5 per cent increase. During the 2004–2005 to 2011–2012 period, the lower middle class population increased from 237.76 million to 446.32 million, while in the earlier 1999–2004–2005 period, this increase was really marginal, from 236.32 million to 237.76 million. The upper middle class underwent a very substantial increase in size during 2004–2005 to the 2011–2012 period, increasing from 21 million to nearly 50 million. In the earlier period, this class had increased from 14.66 million to 21 million. The upper class too increased in both the periods, from 3.76 million to 7.53 million in the first period and from 7.53 million to a whooping 22.87 million in the second period. The biggest difference between the two periods was what happened to the lower classes. In the first period, the absolute size of the lower classes actually increased from 707.5 million to 777.30 million, while in the later period, it declined to 574.84 million. Thus, it seems fairly clear that during the second period, we see an upward mobility for the lower classes that is quite unprecedented in the earlier data. An important transition, where the poor move up to the lower middle class, the lower middle class move further up and so on seems to have started in this period. This was not the case earlier, where only size of the upper classes was increasing, but so was the size of the lower classes. A period of upward mobility for the poor and the middle classes seems to be the distinguishing characteristic of the period 2004–2005 to 2011–2012, unlike the earlier period.

As argued above, the process of economic reforms started in 1991. Several commentators have assumed that the process would automatically result in the expansion of the middle class; however, that is far from true. There seems to have been some small increase in the urban middle class, but the statement is not true for the entire period at an all India level. Therefore, it is really hard to conclude that globalization automatically leads to an expansion of the middle classes. At the very best, it can be said that there might be a substantial lag between the onset of market-led economic processes and the onset of expansionary processes for the middle class. This is also corroborated by the changes in the number of people below the poverty line (Planning Commission 2013). Between 1993 and 2004, there was a very small decline in the number of people below the poverty line in rural India, from 328.6 million in 1993 to 326.3 million in 2004–2005. However, from 2004–2005 to 2011–2012, this number declined to 216.5 million. In urban India, the number of people under the poverty line actually increased from 1993 to 2004–2005, from 74.5 million to 80.8 million. But during 2004–2005 to 2011–2012, this number declined to 52.8 million. In rural India too, the earlier period saw an increase in the absolute number of people below the poverty line from 403.7 million to 407.1 million, but during the latter period, this number declined to 269.3 million.

What could have been the potential role of outsourcing activities in this transformation? If one goes by the estimates presented in the introduction during 2006–2010, 353,000 new jobs were directly generated by the sector, including those in IT services and exports, BPO exports and domestic market. Going by the estimate of 3.2 indirect jobs for every new direct job created, the total number of jobs created during this period would lie somewhere around 1.1 million. Making a generous allowance for the years from 2004–2011–2012, this number could be broadly pegged at an upper limit of 1.5 million. This is a very small magnitude, compared to the 300 million people who have joined the middle classes during this period, or the 210 million who swelled the ranks of the lower middle classes. Even when compared to the decline of about 110 million in the number of those below the poverty line, these figures pale into insignificance. From these data, it can be firmly concluded that the role of the outsourcing sector in 'creating' a new middle class is marginal at best.

The more probable candidate is the fast economic growth that happened in the latter period, especially during the period 2005–2006, 2006–2007 and 2007–2008.

During these three periods, the economy grew by 9.51 per cent, 9.74 per cent and 9.00 per cent respectively leading to a 29 per cent increase in the GDP in a short span of three years. In contrast, the period 1999–2004–2005 saw relatively sedate growth. 1999–2000 saw a growth rate of 6.44 per cent, followed by a sharp deceleration to 4.34 per cent in the following year. Growth revived a little in 2001–2002 to 5.81 per cent, but fell sharply to 3.83 per cent in the following year. There was a drastic increase in 2003–2004 to 8.51 per cent, but again a marginal fall to 7.46 per cent. In spite of the fall, the last two years were periods of rapid growth. These two years were followed by another three years of very high growth. The five years of sustained high economic growth have led to increase in income and expenditure across all population segments (Dutta and Manoj 2014), creating the potential for the observed upward mobility. The period of unprecedented high growth also saw a fairly broad-based distribution of the benefits of economic growth (Planning Commission 2013). In spite of this conjecture, the onset of an economy-wide process of upward mobility needs a far more detailed investigation, but it seems fairly obvious that the outsourcing sector has not made a significant contribution, at least in quantitative terms, in a direct way, to the creation of the new middle class.

Who are the new middle classes? In order to answer the questions raised in the introduction, we need to take a detailed look at the set of people who constitute the expenditure class that corresponds to being lower middle class. We choose to focus on the lower middle class since that class seems to be the most likely one to contain individuals and groups who have moved up from poverty in the more recent past.

The new middle class: a case study

This section presents the results of a survey of 789 households from the city of Mumbai (previously Bombay) that were primarily engaged in the unorganized sector. The sample is not a representative sample in the sense that being confined to those working in the unorganized sector, it is unlikely to be representative of the wider Mumbai population. In particular, it would exclude those who are working in the organized offshoring services sector. However, we have chosen this segment for a reason. The Indian economy has a very large unorganized manufacturing and services sector. The terms ‘unorganized’ and ‘informal’ sectors are often used interchangeably. The informal sector may be broadly characterized as consisting of units engaged in the production of goods or services with the primary objective of generating employment and incomes to the persons concerned. These units typically operate at a low level of organization, with little or no division between labour and capital as factors of production and on a small scale. Labour relations – where they exist – are based mostly on casual employment, kinship or personal and social relations rather than contractual arrangements with formal guarantees (National Statistical Commission 2012). This segment constitutes 92 per cent of the Indian workforce (National Commission for Enterprises in the Informal Sector 2007). The unorganized sector offers jobs that are low skilled and without any social or job security. In a system characterized by upward mobility for the poor, the unorganized sector plays a very important role. Those who are moving out of poverty are most likely to find their first opportunities in the unorganized sector characterized by relatively few barriers to entry. However, the organized sector is characterized by barriers in terms of higher skill requirements as well as labour legislation and trade unions. In general, India has seen an informalization of the labour market (Goldar and Aggarwal 2010). Hence, when looking for those who are transiting out of poverty, the informal sector is the most likely place to find them. Among the informal sector, however, our sample is chosen by randomizing, and hence is likely to be quite representative.

We identify a clear 'lower middle class' among this section using the criteria of $4 to $6 per capita expenditure PPP that has been used by Bannerjee and Duflo (2007), and attempt to distinguish that section from those 'not poor and poor', that is those who spend less than $4 per capita. About 75 per cent of the surveyed households fall in the category of lower middle class, while the rest belong to the poor and non-poor category. There is no household above the lower middle class in our sample. Table 12.5 presents data on various occupations that the new middle class is engaged in.

As can be seen from the data, street vending is the commonest occupation among the lower middle class as well as the non-poor and poor. The interesting category is 'data entry', which one finds among the urban middle class. This is an IT-related occupation, but only about 2 per cent of the respondents were engaged in that activity. The data do not allow the identification of any other direct IT-related activity among the urban lower middle class. From the data, there does not

Table 12.5 Occupational structure of the lower middle class and the poor and the not poor

Occupational structure of the lower middle class	*%*	*Occupational structure of the poor and non-poor*	*%*
Vendors	30	Vendors	34
Food industry	13	Construction work	11
Leather work	8	Leather work	7
Painters/carpenters	7	Welding and repairing	6
Construction	6	Not specified	6
Miscellaneous	7	Food industry	5
Cloth shop/washing	5	Domestic work	5
Security services	5	Miscellaneous services	5
Unspecified	4	General stores	5
Welding and repairing	4	Painter/carpenter	4
Cable/electrical works	2	Incense stick rolling	3
Driver/transport services	2	Toy making	3
Data entry	2	Driver	2
Imitation and zari*	2	Garment making	2
Bangle works	2	Decoration	2
Total	100	Total	100

Note: Imitation is the production of imitation jewellery. Zari is gold brocade work for sarees.

seem to be any significant difference in the occupational structure of the lower middle class and the poor and non-poor category. It is not possible in this table to examine the occupational structure of the middle middle classes and the upper classes since they are not to be found in the unorganized sector. However, we have some data from the NCAER (2010) that demonstrates that the middle middle classes and the upper classes have more skilled based and better paying jobs. However, such jobs are not to be found in the urban unorganized sector. Transiting from the low skilled low paying jobs in the urban unorganized sector to high-skilled, high-paying jobs is a part of the transition from being perhaps lower or middle middle class to being middle middle class and upper middle class to upper classes. Therefore, that question is not generic to the process of formation of the middle class.

Even though the occupational structure based on our sample does not seem to vary much across the two categories, expenditure on basic food, education and major durables differ significantly at an all India level between the lower and the middle classes.

As one can see, there is steady decline on the percentage of expenditure that is made on basic food as one moves up the class structure. This frees up resources for spending on other goods and services. The lower middle class spends significantly more that the lower classes on consumer services and conveyance, on education and medical matters and major durables. The same pattern is repeated for rural and urban India, as one can see from Tables 12.7 and 12.8. There seems to be a clear difference in aspirations among the lower classes and the lower middle classes. This means that though people in our sample are doing the same type of jobs, their material aspirations seem to be quite different from each other. A plumber belonging to the lower class is a very different person from another plumber belonging to the lower middle class.

Table 12.6 Expenditure shares on various goods and services by various classes, all India 2011–12 (per cent)

Item	*All India*	*Lower class*	*Middle class*	*Lower middle class*	*Upper middle class*	*Upper class*
Food-basic	34.00	45.11	33.34	37.98	23.01	13.21
Beverages and refreshments	8.16	8.40	7.96	7.95	8.30	8.80
Meat, egg and fish	3.17	3.62	3.28	3.61	2.52	1.5
Clothing, bedding, footwear	7.47	8.66	7.40	7.85	6.44	5.17
Fuel	8.40	11.28	8.00	9.00	5.96	4.15
Consumer services and conveyance	11.11	6.81	11.60	10.00	15.17	18.02
Education and medical	12.42	7.22	13.36	11.26	17.22	18.75
Entertainment	1.40	0.85	1.56	1.48	1.70	1.65
Minor durables	4.77	5.17	4.90	5.17	4.27	3.16
Major durables	5.25	2.27	4.78	3.37	8.27	14.77
Rent and taxes	3.75	0.57	3.80	2.26	7.08	10.78

Source: Computed from NSSO, 68th Round.

Table 12.7 Expenditure shares on various goods and services by various classes, rural India 2011–12 (per cent)

Item	*All India*	*Lower class*	*Middle class*	*Lower middle class*	*Upper middle class*	*Upper class*
Food-basic	38.98	45.39	36.24	39.08	24.00	12.20
Beverages and Refreshments	8.13	8.55	7.94	8.05	8.60	6.82
Meat, eggs and fish	3.54	3.62	3.57	3.70	3.07	2.18
Clothing, bedding, footwear	7.88	8.74	7.56	7.94	5.96	3.46
Fuel	9.19	11.25	8.20	8.97	5.18	2.60
Consumer services and conveyance	9.21	6.81	10.71	10.00	13.08	9.85
Education and medical	11.31	7.13	13.28	11.33	19.73	25.01
Entertainment	1.11	0.77	1.32	1.32	1.24	1.23
Minor durables	4.91	5.15	4.90	5.14	3.89	2.03
Major durables	4.97	2.33	5.25	3.73	13.06	32.41
Rent and taxes	0.77	0.27	1.02	0.74	2.18	2.21

Source: NSSO, 68th Round.

The data above raise an interesting question. We have argued above that a plumber from the lower class is a different person from the plumber in the lower middle classes, despite the occupational commonality. This is because the aspirational expenditures seem to be different. Indeed, the structure of asset holding in our sample brings out the difference well.

As can be seen from Table 12.9, the lower middle class households have significantly more assets compared to the lower class. What makes this possible? What could be the reason behind the relative affluence of the lower middle classes,

Table 12.8 Expenditure shares on various goods and services by various classes, urban India 2011–2012 (per cent)

Item	*All India*	*Lower class*	*Middle class*	*Lower middle class*	*Upper middle class*	*Upper class*
Food-basic	27.70	43.44	30.19	35.94	22.67	13.40
Beverages and refreshments	8.21	7.58	8.00	7.78	8.19	9.18
Meat, eggs and fish	2.70	3.70	2.99	3.46	2.34	1.37
Clothing, bedding, footwear	6.93	8.19	7.21	7.68	6.61	5.50
Fuel	7.37	11.45	7.78	8.99	6.23	4.45
Consumer services and conveyance	13.60	6.82	12.58	10.11	15.92	19.55
Education and medical	13.87	7.76	13.45	11.16	16.35	17.58
Entertainment	1.77	1.36	1.82	1.79	1.87	1.73
Minor durables	4.61	5.33	4.90	5.24	4.41	3.37
Major durables	5.61	1.92	4.27	2.71	6.59	11.48
Rent and taxes	7.64	2.45	6.80	5.14	8.81	12.38

Source: NSSO, 68th Round.

especially if they are doing the same kind of jobs that the lower classes do? The reason could lie in larger intensity of work for the lower middle class household relative to the lower class household. An interesting possibility is that lower middle classes are more affluent compared to the lower classes not because they do different things, but because more members of the lower middle class household are engaged in economic activities compared to the lower classes, even when the nature of the activities is the same. Thus, from an occupational structure point of view, the difference could be about the quantity of work that is available, rather

Table 12.9 Percentage of households holding various assets

Item	*Percentage of households among lower middle class holding that item*	*Percentage of households among the poor and non-poor class holding that item*
Cell phone	81	31
Clock/watch	85	34
Stove	20	2
Gas stove	34	11
Electricity connection	71	52
Fan	63	46
Colour TV	57	38
VCR/VCD	21	11
Radio/stereo	28	32
Sewing machine	22	7
Car/jeep	0.17	0
Bicycle	12	8
Motorcycle	4	0
Auto rickshaw	0.3	0
Tempo	0.6	0
Pushcart	3	0
Pressure cooker	57	38
Dosa tawa (for making dossas)	25	6
Brass utensils	25	4
Steel utensils	53	11
Chair/stool	57	44
Cot/bed	19	11
Double cot/bed	5.1	0
Sofa set	10	3
Iron safe	18	4
Table	55	42
Sarees/salwar	59	20
Silver jewelry	41	16
Gold jewelry	54	29
Refrigerator	7	3
Computer	0.7	0.6

than the quality. Indeed, the following tables (Tables 12.10 and 12.11) corroborate this point.

The majority of the lower middle class households have two earning members. Table 12.11 gives the same information for the lower group.

The difference is clear. An overwhelming majority of the lower class households have only one member working. This must be seen in the context of larger household size among the poor and non-poor, implying a larger dependency load in the lower class compared to the lower middle class.

These findings imply that the difference between lower middle class and lower class households is quantitative, rather than qualitative. Lower middle class households earn better, not because they are engaged in different occupations compared to the lower classes, but simply because they have been able to get more of their family members to do the same things that the lower classes do.

From the data presented in this section, the lower middle class as identified by the consumption expenditure criteria seems to be just a quantitative expansion of the incomes and assets of the classes directly below them. That expansion seems to be driven not by a change in the occupational structure, but by relatively more household members doing the same type of work done by the poor and the non-poor. What seems to be important in the transition from lower to lower middle classes is the access to and availability of employment. As the household level income goes up, one sees an expansion in aspirational spending as well as on spending on education and health.

Table 12.10 Distribution of earning members in lower middle class households

Number of earning members	*Distribution of households (per cent)*
1	46.75
2	52.21
3	0.85
4	0.17

Table 12.11 Distribution of earning members in lower class households

Number of earning members	*Distribution of households (per cent)*
1	73.25
2	25.26
3	1.57
4	0.00

Conclusion

The middle class in India has substantially expanded during 2004–2005 to 2011–2012. This period has seen unprecedented upward mobility among urban as well as rural Indians. There is definitely a shift in aspirations along with this economic transition. At least 600 million Indian are now middle class, and are spending substantially more on education, health, consumer services and major durables than they did earlier. In that sense, Indian society is on the cusp of a major transformation. In an important sense, a much larger number of Indians are now able to access the kind of cultural capital that allows them to transit to the cultural markers of a middle class. But at least in quantitative terms, the contribution of the offshoring sector to this middle class creation is marginal at best. At a very conservative estimate, around 110 million Indians have ceased to be poor during 2004–2005 to 2011–2012, while the ITES-BPO sector has created at the most 1.5 million jobs in the same period, both directly as well as indirectly. The potentialities of the offshoring sector in creating a middle class in the future are further hampered by the possible limitations of its future growth arising from international competition. Our primary data from the Mumbai sample survey show that the initial trigger for the transformation from being poor to being lower middle class is likely to be a quantitative expansion of employment opportunities available to the poor rather than a qualitative shift, as envisaged by the 'offshoring creates a middle class' argument.

References

Banerjee, Abhijeet and Duflo, Ester (2007) *What is Middle Class About? The Middle classes Around the World*, MIT, Department of Economics, Working Paper No. 07–29. Cambridge, MA: MIT.

Dutta, Bhaskar and Manoj, Panda (2014) Social welfare and household consumption expenditure in India: 2004–05 to 2011–12. *Economic and Political Weekly*, XLIX (31), 2 August..

Fernandes, Leela (2006) *India's New Middle Class, Democratic politics in an Era of Economic Reform*. University of Minnesota Press: Minnesota.

Fukuyama, Francis (2012) The middle class revolution. *Poverty in Focus*, 26, International Policy Centre for Inclusive Growth, Poverty Practice, Bureau of Development Policy, UNDP: New York.

Goldar, Biswajit and Aggarwal, Suresh Chandra (2010) *Informalisation of Industrial Labour in India: Are labour market Rigidities and Import Competition to Blame*. Institute of Economic Growth: New Delhi.

NASSCOM (National Association of Software and Service Companies) (2010) *IT-BPO Sector in India: Strategic Review 2010*. NASSCOM: New Delhi.

NASSCOM (2014) *The IT-BPM Sector in India: Strategic Review 2014*. NASSCOM: New Delhi.

National Commission for Enterprises in the Informal Sector (2007) *Annual Report 2007–08*. Government of India: New Delhi.

National Statistical Commission (2012) *Report of the Committee on Unorganised Sector Statistics*. Government of India: New Delhi.

NCAER (National Council of Applied Economic Research) (2010) *Survey, 2010*. NCAER: New Delhi.

NSSO (National Sample Survey Organisation) (2000) *55th Round*, National Statistical Organisation, Ministry of Statistics and Programme Implementation. Government of India: New Delhi.

NSSO (2005) *61th Round*, National Statistical Organisation, Ministry of Statistics and Programme Implementation. Government of India: New Delhi.

NSSO (2011) *68th Round*, National Statistical Organisation, Ministry of Statistics and Programme Implementation. Government of India: New Delhi.

Planning Commission (2013) *Press Note on Poverty Estimates 2011–12*, Government of India: New Delhi

Rastogi, G. and Pradhan, B. (2011) *Offshore: How India Got Back on The Global Business Map*. Portfolio Penguin: New Delhi.

Sandhu, A.S. (2008) *Globalization of services and the Making of a New Global Labor Force in India's Silicon Valley*. University of California: Santa Barbara.

Wilson, Dominic and Dragusanu, Raluca (2008) The expanding middle: The exploding world middle class and falling global inequality, *Global Economics Papers*, 170, Goldman Sachs: New York.

13 How the BPO industry contributes to the formation of a consumerist new middle class in Mumbai

Sandhya Krishnan

Introduction

The last few years have seen an emergence of interest in the new middle classes in the Global South as its consumption demand has been resilient in spite of the economic crisis of 2008–2009. These new middle classes are expected to assume the traditional role of the American and European middle classes as global consumers and play a key role in rebalancing the world economy (ADB, 2010; Kharas, 2010; Wilson and Dragusanu, 2008). India is one of the emerging market economies where the new middle class is exploding in numbers. It is predicted that by 2025, India's new middle class will account for 59 per cent of the country's spending power and moreover, India will surpass Germany as the world's fifth largest consumer market (Ablett *et al.*, 2007).

Existing research on the new middle class in India can be divided into three categories based on their focus of study. The first category deals with measuring the size of the new middle class and studying the impact of the emergence of the class on economic inequality and marginalization (see ADB, 2010; Banerjee and Duflo, 2008; Meyer and Birdsall, 2012; Wilson and Dragusanu, 2008). The focus of the second category lies in studying which social groups constitute the new middle class (see Fuller and Narasimhan, 2007; Upadhya, 2008). The third type, taking a socio-cultural account of the subject, explores qualitative changes in consumption practices and lifestyles of the new middle class (see Brosius, 2013; Fernandes, 2006; Lakha, 1999). This chapter contributes to literature in the third category. Existing studies in this category, however, concentrate on changes in consumption practices brought about by the processes of globalization and liberalization on the Indian new middle class in general. Because different outcomes of globalization and liberalization have varying impacts on different groups of people (Fernandes, 2006: 90), it is necessary to study specific outcomes in isolation. This chapter hence investigates the changes in consumption practices of employees of the business process outsourcing (BPO) industry in Mumbai.

The offshore service outsourcing industry, which comprises the BPO and information technology (IT) services, is widely acknowledged as one of the important sectors contributing to the formation of a new middle class in India (see for example, Fernandes, 2006: 114–118; Fuller and Narasimhan, 2007; Murphy, 2011; Upadhya, 2008). There exists a fair amount of research undertaken on IT workers in India and their new middle class identity (see Fuller and Narasimhan, 2007; Upadhya, 2008), but it does not look into their consumption practices. Research on BPO workers in India is limited to investigating the work conditions and turn-over rates of call-centre agents (Taylor *et al.*, 2013; Vira and James, 2012). Murphy's (2011) work, which explores social identification of call-centre workers stands as an exception, but it fails to explain the link between workers' participation in the call-centre industry and their changing consumption practices. This chapter studies a more representative sample of BPO workers that includes those participating in low-end activities such as back-office jobs and call-centres as well as those involved in high-end activities such as accounting, web-designing, analytics and market research. It further investigates the nature of changes in consumption practices witnessed by employees of the industry after they get into the job and brings to light various factors within the industry that influence those changes. Mumbai is one of the most favoured destinations for BPO companies to set up their offices (Tholons, 2013),[1] but surprisingly, in the context of the BPO industry it has been studied quite sparsely compared to other Indian cities, such as Bangalore, Chennai and New Delhi, which have also benefitted from service outsourcing activities. The city hence is an interesting place to investigate the emergence of the BPO industry and assess its contribution to the formation of a consumerist new middle class.

The following section lays down the theoretical framework to analyze the new middle class with a focus on its consumption practices. The chapter then explains the data and research methodology, and it then presents the empirical findings. The last section concludes with a discussion of the results and recommendations for further research.

Theorizing the consumerist new middle class

Until the 1980s, work on the middle class in India was concentrated on its professional occupations and political participation, with little attention paid to its consumption practices (Haynes and McGowan, 2010). With the opening up of the Indian economy in the late 1980s and early 1990s, a new ideology emerged that welcomed consumption by the middle class as integral to the project of development (Fernandes, 2006: xv; Haynes and McGowan, 2010). This is reflected in the large body of recent empirical studies on the Indian middle class and its changing consumption practices. Lakha (1999), for example, observes that global consumer icons and western style consumerism are on the rise among the middle class in globalized India. Fernandes (2006: 41–65) shows the transformation in advertising images of liberalized India that reflect new practices of middle class consumption. Nijman (2006) in his empirical work on the middle class in Mumbai finds a significant increase in middle class credit-based consumption and asserts that consumption has become the marker of middle class status in liberalized India. Kharas (2010) notes that consumption patterns of the new middle class are guided by the class' consumptive desires, rather than driven by the necessities of life. Brosius (2013), who studies the sites of new consumption practices of the middle class in India, finds evidence of conspicuous credit-driven and debt-laden consumption. Even quantitative studies on the middle class by Banerjee and Duflo (2008) and Ravallion (2010) define new middle classes in developing countries based on their consumption expenditures. This shift in class analysis from a Marxian, production-based view to a consumption-based view is also demonstrated in modern theories on social class.

In the late twentieth century, employing the concepts of cultural and symbolic capital, Bourdieu arguably pioneered the analysis of social class using the lens of consumption. Several empirical studies on consumption and the new middle class are based on Bourdieu's class framework (see for example, Fernandes, 2006; Murphy, 2011). A more recent theoretical framework to analyze class structure, which is yet relatively unknown, is that proposed by Philip Kelly. Kelly's (2007) class typology borrows ideas of class structure from different schools of thought and can be seen as a comprehensive summary of all major class theories. He analyzes class structure using four inter-related dimensions: position, process, performance and politics. Of these, class as performance is the most relevant tool for understanding the new middle class from the perspective of its consumption practices. According to Kelly (2007), class as performance is that part of class which is played out or performed in a variety of settings. Consumption is an important dimension of class performance. Classed consumption relates to the forms of consumption that are seen as marking a person's class in the productive sphere and used to articulate one's class identity. These include, for instance, knowing one's way around an expensive clothing boutique or a restaurant menu. Kelly further argues that classed consumption is not unrelated to other dimensions of class such as position (the position that one belongs to in the labour market or the economic position one holds) as it determines the material resources available in order to engage in various forms of consumption. Thus, though consumption practices are the defining identity of the new middle class, they are also linked to other dimensions of class such as labour market position and income. Empirical evidence in the following sections of the chapter will show how the dimensions of class position and performance, that is, working in the BPO industry (labour market position), the income earned therein (economic position) and the consumption habits picked up (performance) interact with each other to produce a consumerist new middle class identity.

Data and methodology

This study uses a mixed research method that draws on primary data gathered via semi-structured interviews and a survey. Twenty-four interviews were conducted with current and former employees and industry experts of the BPO sector in Mumbai during October 2012 to March 2013 (see Table 13.1). Employees refer to only those workers who are directly involved in the revenue-generation process of the firm and exclude ancillary activity staff like security guards and senior managerial-level workers. Typical educational backgrounds of these employees range from higher secondary schooling to a master's degree depending on the type of outsourcing activity they are involved in. Industry experts mean persons at a senior level who are familiar with the overall working of their firm. In an industry very wary of leakages of confidential data, entry into the premises of the company offices was restricted for strangers, and workers were often hesitant or too tired to talk to strangers after long hours of working in shifts. On account of inaccessibility to workers, potential interviewees could not be chosen by a random sampling method and were contacted via the author's personal networks. Of the 24 interviewees, 21 were reached via the author's personal contacts and the contacts of 3 interviewees were given by the earlier respondents.

In addition to the interviews, a survey of 322 employees of the BPO industry was undertaken. Again, on account of the problem of access to workers, the task of administering the survey was outsourced to a market research firm. The firm collected 303 responses during the period August to September 2013 and 19 responses were collected online by the author during the period July to September 2013. In order to validate the data collected by the firm, responses of a random sample of the survey participants were verified over the telephone. Using stratified sampling method, a gender distribution of approximately 70 per cent males and 30 per cent females was maintained in the sample. This is in accordance with the data released by NASSCOM (2013) that claims that women constitute 30–35 per cent of the workforce in the industry.

Questions in the interviews and the survey pertained to the respondents' consumption habits and the factors within the industry that influence them. To ensure that respondents felt free to share their experiences, theirs as well as their firm's identities were promised to be kept confidential. In the following analysis of empirical results, a single letter is used to identify respondents.

Table 13.1 Sample summary

	Interviews			*Survey*
	Employees	*Industry experts*	*Total (Employees + experts)*	*Employees*
Sample size	18	6	24	322
Male	14	6	20	220 (68.3%)
Female	4	0	4	102 (31.7%)
Current employees	14	NA	NA	249 (77.3%)
Former employees	4	NA	NA	73 (22.7%)
Average age while joining the industry (years)	22.5	NA	NA	22.3
Average experience in the industry (years)	6.4	NA	NA	2.3

New middle class consumption

> Smart phones, watches, Levi's jeans, branded shoes … The new middle class is about going to places and doing things that possibly the last generation could not and having the spending power to do it as well.
>
> (B, male, 21, Call-centre agent, December 2012)

The above quote points at two central features of the consumerist new middle class. First, the new middle class is recognized for its new consumption practices, something the earlier middle class in India was not identified with. Second, the new middle class has more purchasing power than the earlier middle class, enabling it to indulge in its new consumption practices. The next two sections respectively discuss the role of the BPO industry in contributing to these two key identifying features of the new middle class: its spending power and new consumption practices.

Income and expenditure of the new middle class

There are several definitions of the middle class in developing countries based on its consumption expenditure and income, reflecting its purchasing power. Here we use the income-based definition of the middle class given by Meyer and Birdsall (2012) and a consumption expenditure-based definition of Banerjee and Duflo (2008). Meyer and Birdsall (2012) define the middle class in India as those whose daily per capita income lies between US$10 and $50 measured in 2005 PPP (purchasing power parity). Though this interval is slightly higher than other income-based definitions such as that by the National Council of Applied Economic Research (NCAER) (Shukla, 2010), it is chosen for specific reasons. The new middle class in India is looked upon as a driver of consumption demand and growth in the long run and is expected to be somewhat resilient to economic shocks. Meyer and Birdsall (2012) find the lower limit of $10 to be high enough to imply minimum vulnerability from global economic and political shocks and enough for being middle class in today's globalized world. The choice of the upper limit of $50 is based on the finding that those with incomes higher than this consider themselves to be rich (Birdsall, 2012). Banerjee and Duflo (2008) define the middle class in developing countries as those whose daily per capita consumption expenditure lies between $2 and $10, measured in 1993 PPP. They further define the lower middle class as those whose daily per capita expenditure lies between $2 and $4 and the upper middle class as those with daily per capita expenditure between $6 and $10. This definition of the middle class is chosen over other comparable definitions such as that of ADB (2010) and Ravallion (2010), as it uses a relatively higher lower bound, thus ensuring higher resilience to economic shocks.

Figure 13.1 shows the kernel density estimation of daily per capita income of BPO employees in Mumbai in 2013, converted to 2005 PPP dollars to facilitate comparison with Meyer and Birdsall's (2012) calculations. The area under the curve between any to points on the x-axis denotes the probability that the income of the employees lies within that interval. The two vertical lines in the figure correspond to income levels of $10 and $50 respectively, representing the middle class income range. The figure shows that most BPO employees (about 87 per cent) earn middle class level incomes, more than 10 per cent earn above middle class level incomes and barely 2 per cent employees earn less than $10 a day. Using the same definition, Meyer and Birdsall (2012) found that less than 10 per cent of India's population belonged to the middle class in 2009–2010. We can hence conclude that the BPO industry pays its employees incomes far higher than what an average Indian earns.

BPO employees in Mumbai also spend more compared to the rest of India. Figure 13.2 shows the kernel density estimation of consumption expenditure of BPO employees in 2013, measured in 1993 PPP dollars. The vertical lines in the figure corresponding to expenditure levels of $2 and $4 represent the boundary limits of the lower middle class and the $10 line represents the maximum limit for the upper middle class, as defined by Banerjee and Duflo (2008).

Figure 13.2 shows that modal consumption expenditure for BPO employees is well above the middle class range. A negligible proportion of employees have consumption expenditures below $2 a day. In contrast, consumption expenditure data from the National Sample Survey (NSS) for 2011–2012 shows that although half of India falls in the middle class expenditure range, three-fourths of them belong to the lower-middle class category, spending only between $2 and $4 every day. Further, over 47 per cent of the population lives on daily expenditures below $2 and barely 2 per cent Indians have expenditures exceeding the middle class range.[2] In terms of income and consumption expenditure patterns we can thus claim that BPO employees in Mumbai not only belong to a privileged section within the Indian middle class, but some of them also comprise the elite of the society.

Consumption practices of the new middle class

While income and expenditure reflect the consumption capacity of the new middle class, consumption practices depict the manner in which new middle class identity is played out. Of the several consumption habits, a large number of survey respondents believed that their food and dressing habits in particular underwent a

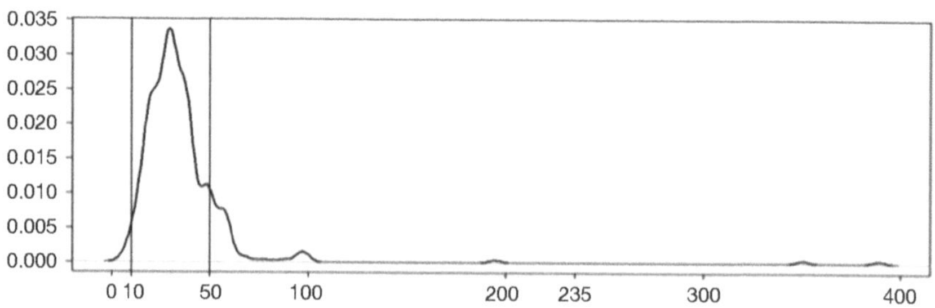

Figure 13.1 Distribution of daily per capita income of BPO employees (2005 PPP US$) (N=301)

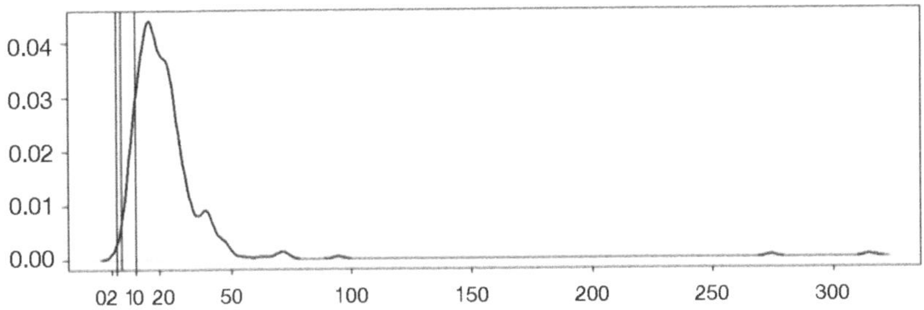

Figure 13.2 Distribution of daily per capita consumption expenditure of BPO employees (1993 PPP US$) (N=301)

transformation after working for the BPO industry. Over 55 per cent of the respondents reported to have become more brand conscious, 43 per cent wear more modern and fashionable outfits after getting into the industry and 37 per cent felt that they have a better dress sense than before. Similarly, 35 per cent of the respondents affirmed that they try new and different kinds of cuisines and 27 per cent eat out at restaurants more often than before. Only about 2 per cent respondents claimed to have not had any change in their consumption habits. Similar results on consumption practices were found during the interviews, where several interviewees described how they picked up new dress and food habits after getting into the industry. A young male BPO employee for instance noted:

> In companies like my previous job [a private coaching institute], no one really looks (at your clothes). When you come to a BPO, you see people wearing different clothes, the way they wear it, the combination... so it changes. Earlier I used to buy clothes from Fashion Street [a popular street in Mumbai that sells fashionable wear at low prices]. Now I do not like the clothes there. Now I only buy from Westside [a domestic private retail chain].
>
> (E, male, 22, Back-office executive, January 2013)

A slightly older employee reported on his changing dining behaviour:

> Earlier going out would mean visiting an Udipi restaurant [a modest Indian vegetarian restaurant] and having a roti [Indian bread], sabji [vegetable] and a dessert. In the evening you would go and have some chaat [a snack]. Now, you want to try new places. So you may go to a Pizza Hut or you may try Mexican or Thai food. Once in a while we also splurge and go to a Mainland China or a Taj restaurant.
>
> (J, male, 35, supervisor, February 2013)

These narrations show that changes in dressing imply both having a better dress sense as well as being more brand-conscious. Changing food habits among the new middle class consist of both going to more expensive places to eat and experimenting with multicultural cuisines. While the higher than average income that BPO employees earn plays a role in bringing about these changes, the environment within the industry is also an important influence. As respondent *E* describes, his dress sense changed after looking at others in his workplace who wore better clothes than him and the realization that his way of dressing was being observed.

Amenities within the outsourcing companies and performance-based incentives given to employees introduce them to new forms of consumption practices. Since employees in the BPO industry generally work in shifts, they are provided with free pick-up and drop-off services by cars or comfortable buses. Consequently, they tend to travel in such comfortable and relatively expensive modes of transport even outside of work. Further, several companies have multinational food outlets and cafes such as McDonalds, Pizza Hut and Starbucks located within their premises. Shopping malls housing similar outlets also strategically locate themselves around outsourcing companies. Not surprisingly, employees tend to visit similar places in their leisure time. In fact, as entry into the office premises is restricted to outsiders, most interviews conducted for this research took place in cafes located in shopping malls around the respondents' workplaces.

Results from the survey show that 67 per cent of the employees get free transport facilities; 31 per cent are given credit or debit cards on joining the company, 29 per cent have multi-cuisine cafeterias in their office premises and 34 per cent have either gymnasium or sport facilities or both. Only 17 per cent of the employees do not get any such facilities. The work environment in the BPO industry thus introduces its employees to new and expensive consumption habits. Both employees and industry experts confirmed this during the interviews.

> Earlier only a general manager would be sent a car to be picked up. Today, all these guys are being sent cars. And if the driver is even ten minutes late, they abuse him. Standards and expectations have risen.
>
> (U, male, human resources head, October 2012)

> In general Indian companies, not the really big ones, but in an average company, you would have to pay for your coffee, tea, lunch, etc. In BPOs, you have nice coffee vending machines, machines for soft drinks, etc. You have to pay for them, but they are subsidised.
>
> (P, male, 29, recruitment team member, March 2013)

> We have a gym, a cafeteria, a beauty salon and a library in our office. We have to pay for the services, but they are much cheaper. If you come to my office, you can see people going to KFC or McDonalds every day. Right now, if you roam here [in the mall], half the people are from my company, or they may be in Inorbit [another mall in the vicinity].
>
> (L, female, 32, knowledge coach, December 2012)

Besides the facilities, the industry also offers several perks to its employees. Though perks have been historically provided in the Indian public sector too, the BPO industry has transformed the status implications of these perks by linking them to new patterns of consumption (Fernandes, 2006: 94). While the Indian public sector provides its employees with standard benefits such as insurance, medical facilities, provident fund and so on, BPO companies, besides these standard benefits, also offer monetary and non-pecuniary benefits such as smart phones and home appliances, which are typically attractive to the young, who are found in majority in the industry. Survey results showed that 70 per cent of the employees get performance-based monetary rewards, 30 per cent get non-monetary rewards in the form of gifts such as mobile phones, laptops, home appliances, etc., 54 per cent get standard benefits such as provident fund, and only 6 per cent do not get any form of additional incentives. The BPO industry thus provides its employees with exposure to a variety of quality goods and services and introduces them to new forms of consumption behaviour.

However, not all respondents believe that the BPO industry is responsible for bringing about changes in their consumption practices. The advent of liberalization in India has enabled the entry of multinational retail chains into the country, increased penetration of digital television and brought about similar other changes that influence consumption practices of the middle class. One interviewee exclaimed:

> I would not say that it is because of the outsourcing industry that such things are happening. It is because of the way India is growing. Earlier I would buy clothes from a local supplier and now we buy branded clothes. But people would not know what to wear if such things were not made available in the market. There were no brands or branded shops before in India. Availability of goods in India is more important.
>
> (G, male, 30, sales executive, February 2013)

It is difficult to delineate the specific factors influencing new consumption practices of the BPO employees. Nonetheless, from the empirical evidence provided here, we can conclude that though several factors may influence consumption practices of BPO workers, the BPO industry itself is certainly among them and likely one of the more important factors. The industry influences consumption practices of its employees via two main channels. First, it pays its employees relatively high salaries such that they have enough purchasing power to be spent on discretionary consumption. Second, the nature of work and work environment in the industry is such that it exposes its employees to new forms of consumption practices. Consequently, employees tend to indulge in these new forms of consumption even outside their workplaces. Domestic Indian industries lack such opportunities, making modern industries like the outsourcing sector a vital catalyst for the emergence of new forms of consumption habits.

Conclusion

Impressive economic growth, backed by globalization and liberalization, has given rise to a new middle class in emerging market economies such as India. Workers in the BPO industry are representatives of this newly emerging consumer class. This chapter analyzed how the BPO industry in Mumbai is enabling the process of the formation of a consumerist new middle class. The primary contribution of this chapter lies in bringing out the nature of changing consumption practices of the new middle class and the factors within the BPO industry that influence these changes. It was found that employees in the BPO industry in Mumbai have witnessed several changes in their consumption practices, such as being more brand conscious, trying new and different forms of cuisines and using more luxurious modes of transport. The changes in consumption habits do not strictly imply westernization of consumption as is argued in some existing studies (see, for example, Lakha, 1999), but rather entail consumption of more expensive and new forms of goods and services. Changing food habits, thus, do not imply a switch from Indian to American cuisine, for instance, but consist of eating out more frequently at posh restaurants and trying cuisines that were hitherto unavailable or unheard of. Similarly, increasing brand consciousness involves being more meticulous about one's dress sense and purchasing better quality clothes from both Indian and non-Indian brands. A part of these changes in consumption practices can be ascribed to the wider availability of goods and services in India post liberalization and privatization, and the tremendous growth of various forms of media that create consumerist aspirations. However, empirical evidence presented in this chapter points out that the BPO industry too plays a vital role in bringing about changes in consumption practices and contributing to the formation of a new middle class. The industry provides a first-hand experience to its employees of new forms of consumption practices via various means. Several modern amenities such as cafes, gyms, beauty salons and sport complexes are available to the employees within their office premises at subsidised rates or for free. Perks in the industry include the latest gadgets, home appliances, credit cards, etc. besides standard benefits like insurance and provident fund, which are also provided in public sector jobs. Further, our analysis also showed that the remuneration paid to BPO employees is far higher than the average income in India, making them a privileged group in the society. The higher remuneration enables them to purchase the newly available goods and services that they are exposed to in the industry. The new middle class in the BPO industry can thus be understood as a privileged section within the middle class itself, identified by its new and expensive forms of consumption.

Theoretically, the concept of class, and especially the middle class, remains ambiguous. The empirical evidence provided here helps in reducing that ambiguity to some extent by bringing out the forms of consumption behaviour that determine new middle class identity. This research shows that while factors such as occupation and education primarily determined middle class identity in India earlier, consumption practices are the key determinants today. Class *performance*, in terms of classed consumption, is thus integral to modern analyses of class identities and structures. This is not to say that the former factors have lost relevance in contemporary class studies. As seen here, economic *position* continues to determine class membership even today.

It is essential also to study factors other than consumption and income that determine new middle class identity, which were beyond the scope of this chapter. In the case of India, it would be interesting to study if forces of globalization like the outsourcing industry are helping transcend historical social boundaries like caste and gender in determining class membership. Further, the middle class is generally looked upon as the driver of economic development via its investment in human capital and savings and active political participation (see Easterly, 2001). Does the new middle class continue to play this role, or does it drive development only via consumption? Moreover, the empirical evidence here shows the new middle class to be a privileged section of the society. Does this imply that benefits of globalization and liberalization accrue to only a small, privileged section of the society? It also remains to be seen whether, along with replacing the western middle classes in driving global consumption demand, the new middle class in emerging economies is also converging with them in terms of socio-cultural consumption practices. Is the emergence of the new middle class synonymous with the rise of a global middle class and a global consumer culture? These questions need further research in order to reach a more comprehensive understanding of the impact of globalization on the emergence of a new middle class.

Notes

1 Mumbai is placed in the third position, behind Bangalore (first) and Manila (second) in the overall rankings of the top global outsourcing destinations of 2014 by Tholons (2013).

2 Based on author's calculations using the NSS survey data on Household Consumer Expenditure in India, 68th round, 2011–2012.

References

Ablett, J., Baijal, A., Beinhocker, E., Bose, A., Farrell, D., Gersch, U., ... Gupta, S. (2007). *'The Bird of Gold': The Rise of India's Consumer Market.* India: McKinsey & Company.

ADB (Asian Development Bank). (2010). *The Rise of Asia's Middle Class, Special Chapter, Key Indiacators for the Asia and the Pacific.* Asia and Pacific: Asian Development Bank.

Banerjee, A. and Duflo, E. (2008). What is Middle Class About the Middle Classes Around the World. *The Journal of Economic Perspectives: A Journal of the American Association 22*(2), 3–28.

Birdsall, N. (2012). A Note on the Middle Class in Latin America. *Inequality in Asia and the Pacific.* Manila: Asian Development Bank.

Brosius, C. (2013). *India's Middle Class: New Forms of Urban Leisure, Consumption and Prosperity.* London: Routledge.

Easterly, W. (2001). The Middle Class Consensus and Economic Development. *Journal of Economic Growth 6*, 317–335.

Fernandes, L. (2006). *India's New Middle Class: Democratic Politics in an Era of Economic Reform.* Minneapolis, MN: University of Minnesota Press.

Fuller, C. and Narasimhan, H. (2007). Information Technology Professionals and the New-Rich Middle Class in Chennai (Madras). *Modern Asian Studies 41*(1), 121–150.

Haynes, D. and McGowan, A. (2010). Introduction. In D. Haynes, A. McGowan, T. Roy and H. Yanagisawa, *Towards a History of Consumption in South Asia.* (pp. 1–25). India: Oxford University Press.

Kelly, P. (2007). *Filipino Migration, Transnationalism and Class Identity.* ARI Working Paper Series No. 90, http://ssrn.com/abstract=1317153. http://ssrn.com/abstract=1317153.

Kharas, H. (2010). *The Emerging Middle Class in Developing Countries.* OECD Development Centre, Working Paper No. 285.

Lakha, S. (1999). The State, Globalisation and Indian Middle-Class Identity. In M. Pinches, *Culture and Privelege in Capitalist Asia* (pp. 252–276). London: Routledge.

Meyer, C.J. and Birdsall, N. (2012). *New Estimates of India's Middle Class.* Washington, DC: Center for Global Development.

Murphy, J. (2011). Indian Call Centre Workers: Vanguard of a Global Middle Class? *Work, Employment and Society 25*(3), 417–433.

NASSCOM. (2013). *NASSCOM.* Indian IT-BPO Industry. www.nasscom.in/indian-itbpo-industry

Nijman, J. (2006). Mumbai's Mysterious Middle Class. *International Journal of Urban and Regional Research 30*(4), 758–775.

Ravallion, M. (2010). The Developing World's Bulging (but vulnerable) Middle Class. *World Development 38*(4), 445–454.

Shukla, R. (2010). *How India Earns, Spends and Saves: Unmasking the Real India.* India: SAGE Publications.

Taylor, P., D'Cruz, P., Noronha, E. and Scholarios, D. (2013). The Experience of Work in India's Domestic Call Centre Industry. *The International Journal of Human Resource Management 24*(2), 436–452.

Tholons. (2013). *2014 Tholons Top 100 Outsourcing Destinations: Rankings.* Tholons.

Upadhya, C. (2008). Rewriting the Code: Software Professionals and the Reconstitution of Indian Middle Class Identity. In C. Jaffrelot and P. van der Veer, *Patterns of Middle Class Consumption in India and China* (pp. 55–87). New Delhi: Sage.

Vira, B. and James, A. (2012). Building Cross-sector Careers in India's New Service Economy? Tracking Former Call Centre Agents in the National Capital Region. *Development and Change 43*(2), 449–479.

Wilson, D. and Dragusanu, R. (2008). *The Expanding Middle: The Exploding World Middle Class and Falling Global Inequality.* Goldman Sachs, Global Economics Paper No. 170.

14 Service outsourcing to smaller cities in the Philippines

The formation of an emerging local middle class

Niels Beerepoot and Emeline Vogelzang

Introduction

In the past few years, considerable attention by the popular press and by international agencies has been given to what is considered the 'new' middle class in developing countries (see e.g. World Bank 2007, Asian Development Bank 2010). As part of shifting global economic power structures a new group of Southern beneficiaries of globalization has become more visible and has gained growing international attention. This 'new' or 'Southern' middle class is often used as a term to describe how the benefits of globalization reach larger parts of the population in the Global South (see e.g. Fernandes and Heller 2006, Kharas 2010). Research on this new, Southern, middle class has so far mainly been within the realm of the work of international agencies, consultancy firms and international banks. Academic research on the emergence of a new middle class in developing countries is, with some exceptions, still limited. Some studies have noted that members of the new middle class are mostly working in knowledge-intensive jobs in the private sector: information technology (IT), the banking sector or other business services (see Fuller and Narasimhan 2007, Murphy 2011, Krishnan in this volume). In the Philippines, the country occupying centre stage in this chapter, the sustained growth of the ITES-BPO (IT-enabled business process outsourcing) sector has been perceived to fuel the growth of a new middle class that drives private consumption, notably the consumption of non-essential miscellaneous goods and services (World Bank 2013).

Of even more recent date is the growing attention for the spread of the ITES-BPO sector to smaller provincial cities in the Philippines (see Beerepoot and Hendriks 2013, Kleibert 2014, Laysiepen 2014). Many second-tier cities within the timespan of only a few years have seen the emergence of a sizeable service outsourcing sector that (as in the case of e.g. Iloilo, Baguio and Bacolod) has created around 8,000–10,000 jobs per city. These cities essentially skip the industrial stage of development and instead become part of global services production networks. Given that these cities usually have much smaller and less diverse economies (Andriesse *et al.* 2011), the impact of the emergence of the service outsourcing sector is more profound here than in large metropolises such as Metro Manila and

Mumbai. Employment opportunities for college graduates have so far been limited in smaller cities in the Philippines. With the rise of the service outsourcing sector, better-paying employment is available, stimulating young people to stay longer in smaller cities instead of moving to larger cities such as Manila or Cebu or going abroad. This chapter examines how in one smaller city in the Philippines (Iloilo) the expanding service outsourcing sector is leading to the formation of a new middle class and whether workers perceive themselves to be 'new' middle class. Particular attention will be given to their consumption practices as these have become *the* way to understand the middle class (see Fernandez and Heller 2006, Jaffrelot and van der Veer 2008, Guarin and Knorringa 2014). Consumption is of particular importance in the identity formation of the new middle classes in developing countries (Murphy 2011). It is consumption, not income, which has become the marker for middle class status in common parlance (Nijman 2006). Surprisingly, few studies so far have looked into the consumption practices of workers in the service outsourcing sector. Through examining their consumption practices this chapter will add to a further understanding of the local impact of the service outsourcing sector in the recipient locations in developing countries.

This chapter is based on semi-structured interviews with 31 workers and a survey among 554 workers in the ITES-BPO sector in Iloilo carried out in 2013. The next section provides an overview of the literature on the service outsourcing sector and how the sector can add to the formation of a new middle class. The chapter then outlines the methodological framework of the research and then concentrates on the characteristics of the service outsourcing sector in the Philippines and Iloilo. The next two sections respectively provide a profile of the workers in the Iloilo ITES-BPO sector and discuss their consumption patterns in order to examine whether they are a new middle class in the making. Finally the chapter draws some conclusions.

Offshore services and the rise of the middle class

In the past ten years a substantial body of literature has emerged on the service outsourcing sector and the opportunities it provides for developing countries (see for useful overviews e.g. UNCTAD 2005, 2009, Dossani and Kenney 2007, Bunyaratavej *et al.* 2011, Massini and Miozzo 2012). A range of services previously thought to be non-tradable is now being provided electronically over large distances (World Bank 2007). Since the 1980s, outsourcing and offshoring of business services have experienced a remarkable growth and extended from basic software coding and call-centre work to a range of knowledge-intensive business services and back-office functions such as payroll and accounting, financial and legal research, and even tightly regulated activities such as drug development (Massini and Miozzo 2012). Offshore services are still frequently associated with call-centre work, while the sector contains a much wider variety of activities (see Beerepoot and Hendriks, 2013). For developing countries with capable workforces, services relocation offers enormous employment and entrepreneurial opportunities (Dossani and Kenney 2007). The sector is considered to provide the much-preferred white-collar jobs for an increasingly college-educated labour force. The service outsourcing sector holds the potential of generating (highly) skilled jobs, which are often missing or insufficiently available in developing countries (Dayton-Johnson *et al.* 2009). In the Indian case it meant that for the first time a large but extremely poor economy entered global competition on the basis of the labour potential of its middle-class white-collar workers (Dossani and Kenney 2009).

Contribution to a new middle class

Various authors have debated whether (and how) the service outsourcing sector contributes to the formation of a new middle class in developing countries (see e.g. Fuller and Narasimhan 2007, Nadeem 2009, Murphy 2011). The much-vaunted emergence of IT allied to the rapid economic growth rate in India since the mid-1990s has apparently raised increasing numbers of Indians into the middle class (Jeffrey 2008). Key issue in this debate is whether the sector predominately provides employment to the existing middle class, and whether its benefits are internalized by the existing middle class, or it provides new groups in society access to better paying employment. In India, growth in the ITES-BPO sector has created better income opportunities for high- and medium-skilled labour compared to less-skilled or unskilled labour (Raychaudhuri and Das 2012). The economic dynamics of the ITES-BPO sector not only rest on inequality but also tend to reproduce class and other social divisions due to its education requirements bias, thereby excluding a large section of the Indian population (D'Costa 2011). In Mumbai, and elsewhere in urban India, the middle class is pulling away from the poor and low-income classes (Nijman 2006, see also Hatekar and More in this volume).

Irrespective of whether the sector strengthens the existing middle class or facilitates the formation of a new one (by providing new people access to a middle-class status), the key issue remains why this new middle class is important to look at. Here, multiple expectations of what a strong middle can contribute to a society play a role. First, the middle class is an important prerequisite for stronger, more sustainable economic growth and development (Asian Development Bank 2010). Second, the existence of a strong middle class is seen as an essential condition for a country to economically and socially progress 'from within' (Lange and Meier 2009). Third, the middle class is often regarded as a source of entrepreneurship and driver of political and social change (see *Economist* 2011). Fourth, it functions as a powerful idea of an open class of ordinary people who enjoy good incomes from their hard work, and to which everyone can aspire (Ballard 2012). Therefore, in India, the new middle class is seen to symbolize 'modernity' by way of its aspirational lifestyle, consumerism, materialism and adoration of the West (Nijman 2006, Krishnan in this volume).

New middle class consumer practices

The most visible aspect of new middle class status concerns consumer practices. The ascent of hundreds of millions of developing-country nationals into the global middle class will produce a large group of people who can afford, and will demand access to, the standards of living that were previously reserved mainly for the residents of high-income countries (World Bank 2007). Various consultancy and policy reports emphasize how the new middle class above all should be seen as a consumer force (see McKinsey 2007, Goldman Sachs 2008, Asian Development Bank 2010, Credit Suisse 2010, 2011). Because the middle class typically stands at the forefront of consumption demand, a larger middle class will tend to reinforce changes in consumption patterns (World Bank 2011). The surge in the global middle classes must thus be seen both as an economic transformation involving an increase in purchasing ability and discretionary income, and a socio-cultural transformation involving changes in beliefs, attitudes, norms and motivations (Guarin and Knorringa 2014).

Middle class consumerism and its attendant features – marketing, commercial media, malls and shopping culture – is a leading trend across emerging societies (Nederveen Pieterse 2009). As observed by Dupount (2011), Delhi's insertion in the global economy has been conspicuously translated into its urban landscape via the development of modern infrastructure, high-end residential complexes and exclusive shopping malls, in line with the rise of consumerism and middle-class ideology (Dupont 2011). The malls symbolize a fast-growing consumerist culture with window-shopping and spending time in air-conditioned postmodernist environments emerging as a new leisure activity that is *de facto* restricted to the upcoming middle classes (Dupont 2011). By providing decent incomes the service outsourcing sector is often regarded as fuelling the growth of this new middle class. The relatively high incomes of software engineers and other IT professionals place them easily within the upper segments of the middle class by any income-based definition (Upadhya 2008). They command large disposable incomes at a relatively young age, enabling them to engage in high levels of consumption (Upadhya 2008). The higher than average compensation of ITES-BPO employees can lead to increasing personal consumption as this sector's workforce has a higher propensity to consume (Magtibay-Ramos *et al.* 2007). These observations require a closer look at how ITES-BPO employees stimulate new local demand for goods.

Methodology

This research is based on a combination of semi-structured in-depth interviews with key informants (3) and ITES-BPO employees (31), a survey among ITES-BPO employees and the study of secondary materials on the city's outsourcing industry. The data were collected during a ten-week fieldwork period in Iloilo City between late January and early April 2013. The interviews concentrated on issues such as perceptions of employment, future (career) plans, social life/activities, expenditure patterns, social class perceptions and family relations. Among the 14 ITES-BPO firms located in Iloilo City, two granted permission to approach their agents for interviews. From the 31 interviews, 22 were conducted inside a large call centre and nine in a smaller non-voice BPO firm using a convenience sampling method. After the fieldwork, interviews were transcribed and crosschecked in order to compare and contrast data on the discussed topics and for the purpose of identifying inconsistencies in the data.

To incorporate quantitative data, a self-administered survey was distributed among BPO employees. Due to time constraints and the difficulty of finding participating companies, it was decided to conduct a non-probability sampling technique. Respondents were selected on the basis of accessibility. Eventually, 600 questionnaires were distributed among employees in six firms that agreed to participate. With 554 of them returned, a response rate of 91.7 per cent was reached. Afterwards, the survey was entered in SPSS to analyse the data.

The Philippine and Iloilo service outsourcing sector

The Philippines' ITES-BPO sector had its formative years in the early 1990s when a number of foreign data encoding companies settled in the country. The sector gained momentum in the early 2000s with the launch of international outsourcing and offshoring of voice-based services. In recent years, the sector has been able to grow rapidly thanks to the country's considerable output of college graduates with a good command of English. Currently, the service outsourcing sector employs around 800,000 workers (BPAP 2012). Around 70 per cent of the workers are involved in voice-based services. The Americanized English of Filipinos gives the country a competitive edge over India (Friginal 2009). So far, the vast majority of the ITES-BPO companies and jobs (both nearly 80 per cent) are located in Metro Manila. Supply-side constraints in Metro Manila and active promotion of smaller cities (see Kleibert, 2014) have led the sector to expand to other parts of the country. The advantages of smaller cities are the lower operating costs (wage-levels and office rental in particular) and a lower attrition rate. Here, the impacts or the transformative and invigorative effects on the local economy are also perceived to be much bigger as these cities have a less diverse economic structure. A major restriction in these locations is the lack of sizable office space and extra efforts that are required before the agents reach the required level of English (Laysiepen 2014).

The city of Iloilo long served predominantly as a regional trading hub and node in regional inter-island shipping. The city had an entrepôt function in the sugar production and trade that long flourished in the central Visayas. The rise of the service outsourcing sector from the mid-2000s onwards came after a few decades of economic decline caused by the regional sugar industry losing out to the international competition. Currently the city has around 430,000 inhabitants. The position of the city as a regional educational centre (guaranteeing a steady supply of potential workers) has been instrumental to the arrival and growth of the service outsourcing sector. During the research period in 2013 the city hosted 14 ITES-BPO companies, of which six are call centres. Non-voice activities in Iloilo include data entry, teaching English online, medical transcription and web design. The sector employs around 8,500 people (in 2013), most of which work in four call centres that employ between 1,500 and 2,000 workers each. In a related development the city in recent years has emerged as a popular place for South Koreans to study English. About 1,000 of them are currently enrolled in the city's local language schools.

There have been various accounts of how the rise of the service outsourcing sector transforms smaller Philippine cities into 24-hour economies since serving Western clients means working predominately at night (see Hendriks 2010, Laysiepen 2014). Observations in Iloilo make clear how the service outsourcing sector stimulates indirect employment in such domains as catering, retail (malls, leisure shopping) and transport services. As such, many recent economic developments in the city are attributed to the service outsourcing sector, as emphasized in one interview:

> The establishment of the BPO sector is a big factor for Iloilo's economic development. Only in the last two years we have seen new hotels come up, new commercial centres, of which some of them are still being built right now. New investors are coming in and I would assume it is because of the higher purchasing power Illongos have. If you have a pool of 5,000 people who are earning around 12,000 pesos a month, that is a lot of purchasing power.
>
> (Interview, local government counsellor, 7 February 2013)

The purchasing power of ITES-BPO workers is therefore the most often cited, and most visible characteristic of this group, as will be further elaborated below. New people with spending power not just lead to the demand of new goods and services but given the demographic characteristics of the group also to a specific set of consumer goods.

Profiling workers in the Iloilo ITES-BPO sector

The empirical study for this chapter involved a survey among 554 workers in the service outsourcing sector in Iloilo. The vast majority of them were born and raised in Iloilo or the direct vicinity of the city. The average age of the respondents was around 25 years, which reflects the young age that is typical for workers in the sector. Most respondents are college graduates. The main motivation for them to join the ITES-BPO sector is (not surprisingly) the financial compensation that the sector offers. The ITES-BPO sector pays twice as much compared to other sectors such as retail or manufacturing. Basic monthly payment lies between PHP10,000 and PHP15,000 (or US$225–337). Additional benefits that they receive during employment involve a night work allowance, medical insurance, company parties and performance bonus. Other motivations to join the sector include a lack of local alternatives and joining friends who already work in the sector. One respondent emphasized how glad she was having found a job in the ITES-BPO sector, since no other local company would hire her as an undergraduate. The sector stimulates workers to stay in Iloilo, whereas before they would often move elsewhere in search of employment. This was best exemplified in an interview with an ITES-BPO worker:

> Before joining this ITES-BPO company, I planned to work abroad if I couldn't get a job in Iloilo. However, since I got a prominent job now, I plan to stay and study at the same time since I will start my master's degree this June. If eventually there is an opportunity to work abroad, why not? But for now I see myself staying in this company.
>
> (Interview, ITES-BPO worker, 11 March2013)

The quote illustrates that the sector could be instrumental in spreading the economic benefits of service sector growth more widely, as intended at with the Next Wave Cities promotion (see BPAP 2012, Kleibert 2014). Of the surveyed workers, 49 per cent expected to work at least one more year in the ITES-BPO sector while 32 per cent even preferred to work in the sector for an indefinite period. Only a small number of workers (9 per cent) saw their job as a stepping stone towards better ITES-BPO jobs in Manila or Cebu City. Many respondents highlighted the acquisition of generic skills as one of the main benefits of working in the service outsourcing sector (see also Marasigan in this volume). The most often highlighted skills learned during employment included (in this order of importance): self-confidence, concern for quality, communication skills and cooperation with others. As emphasized by one respondent:

> One of the things I have enhanced is my social skills. Prior to this job, I was really introverted. I wouldn't talk to people if they wouldn't talk to me first. Working in the ITES-BPO sector has really improved my self-confidence.
>
> (Interview, call centre agent, 12 March 2013)

Acquisition of generic skills is more often recognized as a key benefit of work in the service outsourcing sector (see Beerepoot and Hendriks 2013). Recently, work in the service outsourcing sector has become evaluated more positively (see Upadhya 2008, Vira and James 2012, Beerepoot and Hendriks 2013, Marasigan in this volume) and seen as a particular stage in peoples' careers during which they have the opportunity to acquire skills that can be used in their further career. The sector strengthens economic independence and self-confidence among its workers. Notwithstanding the positive appraisal and learning opportunities that the sector provides, the respondents do not forget to mention the negative features of work in this sector. Doing monotonous work at night for long periods causes stress and health problems. Still, the lack of local employment alternatives drives them towards this sector.

When asked about what defines new middle class status for them, most respondents named the level of income, stability of income and level of education. When subsequently asked whether since their start in the service outsourcing sector they have experienced a change in class status, many responded positively (see Table 14.1). The main reason why they perceived a change in their class status was because of their higher, and more stable, incomes. It should be noted that these are subjective classifications, based on how respondents evaluated their own situation before working in the sector and at the time of interview. Especially young respondents may have evaluated their BPO position and (their first) income very positively.

Table 14.1 Perceptions of class position of workers (N=538)

Before	*Now*				
	Lower class	*Lower middle class*	*Middle middle class*	*Upper middle class*	*Upper class*
Lower class (N=95)	25	52	13	4	1
Lower middle class (N=206)	1	103	100	1	1
Middle middle class (N=209)	1	8	184	16	0
Upper middle class (N= 4)	0	1	10	13	0
Upper class (N=4)	0	0	0	1	3
Total	27	164	307	35	5

Source: Survey results (2013).

Prevalent are the shifts from lower middle class to a 'middle middle class' status and the preservation of an existing middle class status. This suggests that the ITES-BPO sector predominately stimulates upward movements within the middle class. The job selection criterion of having completed college education is instrumental in these shifts. It confirms perceptions that the service outsourcing sector mainly stimulates upward movements within the middle class (see also Raychaudhuri and Das 2012). As such it could add to perceptions that the ITES-BPO sector strengthens inequality within an urban labour market, which is beyond this chapter to investigate. It also requires a closer investigation of consumption practices to see how those provide a stimulus of local economic growth.

New consumer practices of ITES-BPO workers

A main feature of the ITES-BPO sector is the relatively high salaries that workers can earn. Compared to other jobs such as nursing (US$135), teaching (US$135) and wholesale/retail (US$112), ITES-BPO employees earn on average twice as much per month (US$225 to US$337). With a total pool of around 8,500 workers they form a sizeable local consumer force that reshapes local demand for goods. An often-mentioned example among respondents of how local consumer' demands in Iloilo have recently changed is the establishment of a Starbucks coffee bar. Initially, doubts were raised over whether the Illongos would be willing to pay 200 pesos (or $4.4) for a cup of coffee. But soon the Starbucks became very popular among local citizens and the owners even opened a second one in the city. While essentially anecdotal, this illustrates how local demand for goods is changing and people are willing to spend more money or engage in luxury or conspicuous consumption. Many respondents emphasized how since they worked in the ITES-BPO sector they spent more money on clothes, gadgets and other luxury items. These are illustrations of what the World Bank (2013) regards as consumption of non-essential miscellaneous goods and services driven by the rise of the service outsourcing sector. One respondent highlighted that he can eat out at fast-food chains every day as an example that he now belongs to the middle class:

> It's a luxury to be able to eat at Jollibee every day. Most families can only go there four times a month, but I can go there every day.
>
> (Interview, call centre agent, 14 March 2013)

The importance attached to consumption is deeply woven into the service sector, especially in call centres, in the form of 'aesthetic labour' where the agent's presentation is part of the product: 'sounding right, looking good' (Warhurst and Nickson 2009). One interviewed agent stressed that having a good dressing style is part of the ITES-BPO culture. It is part of the ITES-BPO lifestyle to buy new clothes or a new pair of shoes every payday. Among the respondents, 45 per cent said they cared more about their clothing and looks after getting into the sector. In a similar research on middle-class formation among Indian ITES-BPO employees, it was argued that Indian ITES-BPO workers have become part of an emergent global middle class (Murphy 2011, see also Krishnan in this volume). The phenomena of consumer culture, luxurious lifestyles and social class identity are all vital components of the emerging new middle class that distinguishes itself from other groups in society as they are more influenced by Western values and lifestyles through the global aspect of their job. One of the agents in this research also stressed the need to learn about Western lifestyles for her ITES-BPO job:

> We learn to adapt to different cultures, because we need to learn general information about the country and their manners, like what type of food they are into, what arts they like, music, everything. It is important to learn this so that by the time we communicate and make calls we don't just listen and take their concerns or resolve their issue; we get to engage with the customer.
>
> (Interview, call centre agent, 14 March 2013)

Despite being exposed to a culture of conspicuous consumption, ITES-BPO employees did not appear to spend their money only or even mainly on miscellaneous goods. On the contrary, almost all respondents reported contributing a percentage of their income to their family's income (varying from 20 to 99 per cent). One respondent mentioned that his income enabled two sisters to study nursing. Most workers saw their job as a stable source of income to support their own and their family's expenses. This implies that they contribute to maintaining their own *and* their family's middle class status. These responses are similar to what can be observed among overseas workers who also often highlight the importance of supporting the family with their newly earned income (Asis et al. 2009).

Conclusion

This chapter has looked at how the rise of the service outsourcing sector in Iloilo fosters the formation of a new middle class in this city. Service outsourcing is no longer only impacting primary cities in Southeast Asia, as illustrated in various case studies in this book, but is increasingly driving changes in lower-tier cities as well. In smaller provincial cities in the Philippines the sector provides new local employment opportunities, albeit and in a direct sense only for a selective group of workers. The rise of the service outsourcing sector has stimulated young people to stay longer in Iloilo instead of trying their luck in larger Philippine cities or abroad. The new middle class is often characterized as a new consumer force whose higher spending power is based on new service sector employment opportunities provided through globalization. The service outsourcing sector workers in Iloilo fit in this picture. Their consumption practices are often highlighted as the most visible local transformation due to the rise of the service outsourcing sector. In Iloilo the ITES-BPO sector has enabled workers to make upward movements in class status, though these mainly involve changes within middle class status. Similar to the accounts by Nadeem (2009), Murphy (2011) and Krishnan (in this volume), these workers have become exposed to a culture of consumption that is often stimulated through their peers in the sector. Workers engage in more visible, luxury consumption and perceive that, through their new employment, they have made upward movements in their class status. Still, workers often emphasize their responsibility towards supporting the family income.

Further research could concentrate on the indirect employment generated through the rise of the service outsourcing sector. As emphasized by Kumar in this volume, this involves looking at businesses supporting the growth of the ITES-BPO sector and how they provide employment opportunities to other segments of the urban labour market. Such research provides an input to a more general understanding on the longer-term growth prospects of the ITES-BPO sector in developing countries. As argued by Roubini (2014) eventually technology will replace service jobs in developing countries as well. And soon enough voice-recognition software will replace the call centres of Bangalore and Manila (Roubini 2014). In the Philippines, critical concerns have recently been raised on the 'jobless growth' that the country is currently experiencing (Syed 2013). Despite rapid economic growth (stimulated through the rise of the service outsourcing sector) the national unemployment rate has increased in the recent years. Herewith more fundamental questions can be raised about whether (offshore) service sector growth provides a viable pathway for development of underdeveloped countries, particularly when the sector displays high levels of footlooseness (given its low fixed investments) and just as quick as the sector emerged in places like Iloilo city, it could disappear.

References

Andriesse, E., N. Beerepoot, B. Van Helvoirt and G. van Westen (2011) Regional business systems and inclusive/exclusive development in the Philippines, Thailand and Malaysia In: B. Helmsing and S. Vellema (eds) *Value Chains, Inclusion and Endogenous Development: Contrasting Theories and Realities*. London: Routledge, pp. 151–177.

Asian Development Bank (2010) *Key Indicators for Asia and the Pacific 2010*. Manila: Asian Development Bank.

Asis, M., N. Piper and P. Raghuram (2009) International Migration and Development in Asia: Exploring Knowledge Frameworks. *International Migration*, Vol. 48 (3), pp. 76–1106.

Ballard, R. (2012) Geographies of Development: Without the Poor. *Progress in Human Geography*, Vol. 36 (5), pp. 563–572.

Beerepoot, N. and M. Hendriks (2013) Employability of Offshore Service Workers in the Philippines: Opportunities for upward labour mobility or dead-end jobs? *Work, Employment and Society*, Vol. 27 (5), pp. 823–841.

BPAP (Business Processing Association Philippines) (2012) Philippine IT-BPO Investor Primer. www.bpap.org/publications/research/investorprimer2012.

Bunyaratavej, K., J. Doh, E. Hahn, A. Lewin and S. Massini (2011) Conceptual Issues in Service Offshoring Research: A Multidisciplinary Review, *Group and Organization Management*, Vol. 36 (1), pp. 70–102.

Credit Suisse (2010) *Global Wealth Report*. Zurich: Credit Suisse Research Institute. www.credit-suisse.com/researchinstitute.

Credit Suisse (2011) *Emerging Consumer Survey*. Zurich: Credit Suisse Research Institute.

Dayton-Johnson, Y., A. Pfeiffer, K. Schuettler and J. Schwinn (2009) Migration and Employment. In: OECD (ed.) *Promoting Pro-poor Growth Employment*, Paris: OECD, pp. 149–177.

D'Costa, A. (2011) Geography, Uneven Development and Distributive Justice: The political economy of IT growth in India, *Cambridge Journal of Regions, Economy and Society*, Vol. 4, pp. 237–251.

Dossani, R. and M. Kenney (2007) The Next Wave of Globalization: Relocating service provision to India. *World Development*, Vol. 35 (5), pp. 772–791.

Dossani, R. and M. Kenney (2009) Service Provision for the Global Economy: The Evolving Indian Experience. *Review of Policy Research*, Vol. 26 (1–2), pp. 77–104.

Dupont, V. (2011) The Dream of Delhi as a Global City. *International Journal of Urban and Regional Research*, Vol. 35 (3), pp. 533–554.

Economist (*The*) (2011) The New Middle Classes Rise Up. *The Economist*, 3 September. www.economist.com/node/21528212.

Fernandes, L. and P. Heller (2006) New Middle Class Politics and India's Democracy in Comparative Perspective. *Critical Asian Studies*, Vol. 38 (4), pp. 495–522.

Friginal, E. (2009) *The Language of Outsourced Call Centres: A corpus-based study of cross-cultural interaction*. Philadelphia: John Benjamins Publishing.

Fuller, C.J. and H. Narasimhan (2007) Information Technology Professionals and the new-rich middle class in Chennai (Madras) *Modern Asian Studies*, Vol. 41 (1), pp. 121–150.

Goldman Sachs (2008) *The Expanding Middle: The expanding global middle class and falling global inequality*. Global Economics Paper No 170. New York: Goldman Sachs

Guarin, A. and P. Knorringa (2014) 'New' Middle Class Consumers in Rising Powers: Responsible consumption and private standards. *Oxford Development Studies*, Vol. 42 (2), pp. 151–171.

Hendriks, M. (2010) Local Outcomes of the Changing International Division of Labour: The Emergence of the Offshore Service Sector in Baguio City, The Philippines. MA thesis, University of Amsterdam.

Jaffrelot, C. and P. van der Veer (2008) *Patterns of Middle Class Consumption in India and China*. London: Sage

Jeffrey, C. (2008) Kicking Away the Ladder: Student Politics and the Making of an Indian Middle Class, *Environment and Planning D*, Vol. 26 (3), pp. 517–536.

Kharas, H. (2010) *The Emerging Middle Class in Developing Countries*. OECD Working Paper No 285. Paris: OECD.

Kleibert, J. (2014) Strategic Coupling in 'Next Wave Cities': Local institutional actors and the offshore service sector in the Philippines, *Singapore Journal of Tropical Geography*, Vol. 35 (2), pp. 245–260.

Lange, H. and L. Meier (2009) (eds) *The New Middle Classes. Globalizing Lifestyles, Consumerism and Environmental Concern*. Dordrecht, Heidelberg, London, New York: Springer.

Laysiepen, L. (2014) Socio-economic impact of the business process outsourcing sector: An emerging new middle class in Bacolod (the Philippines). MA thesis, University of Amsterdam.

Magtibay-Ramos, N., Estrada, G.E and Felipe, J. (2007) *An Input–Output Analysis of the Philippine ITES-BPO Industry*. Manila: Asian Development Bank Economics Working Papers. www.adb.org/publications/analysis-philippine-business-process-outsourcing-industry.

Massini, S. and M. Miozzo (2012) Outsourcing and Offshoring of Business Services: Challenges to theory, management and geography of innovation, *Regional Studies*, Vol. 46 (9), pp. 1219–1242.

McKinsey (2007) *The 'Bird of Gold': The rise of India's consumer market*. San Francisco, CA: McKinsey Global Institute.

Murphy, J. (2011) Indian Call Centre Workers: Vanguard of a global middle class? *Work, Employment and Society*, Vol. 25 (3), pp. 417–433.

Nadeem, S. (2009) Macaulay's (Cyber) Children: The cultural politics of outsourcing in India. *Cultural Sociology*, Vol. 3, pp. 102–122.

Nederveen Pieterse, J. (2009) Towards the 21st Century International Division of Labour. In: S. Dasgupta and J. Nederveen Pieterse (eds), *Politics of Globalisation*. London: Sage, pp. 155–179.

Nijman, J. (2006) Mumbai's Mysterious Middle Class, *International Journal of Urban and Regional Research*, Vol. 30 (4), pp. 758–775.

Raychaudhuri, A. and P. Das (2012) *International Trade in Services in India: Implications for Growth and Inequality in a Globalising World*. Delhi: Oxford University Press.

Roubini, N. (2014) Where Will All the Workers Go? www.project-syndicate.org/commentary/technology-labor-automation-robotics-by-nouriel-roubini-2014-12.

Syed, S. (2013) Philippines 'Puzzle': Growing economy fails to create jobs. www.bbc.com/news/business-23598279.

UNCTAD (United Nations Conference on Trade and Development) (2005) *World Investment Report: The Shift Towards Services*. New York: United Nations Conference on Trade and Development.

UNCTAD (2009) *Information Economy Report 2009: Trends and Outlook in Turbulent Times*. New York: United Nations Conference on Trade and Development.

Upadhya, C. (2008) Employment, Exclusion and 'Merit' in the Indian IT Industry, In: Mahendra Dev, S. and K. Babu (eds) *India's Development: Social and Economic Disparities*, New Delhi: Manohar, pp. 145–168.

Vira, B. and A. James (2012) Building Cross-sector Careers in India's New Service Economy? Tracking former call centre agents in the national capital region, *Development and Change*, Vol. 43 (2), pp. 449–479.

Warhurst, C. and Nickson, D. (2009) 'Who's got the look?' Emotional, aesthetic and sexualized labour in interactive services. *Gender, Work and Organization*, Vol. 16 (3), pp. 385–404.

World Bank (2007) *Global Economic Prospects: Managing the Next Wave in Globalisation*. Washington, DC: The World Bank

World Bank (2013) *Philippine Economic Update: Accelerating Reforms to Meet the Job Challenge*. World Bank: Poverty Reduction and Economic Management Unit East Asia and Pacific Region. www.worldbank.org/content/dam/Worldbank/document/EAP/Philippines/Philippine_Economic_Update_May2013.pdf.

15 Conclusions

Offshore services and the road to development

Niels Beerepoot, Bart Lambregts and Robert C. Kloosterman

Emerging insights

This book started with the observation that the rapid rise of offshore services production creates profound changes in the economic, social and even the physical landscape of countries around the world, and in India and parts of East and Southeast Asia in particular. Enabled by the disintegration of services production, emergent global services production networks assimilate new, previously (semi-)peripheral places into the global economy and offer a range of novel opportunities to their economic agents. A new international division of labour can be seen to take shape, influenced by such factors as the local availability of particular skills, cultural affinities and cost advantages. With the number of jobs involved in India, East Asia and Southeast Asia alone currently running in the millions, and with future numbers possibly being multiple times larger than that, it is understandable that there is increasing attention for the potential of services offshoring as a strategy for development for emerging economies.

This book has sought to investigate the local impacts in South and Southeast Asia of this latest wave of globalization. It set out to identify the opportunities created, the transformations triggered, the different development trajectories followed and the major challenges met. The twelve case studies from India, the Philippines, China's Pearl River Delta, Hong Kong and Bangkok yield a wealth of empirically grounded insights into how services offshoring is making an impact in the region. Together these case studies teach us a number of important things.

First, the offshore services industry offers the receiving countries a number of immediate gains. These include direct job creation, expansion of business opportunities for local suppliers of supporting services (creating indirect employment), rents (for those physically facilitating the operations of ITES-BPO firms), which may or may not come to the benefit of local development, and increased consumption by most if not all directly or indirectly involved in the sector (adding in turn to indirect job creation too). These gains are immediate, but also very vulnerable to sectoral dynamics: they are bound to fade away as soon as the industry, which is footloose by definition, finds new competitive locations or becomes subject to increasing automation. The concern, as highlighted by Ofreneo in Chapter 9, is widely shared that services offshoring creates new branch-plants economies that lack local embeddedness and are vulnerable to eventual relocation of production to lower cost locations (see also Phelps *et al.* 2003, Dawley 2011, Kleibert 2015).

Long-term gains, as shown in the study of Marasigan (Chapter 10), include the accumulation of new skills among those working in the industry. These gains increase when industry upgrading takes place and more workers become occupied in higher-level service production. A less favourable situation arises when upgrading does not take place and too many people continue to toil in the production of low-level services without learning useful new skills. This can become a problem when these people otherwise qualify as an economy's best educated and dispose of capacities that, when employed differently, could contribute more meaningfully to a society's economy and development. The importance as well as the complexity of the matter are also demonstrated by Iguchi (Chapter 5). In her chapter on inter-organizational linkages between Japanese manufacturing subsidiaries and local Filipino firms, she shows how the lack of linkage formation between the two is intensively linked to stagnant skill development in the industrial labour force. Here, the government's failure to effectively support the enhancement of the local industrial sector has led to a highly dependent and vulnerable development trajectory.

Another important insight emerging from the case studies is that the offshore services industry has the potential to transform other industries in a local economy. The study by Kumar (Chapter 11) has shown how Mumbai's ITES-BPO industry ups the ante for a supplying sector such as security services. While the arrival of more sophisticated demand for particular products or services is generally seen as a boon for development (e.g. Porter 1998), Kumar shows that it may also entail a threat. In a given local economy it may well be that only the largest or otherwise best-endowed suppliers are capable of stepping up their performance and meeting the new demand, effectively marginalizing other suppliers in the process. Worse still, it may even result in a situation where local players are excluded from the scene at all, with the business that could have been theirs taken by well-endowed newcomers from elsewhere. A substantial part of the security market created by Mumbai's offshore services industry being serviced by global security services firms is a case in point. This chimes with the situation experienced by foreign manufacturers in the Philippines as shown by Iguchi (Chapter 5). In the virtual absence of qualified local suppliers of parts and intermediary services, many of these manufacturers source their more advanced inputs from overseas. While it is true that in the case of Mumbai's foreign-owned security firms the bulk of the jobs are still filled by local staff, part of the value created is captured elsewhere.

A decisive answer to the questions of whether, how and to what degree the services offshoring wave contributes to the emergence of a 'new' middle class in the Global South cannot be given yet. As argued by Hatekar and More (Chapter 12), there is the issue of numbers: while certainly not inconsiderable and still growing, 3 million relatively well-paid ITES-BPO workers of a population of about 1,252 billion (the case of India), or 1 million of a population of 100 million (the

Philippines) calls for modesty about the contribution the sector can make in the short term. Yet, the contributions by Beerepoot and Vogelzang (Chapter 14) and Krishnan (Chapter 13) show that a new consumerist force is emerging in the cities where the ITES-BPO sector locates. Since ITES-BPO firms tend to concentrate in cities large and small where their main resource – qualified labour, consisting mostly of college or university graduates – is plentiful, the industry's contribution to new middle class formation at the local level may be substantial. Especially in smaller towns previously peripheral to the forces of globalization, the arrival of several thousands of relatively well-paid, modern economy ITES-BPO jobs can make quite an impact, as the chapter by Beerepoot and Vogelzang demonstrates. As evidenced by the study of Krishnan, the combination of working in an international ITES-BPO environment and receiving a comparatively quite decent pay does alter the self-image of people, boosts their (consumerist) aspirations and increases their capacity to realize these.

The various chapters also clearly point out that the development of offshore services economies does not follow a singular trajectory. Kleibert's historical comparison between the development of the ITES-BPO in India and the Philippines (Chapter 3) shows that some countries clearly are more firmly en route to capturing the gains of the services offshoring wave than others. Explaining factors include structural forces such as the local availability of specific resources (notably skills), agency (local actors in some places being more intent on capturing opportunities and advancing in the domains of value enhancement and value capturing than in others) and a good measure of serendipity (e.g. timing and the evolution of the opportunity context). With the trend moving away from infancy and towards maturity, future success (for local/regional/national economies) will depend most of all on local agency, with important roles notably for local entrepreneurs, relevant government agencies, industry associations, finance and facility providers and educational institutions. In this respect, Raquiza's (Chapter 4) critical analysis of the rise of the ITES-BPO industry in the Philippines shows that current success offers no guarantee of success in the future if key local actors do not get their act together.

While the majority of the book's chapters dealt with the region's two most established offshore services destinations, the case study of China's Pearl River Delta presented by Zhang (Chapter 6) nicely shows the challenges that relative latecomers face. In the same way that yet-to-industrialize economies have to find ways around the contemporary industrial dominance of China, Chinese cities aspiring to diversify their economies into export-oriented services will have to make inroads in a production landscape that regionally, if not globally, is dominated by India (IT-related services) and the Philippines (contact services). This requires the identification of promising market niches that moreover must match the locally available labour skills and expertise. Pearl River Delta and other cities may derive hope from the cases of Bangkok and Hong Kong as portrayed by respectively Lambregts (Chapter 8) and Sigler and Zhao (Chapter 7). While Bangkok's appeal to Japanese contact centres and their employees shows that the variety of niches virtually has no bounds, Hong Kong's successful transformation from a manufacturing enclave to the region's main merchanting and merchandizing hub demonstrates that there are ample opportunities in services. Yet, both those who aspire to hop on the offshore services bandwagon as well as those who seek to build upon existing positions would do well to heed the sobering message put forward by Ofreneo in Chapter 9. The economic growth generated by South and Southeast Asia's 'offshore services miracle' so far has benefitted only a limited and already relatively privileged part of the population and workforce. Many, and notably those employed in the region's huge informal economy, have little or no access to emerging opportunities. Moreover, hard-won labour rights are all too easily sacrificed for the benefit of promoting growth. For the development gains to be sustainable and inclusive, the interests of the offshore services industry, labour and governments should be properly balanced.

Service-led development in developing countries is, to summarize, neither a bed of roses for all the workers involved nor a guaranteed path to sustained economic development and prosperity. As Kloosterman, Beerepoot and Lambregts argue in Chapter 2, specific locational conditions have to be met for the establishment of export-oriented services. These activities are dependent on a skilled labour force, (foreign) language proficiency, a suitable physical and legal infrastructure and an openness to the wider world. Even if these conditions are fulfilled, the impact of these activities on the wider economy and more specifically as a driver of sustained overall economic growth is anything but given. This is, as mentioned above, obviously linked to the relative size of the export-oriented service sector in the overall economy, but it also contingent on a set of institutional conditions that are basically centred around the governance capacity of the state (at the national and the local levels). To be able to exploit the growth potential of these services, the educational system (a spillover of the export-oriented services through backward linkages), the physical infrastructure and the business climate for domestic nascent entrepreneurs in these services have to be improved on a continuous basis. This presupposes a rather strong but also a responsive state. Even in countries where the initial conditions for the establishment of export-oriented services are met, this may still be a tall order.

Having said that, many developing countries face, as latecomers, a drastic narrowing of the options with the near-complete dominance of China and China-centred supply chains in manufacturing. From that perspective, export-oriented services may offer a suitable and feasible stepping stone for these latecomers. The competences acquired in these services and the spillover effects may subsequently be utilized to upgrade tourism and, arguably, also to upgrade particular forms of agriculture and manufacturing. History has shown that the first rungs of the ladder of economic development are often hard. They go together with severe exploitation of workers – from the young women in the satanic mills of England during the Industrial Revolution to the workers in Korean factories in the 1960s and to those working in the call centres of the Philippines during the night – and with a journey of discovery full of trial and many errors of which activities suit a specific national or local economy.

Avenues for further research

This book presents a number of issues and subjects for further research. These include case studies on new destinations for offshore outsourcing, reaching new groups of workers (e.g. via impact sourcing) and new delivery models (such as microwork). Such topics can be placed within overarching debates on whether the service sector can act as a driver of economic growth and how at global level the tradability of services and growing global competition for jobs lead to increasing convergence between the Global North and South.

Academic discussion will continue between those who argue that services can act as growth escalator for developing countries (e.g. Ghani and O'Connel 2014) and sceptics who claim that a services-led model cannot deliver rapid growth and good jobs in the way that manufacturing once did (Rodrik 2014). These opposing views lie at the heart of the debate on service sector-led development and stand to benefit from further empirical studies on how service sector growth is making an impact beyond primary cities and beyond the sector's traditional beneficiaries of college-educated workers. Whereas Ghani and O'Connel (2014) claim that service-led growth is compatible with greener, inclusive and more gender friendly growth, case studies in this book have highlighted the unevenness of service-led growth. This corresponds with Krishna and Nederveen Pieterse's (2008) concept of hierarchical integration, which emphasizes the uneven terms of integration of different labour segments in contemporary globalization. Further case studies will help to develop a more profound understanding on who has access to the new employment opportunities. This should also involve closer examination of the indirect employment generated. Aside from optimistic projections by organizations such as NASSCOM (2010), few studies have looked in detail at the characteristics and quality of the indirect employment that is generated. As ITES-BPO companies often have limited input–output relations in the domestic economy (Magtibay-Ramos *et al.* 2008) indirect employment is more difficult to identify and measure. Beyond the highly visible shopping malls and condominium complexes, the money that is earned is invested in education (as revealed by Beerepoot and Vogelzang in this book) of which the positive effects for individual and society take longer to materialize.

How the international division of labour in service offshoring further evolves is another subject for investigation. This book has demonstrated how, beyond India and the Philippines, other countries are making efforts to attract international service outsourcers. This will add to further specialization between countries but also to the formation of new networks of production. These networks will not only connect the South to the North (with services typically being delivered from the South to the North) but increasingly also different economies within the South. The maturing of the ITES-BPO sector could also cause the sector's image for workers to change, particularly when it provides them with opportunities for longer-term careers. It also raises questions on how groups of workers other than the traditional pool of college-educated middle class workers can be reached. As part of corporate social responsibility commitments by service outsourcers some initiatives have been undertaken to provide employment to less-privileged groups in society (Gino and Staats 2012, Heeks 2013). The ambition of such impact-sourcing initiatives is to engage the poor and vulnerable, and reach below the easy-to-find, already-trained employees who typically have other employment options (Rockefeller Foundation 2011). Whereas impact sourcing is emerging as an interesting sub-field within service outsourcing (for achieving poverty reduction goals), the criteria for what impact sourcing involves are ambiguous and require further research.

Offshore outsourcing of services as described in this book is still largely based on a traditional model of relocation of service work, which is driven by multinational firms that engage in labour arbitrage to seek the lowest cost location for production. New delivery models in services such as online job marketplaces (see Beerepoot and Lambregts 2015) can stimulate a next wave in service outsourcing as they help to bring outsourcing within the reach of small firms and individuals. This opens new opportunities for expanding the market for service outsourcing and both in India and the Philippines many individuals have already registered as online freelancers working in the highly competitive market for microwork (see also Lehdonvirta and Ernkvist 2011).

Ultimately, global competition for service sector jobs could lead to global convergence in wage levels. While gap closure is not likely to happen soon, it is part of what ongoing globalization could mean for societies and the world as a whole. Stagnant wages in the Western world and rising wages in Asia have already reduced the wage gap (ILO 2013). This could also lead to the reshoring of jobs to the West, so adding a new chapter to the global dynamics in offshore outsourcing of services. Either way, South and Southeast Asia will continue to provide a fertile ground for studying the processes that have been analysed in this book. Various authors stress how Asia will regain its position as economic center of the world in what will become the 'Asian Century' (Mahbubani 2009, ADB 2011). Whether and how this will materialize remains to be seen but for the years to come it will keep our research (and that of many others) focused on the developments in this part of the world.

References

ADB (Asian Development Bank) (2011) *Asia 2050: Realizing the Asian Century*. Mandaluyong City: ADB.

Beerepoot, N. and Lambregts, B. (2015) Competition in online job marketplaces: towards a global labour market for service outsourcing? *Global Networks,* 15 (2), 236–255.

Dawley, S. (2011) Transnational corporations and local and regional development. *In*: A. Pike, A. Rodriguez-Pose and J.J. Tomaney, (eds). *Handbook of Local and Regional Development*. London: Routledge, 394–412.

Ghani, E. and O'Connell, S.D. (2014) *Can Service Be a Growth Escalator in Low Income Countries?* World Bank Policy Research Working Paper 6971, Washington, DC: World Bank.

Gino, F. and Staats, B. (2012) The microwork solution. *Harvard Business Review*, December, 92–96.

Heeks, R. (2013) Information technology impact sourcing. *Communications of the ACM*, 56 (12), 22–25.

ILO (International Labour Organization) (2013) *Global Wage Report 2012–2013*. Geneva: ILO. www.ilo.org/global/research/global-reports/global-wage-report/2012/lang--en/index.htm.

Kleibert, J.M. (2015) Expanding Global Production Networks; The emergence, evolution and the developmental impact of the offshore service sector in the Philippines. PhD thesis. Universiteit van Amsterdam.

Krishna, A. and Nederveen Pieterse, J. (2008) The dollar economy and the rupee economy. *Development and Change*, 39 (2), 219–237.

Lehdonvirta, V. and Ernkvist, D. (2011) *Knowledge Map of the Virtual Economy: Converting the virtual economy into development potential*. Washington: IBRD.

Magtibay-Ramos, N., Estrada, G. and Felipe, J. (2008) An input–output analysis of the Philippines BPO industry. *Asian-Pacific Economic Literature*, 22 (1), 41–56.

Mahbubani, K. (2009) *The New Asian Hemisphere: The irresistible shift of global power to the East*. New York: Public Affairs.

NASSCOM (2010) *Impact of the IT-BPO Industry in India – A Decade in Review*. New Delhi: NASSCOM.

Phelps, N.A., MacKinnon, D., Stone, I. and Braidford, P. (2003) Embedding the multinationals? Institutions and the development of overseas manufacturing affiliates in Wales and North East England. *Regional Studies*, 37 (1), 27–40.

Porter, M.E. (1998) Clusters and the new economics of competition. *Harvard Business Review*, 76 (6), 77–90.

Rockefeller Foundation (2011) *Job Creation Through Building the Field of Impact Sourcing*. Working Paper June 2011. New York: Rockefeller Foundation.

Rodrik, D. (2014) Are services the new manufactures? 13 October. www.project-syndicate.org/commentary/are-services-the-new-manufactures-by-dani-rodrik-2014-10.

Index